The Dog Trainer's Complete Guide

to a

Happy, Well-Behaved Pet

Contents

The Dog Trainer's Complete Guide

to a

Happy, Well-Behaved Pet

Jolanta Benal

St. Martin's Griffin New York

www.stmartins.com

Photographs courtesy of the author

Text design by Meryl Sussman Levavi

Library of Congress Cataloging-in-Publication Data

Benal, Jolanta, 1958–
    Dog trainer's complete guide to a happy, well-behaved pet / Jolanta Benal. — 1st ed.
        p. cm.
    Includes bibliographical references and index.
    ISBN 978-0-312-67822-7 (alk. paper)
    1. Dogs—Training.   I. Title.
    SF431.B417 2011
    636.7'0887—dc23

                                                              2011026767

First Edition: November 2011

10 9 8 7 6 5 4 3 2 1

Whatever is done against one's will, under the threat of force, is like an arrow artificially tied back, or a river dammed in on every side of its channel. Given the opportunity it rejects the restraining force. What is done willingly, on the other hand, is steadfast for all time. It is made fast by the unbreakable bonds of love.

—Gregory of Nazianzus, ca. 329 C.E.–ca. 389 C.E.

[Dogs are,] and this is important, perfectly obedient to the laws of learning.

—Jean Donaldson, *The Culture Clash*

The Dog Trainer's Complete Guide

to a

Happy, Well-Behaved Pet

Introduction

A DOG MANIFESTS HERSELF

Once upon a time, I didn't like dogs. Then there came a period of spousal arm-twisting ("Look how cute that dog is" and the like), at the end of which my partner, Sarah, and I were standing in a veterinarian's office looking at a medium-size yellow dog. She had been found on the street the day before and she was wobbly on her feet because she'd been spayed that morning. She appealed to my eyes not at all. The date was May 8, 1998.

For some reason I wanted to know how it felt to walk a dog, so I leashed the yellow dog and walked with her the few blocks home while Sarah took the car. The yellow dog pulled on the leash.

Back at our apartment, Sarah and I offered the yellow dog a bowl of water. "Well, Isabella, how do you like your new home?" I asked. It had been only a few hours since the surgery. Isabella immediately regurgitated the water all over our hall floor.

Sarah looked at me. "'Isabella'?"

I shrugged.

Isabella baffled me in every possible way. I was used to cats. She was much larger than a cat. She followed me from room to room, breathing and taking up space. The first time I left her alone in the apartment, I leashed her to a sofa leg because I was afraid she might chase our cats. When I came home, she had scratched the finish off the floor trying to escape. Also, she had defecated.

I had agreed to a dog only on condition that it (it!) stay off the furniture. And, especially, off the bed. Our apartment was a mostly open-plan space, so we put Izzy in our small home office, which had a door. The first night, she was groggy and went to sleep. The second night, she howled and scratched at the door. The racket was terrible, but wouldn't it be catastrophic to give in? Wouldn't that teach her that she, not we, was Maximum Leader here? We called Sarah's sister, who'd had dogs all her life. What should we do? Penny was quite patient, all things considered. "The dog is lonely. *Let her out*," she said.

Obviously, I had no clue.

I went to the library, as I always do when I have no clue. Also, in 1998 there was very little Googling. I looked at every single dog book on the shelves. One included a chapter on how to respond if a "humaniac" called the cops on you because you had swung your dog in a circle in the air by the choke chain around her neck and made her scream and pass out. The writer's bio said he'd worked on Disney films. Large swaths of my childhood had apparently been more sinister than I realized at the time.

Another book explained that it was undesirable for dogs to vocalize in their crates. If your dog made noise in the crate, you should bang on the top of the crate until the dog shut up. This, the author promised, would result in a well-balanced dog. I had some trouble seeing how scaring Isabella would accomplish this.

Still other books spoke of rewarding appropriate behavior with treats and in general gave more of an impression that their authors might actually kind of like dogs, or at least not want to make their lives completely miserable. Two things the books had in common, though: (1) they all gave reasons why you should jerk on the dog's neck; (2) as the neck-jerking might suggest, the relationship between trainer and dog was understood as, at bottom, adversarial. Sooner or later the dog was going to blow you off or defy you, and then you'd have to get tough. Though you should always be "fair," whatever that meant, and of course there were certain very sensitive dogs with whom you shouldn't get *too* tough.

It was nice to know I wasn't going to have to jerk on Izzy's neck that much. But I resolved to do it firmly whenever I needed to.

So I taught Izzy a bunch of things. (Notice that I had somehow become her primary caretaker and trainer.) I taught her to sit, to lie down, to stay, to jump through a hoop, to jump onto a low wall and walk along the top, to come when called. No matter how much I jerked on her prong collar, though, I couldn't quite get her to stop pulling on leash, or to stop barking and lunging at certain other dogs on the street. (A prong, or pinch, collar is one of those metal collars with prongs on the inside that dig into the dog's neck when you jerk the leash.) Off leash, Iz got along well with other dogs, so we went to Brooklyn's Prospect Park every morning to exercise her. I met other people and their dogs and, thanks to the exercise, Izzy stopped licking the finish off our apartment floors. She never chased our cats. She was pleased to see me when I came home, she stopped defecating on the floor when left alone, and she no longer seemed to take up quite so much space. Possibly by now I had even admitted that the world wouldn't end if she sat on the couch with us while we watched movies.

On the whole, having a dog was copacetic.

A bit more than a year later, the dog who became Muggsy Malone was left tied up on our block. I'm ashamed to say it didn't occur to me to bring him home; the idea of having two dogs was beyond me. Sarah, however, marched out, collected him, and marched back in. Izzy and Muggsy fell in love at first sight. As for Sarah and me, he was our introduction to Pit Bulls (cute! funny! gator mouths!) and also to serious behavior problems. The two don't inevitably go together, by the way.

Muggsy lunged and snarled at many people who were not us. Tall people, UPS people, postal people. Police people. If anyone but Sarah or me bent over him, he lunged and bit them in the face. He never did serious damage—a couple of small punctures, at most—but still. Pit Bull! Biting the face! We needed help and we knew it.

We asked around for names and everyone mentioned the same fellow. We hired him.

Famous Local Trainer taught us to fill a plastic bottle with pennies and throw it at Muggsy whenever Muggsy was about to lunge, and, sure enough, that shut down the lunging in no time, but even though it seemed to work, the "rattle of justice," as FLT called it, made us feel unhappy and weird. FLT had said that the lunging would come back if we didn't keep rattling, but somehow or other we stopped carrying the penny bottle anyway, and somehow or other we never managed to find the time for another session after our first two, though we'd bought a package of five. Besides, something peculiar had happened during FLT's first visit to our apartment.

Izzy was a quiet dog, but not one of those quiet dogs who make the sweat run down your spine. We'd held a party the summer after we got her and she mingled like a champ. She had never reacted aggressively to any person, as far as we could see. But when FLT sat down in our living room, Izzy stationed herself on the other side of the coffee table and directly facing him, and she growled.

"Have you ever had any trouble with this one?" FLT asked.

No, we hadn't, we replied, winching up our jaws. I don't remember what we did about Izzy then; just put her in another room, maybe.

Though we had initially contacted FLT about Muggsy, Izzy's barking and lunging at other dogs while on leash seemed to be getting worse. I tried diligently to "correct" it, sometimes jerking her right off her feet, just the way the books said I was supposed to do. One book told me that I should become exceptionally "demanding" when other dogs were present, which seemed to mean I was supposed to issue many commands. That would teach Izzy to pay attention to me instead of to the other dogs. The photo that accompanied these instructions depicted a dozen dogs passing one another on an outdoor staircase. I studied it carefully for further clues, but Izzy barked and lunged no matter how "demanding" I got. We needed the cavalry again—but, we surmised, since Iz disliked FLT so much, maybe we should get *different* cavalry. I asked around some more. Well, a dog walker told me, there *was* somebody else. She was a little weird in her approach. Her name was Polly.

Cue the "Ode to Joy."

Polly was a tiny, unassuming woman with a bad scar on her face from a car accident. Her weird approach involved having me feed Izzy chicken whenever we passed another dog; eventually, Polly said, when Izzy saw another dog, she wouldn't stiffen, bark, and lunge but instead would look automatically for her chicken.

Holy cow, it worked. It worked *fast*. I developed a strong interest in everything Polly had to say.

Polly said I might want to trade in my prong collar for a piece of headgear called a Halti.* First, though, I had to prove to Iz that the Halti was a good thing. This I'd do by showing Izzy mad love and playing with her whenever the halter went on, then ignoring her briefly after the halter came off.

Huh. Okay, that worked too. No more jerking on Izzy's neck. On the rare occasions when she came near lunging, I could hold the leash near where it attached to the Halti; this gave me enough leverage to keep all her feet on the ground.

---

* I don't use halters much anymore; most dogs dislike them, and front-clip harnesses serve a similar purpose. Back in the day, though, the halter seemed like a godsend.

Then Polly put a little plastic object in my hand. A child's toy. A clicker. How big an impression it made on me, you may judge by the fact that I've given clickers a chapter of their own. Oh, and there was a book she thought I should read, *The Culture Clash,* by one Jean Donaldson. Donaldson's name didn't appear in any of the library books I'd read, I'd never heard of her publisher, and the book had about the worst-looking cover I'd ever seen. Also, it was badly proofread.

It knocked my socks off. Everything I thought I knew about dogs—the need to be alpha, the defiance, the importance of "correcting" them by yanking on their necks—Donaldson turned upside down. And everything she said was so logical, so obviously grounded in close observation, that I could see she was right. How can I describe the experience of reading *The Culture Clash* for the first time? Evolution happens. The earth revolves around the sun. Dogs are perfectly obedient to the laws of learning. Oh, *yes.*

But what about Muggsy? Polly had a few things to say about him, too. If it was easy to teach Iz that passing dogs = chicken, what could we teach Muggsy about people in uniform? A kind cable repairman let me walk Muggsy back and forth, back and forth, back and forth, stuffing chicken in his face while the repairman repaired cable. I don't think it occurred to me that the repairman might feel a bit nervous with me walking my admittedly aggressive Pit three feet behind him for half an hour. Our mailman forgave all and threw chicken at Muggsy; result, butt wiggles. I can't remember anymore how long it took Muggsy to decide our UPS man was his best friend, but I do remember an illicit visit to the back of the brown truck, again involving chicken and, yes, butt wiggles.

That progress aside, Muggsy still had a problem with people's faces. Namely, he really had to stop lunging at them. I could get in his face, so I did. I bent over him and gave him a piece of chicken. I bent closer and gave him a piece of chicken. I bent closer yet and gave him a piece of chicken. Repeat, repeat, repeat. This was almost as boring to do as it is to read about.* However, some time shortly afterward my friend Jon swung Muggsy into his lap and bent over his face to kiss him, too fast for me to say *Ohmygodnodon't,* and as the cold sweat sprang out all over my body Muggsy grinned up at Jon and licked him.

---

* Very Important Point: Watching good behavior modification take place is like watching paint dry, assuming you have no special interest in paint.

Now, I have to put in a disclaimer here. Not only is this the short version of the work Sarah and I did with Muggsy, but also, of all the behavior modification I have ever done with any dog, Muggsy's was the quickest and easiest. (Even so, see the footnote here with the reference to drying paint.) Who knows why? If I were more paranoid, I'd be tempted to say the universe was pulling a bait-and-switch on me: "Hey, Benal! Check this out—it is so fun and rewarding to turn scary dogs into friendly ones, and it's barely the work of a moment! You *totally* want to do this for a living!"

Muggsy broke our hearts by dying less than two years after we got him, of leptospirosis, a bacterial infection contracted from a rat he caught in the park one night. He had spent the last year of his life as a babe magnet (women would *stop their cars and get out* to say hi to him), clicker-training star, and all-around friendly guy. We warned the vets and techs who tried to save him that he had a history of biting, but he never gave them a reason to believe it. The last trick I taught him before he got sick was "Bang! You're dead." When I pointed my index finger at him, he'd drop flat on his side; after a few seconds, he'd open one eye to see if he'd been dead long enough yet.

It was a year before we could even think about getting another dog. But in the autumn of 2001, friends of ours were fostering a stray Pit Bull from the Bronx who had been diagnosed with false pregnancy. The false pregnancy turned out to be seven puppies, born on December 4. The temptation was too much; Sarah and I agreed to, you know, just think about adopting one.

Being *terribly* sophisticated about dogs by then, I visited the litter and administered a puppy "temperament test." You hold a puppy upside down, call him to you, make a loud noise, and so on; the idea is that these little experiments will reveal the puppy's personality. Juniper's responses were completely ordinary in every way. We brought him home on February 1, 2002, at eight and a half weeks old, and a few days later he jumped the first puppy he had a play date with and pinned her to the ground. Then he did it again. By the way, what little research there is suggests that puppy temperament tests have almost exactly zero value.*

---

* This isn't true, however, of the behavior evaluations conducted at shelters. The short version is that behavior is most fluid in very early life, and much less so in adulthood. Consequently, the snapshot you get of an adult dog's behavior has decent odds of being representative, whereas the seven-week-old who acts one way on Thursday may respond quite differently to the same situations on the following Tuesday.

Here's Juni with a happy, relaxed face. Notice his open mouth with corners of the lips retracted, his soft facial muscles, and his generally "smiley" look. His ears are pulled back: In context with his overall expression, this is a sign of relaxed, deferential friendliness. If his face and body looked tense and his tail were low, pulled-back ears would signal anxiety or outright fear.

Walking with Juni feels like holding hands. See Chapter 8, "Polite Leash Walking."

Which of these dogs is not like the others? Clockwise starting from bottom right: Elliott (a friend's dog), Izzy, Juni, and Timothy M. Small. See Chapter 3, "Anything but 'Obedience.'"

Izzy, my first dog, enjoys an old-lady nap. She was welcome to the sofa, but she also liked her big pile o' quilts. If you don't want your dog on the furniture, give her a comfy bed on the floor as an alternative.

We were in trouble, but I had no idea yet how much. Our puppy's problems turned out to be severe; to save his life, I would have to learn as much as I could about training and behavior, as fast as I could. This book is one result of that process.

As for Juni . . . well, you'll have to read the Conclusion to find out.

So Many Dogs, So Little Time
HOW TO CHOOSE THE RIGHT DOG

The odds that you and your dog will live happily together for his whole life go way up if you, the smart human, the one with all the choice in this situation, give at least as much attention to the characteristics you want in a dog as you would to picking a date on Match.com, and then try to pick a dog who kind of sort of fits the bill. You can get a terrific dog by dumb luck—I know, because twice now I've adopted dogs who just happened to show up at the right moment—but really, it's not the best strategy.

The Internet's rich in quizzes and checklists that offer to tell you what kind of dog to get. I tried a couple while I was working on this chapter. I was afraid they'd be silly, and they are. They ask stupid questions—for example, "Do you want a guarding dog?" How can I put this? *You don't want a guarding dog.* Dogs bred and reared to be suspicious of strangers make, let's say, problematic family pets; for one thing, they can't distinguish among burglars, your dinner guests, and a bunch of EMTs. You *might* want a good-size dog who can bark on cue, but I promise you that's about all the guarding you need.

As for the quiz results, they were loopy. One told me I should get a "Faux French Bulldog," whatever that is (is it made of polyester?), or one of several other currently popular designer mixes. Another suggested a mixed-breed (so far, so good) or a Field Spaniel as my two best choices. Oh, lord. I have lived with several dogs and worked with hundreds, so I kind of know what I like. I like whip-smart, athletic, sociable, better-keep-me-busy-or-I'll-get-annoying dogs, and although I can handle springtime shedding, the thought of grooming a dog regularly all year round makes me want to disembowel myself.* I'm a sucker for Pit Bulls

---

* Forget paying a groomer, either: $45–$150 every six to eight weeks. That money could be spent on dog-training seminars, Laphroaig, and MP3 downloads.

and Pit Bull mixes. I really like herding-dog mixes. And—wild card here—I am a pushover for a nice Chihuahua. Spaniels . . . People, I know some great spaniels, but they're not the right dogs for me. As for supporting the puppy mill/designer mix industry—no. Just no.

The results were not only way off base in terms of my actual preferences, they were also way too specific. Not that it doesn't make sense to consider breed *type*—it does, because breeds and groups of breeds (and their mixes) tend to show behavioral similarities. But a list of five or seven or a dozen breeds implies "Get one of these and you're set." It's not so simple. When you get a dog, even a dog who belongs to a known breed, you don't get a *breed;* you get an *individual dog,* who may or may not have read the breed description (which may or may not be worthless, anyway; see "What If You're Looking for a Particular Breed?," p. 18). Work the other way around: Consider what qualities you want in a companion dog, and then look for those qualities. Breed and breed group can narrow your search, but the dog you're looking for may turn up pretty much anywhere.* This is the beauty of the behavior descriptions and matchmaking paradigms some shelters use—they focus on the qualities of individual dogs and try to pair human adopters with compatible dogs.

And, oh, yes, then there's love. Love is not so predictable. You may fall in love with a completely inappropriate dog. It happens. Frankly, all my dogs have been more or less inappropriate in one way or another. If you thought you wanted a sweet, soft spaniel mix but then fell head over heels for a fast, independent Jack Russell Terrier, fine! But, having chosen that JRT, you must now live up to her; no getting mad when she'd rather learn new tricks than cuddle. As the great trainer Leslie Nelson has said, "Love the dog you have, not the one you wish you had."

Falling in love with a dog who's not your type is not necessarily bad; you thought you wanted to cuddle on the couch all evening, but hey, teaching a new trick every other day turns out to be a blast, it gives you a huge sense of accomplishment, and you're crazy about your brainiac dog. Excellent. Purposely adopting a behaviorally troubled dog is quite another matter. *Don't do it.* Shy dogs, scared dogs, fear-aggressive dogs will pull at your heartstrings—of course they will. Then they may

---

* And I'm going to wind up with a Cavalier King Charles one of these days, as penance for scoffing at spaniels.

refuse to set foot outdoors, or may growl and snap at children or visitors, or may send other dogs and people to the hospital; and then you have to pay someone a lot of money to help, and have I mentioned yet that no ethical trainer will guarantee a happy result?* A really difficult dog may also turn *you* into a trainer specializing in behavior modification, which is what happened to me. Not that it hasn't been great, but there are less emotionally trying routes to a new career. Behaviorally healthy, "easy" dogs also deserve loving homes. They really really do.

How to Decide What Kind of Dog You Want

Dogs take a lot of time and work, so start by walking yourself and your family through a typical day and see how—and whether!—a dog would fit in. Consider the following questions.

- Can you easily see when you'd exercise the dog?
- How will you manage to get a nine-week-old puppy outdoors to pee and poop every hour or two for his first week in your home, and with gradually decreasing frequency afterward?
- On what weekday evenings can you and your partner reliably attend that basic manners class?
- If you work long hours, who'll give the dog a break or two so she isn't crossing her legs all afternoon and into the evening?
- Do you come home from work wiped out? Your puppy or dog will need attention, care, and training regardless.
- If you have children, are they mature enough to understand that animals are not toys—that they feel pain, need rest, and sometimes want to be left alone?
- Who will supervise the puppy/dog during your kids' playdates and make sure the children don't overwhelm him, or vice versa?
- Are your children mature enough to participate in care for your dog?
- If you have other animals, how are they likely to respond to the new adoptee? If they are old or ill, can you realistically and humanely expect them to adapt?

---

* Behavior is simply not 100 percent controllable or predictable. Ethical trainers guarantee that our work is as scientifically sound as we can make it and in keeping with the state of the art. Period.

If, on reflection, a puppy would be more work than you and your family can manage right now, but you long to have a dog, seriously consider adopting an adult from a shelter or a rescue group. I'm not necessarily talking about an adolescent or young dog, either; she'll be almost as much work as a puppy, at least for a little while. Think "mature adult" or even "senior citizen."

MATCH UP NEEDS AND PERSONALITY

So you've decided that your life has room for a dog, and you have some idea of whether you're up for the challenge of a puppy or might do better adopting an adult. Now it's time to match personalities.

Though online quizzes are useless or worse, certain shelters describe their charges' behavior in a way nicely adaptable to your search whether you're adopting or buying. They rate aspects of doggy personalities on a continuum—"shy" to "bold," for instance, or "affectionate" to "aloof."

A True Dog Story: Charlie

One of the sweetest dogs I've ever met turned up at the Brooklyn branch of the New York City municipal shelter some years ago, brought in as a stray. Charlie was a big (90+ pounds) black mixed-breed, not much to look at and grizzled in the face. He'd come out wagging for walks, then droop when I put him back in his kennel. He wasn't the most interactive fellow in the world, but he had a big neon sign over his head saying "I Am a Depressed Old Dog," so I crossed my fingers and did a formal behavior evaluation (see the section on shelters and rescue groups, later in this chapter, for more about these). Charlie did just fine, not that anybody wanted to adopt a huge, old, not-super-responsive mixed-breed dog. And then he developed kennel cough (bordetella), turning himself into a huge, old, not-super-responsive, *sick* mixed-breed dog. New York's municipal shelter system must by law accept every animal brought in, so the facilities are chronically short on space. When room has to be made, the less adoptable dogs die first. I did something I never, ever do: I leaned hard on two friends of mine who had recently lost a beloved dog. They didn't want to adopt; they needed time to grieve. Tough, said I.

You know how this ends, right? My friends came to the shelter. They left with Charlie. He lived five more years and became a certified therapy dog. And my friends forgave me my arm-twisting. Scout's honor.

You can turn that strategy around to help you decide what kind of dog you'd get along with best. Are you . . .

energetic ——————— laid-back?
If you're on the laid-back end of the spectrum, the questions about how a dog would fit in to your life may already have steered you away from a puppy. Remember, adult dogs vary in energy level too!

impatient ——————— patient?
Impatient people may do best with adult dogs who don't need a lot of training and who don't have problem habits to repair.

anxious ——————— calm?
Anxious people, do yourselves a favor and don't get barky, reactive dogs—they'll make you nuts.

interested in grooming ——————— okay with brushing out the winter coat ——————— bored to tears by grooming?
Say you're bored by grooming but willing to deal with the winter coat, up to a point. No Huskies, Malamutes, or Poodles for you, unless you want to shell out big bucks for grooming.

fastidious ——————— a mudpuppy?
Dogs are filthy, okay? They eat feces and roll in dead things. Accept this. If you're going to need to wash the dog a lot, please also take the time to teach her to enjoy being bathed.

physically affectionate ——————— hands-off?
If you like cuddling with dogs, look for a dog who likes cuddling; you'll be sad if you adopt one who has handling issues or who prefers nearby floor space to the spot next to you on the couch. Also, be aware that small doesn't equal cuddly; people tend to force touch on small dogs, and it makes the dogs crazy.

fascinated by training ——————— bored to tears by training?
If you're bored by training and you get a smart, energetic dog, neither of you is going to be happy.

athletic ——————— a couch potato?
Couch potatoes, how about a nice middle-aged or old dog who's been displaced by the recession or a family illness? Leave the adolescent Pit mixes and the field-bred hunting dogs for people who won't want to kill them two days after bringing them home.

robust ——————————— frail?

Say you have osteoporosis and being knocked down could cost you a broken hip. Pass on the body-slamming adolescent Lab mix and go for a smaller, quieter adult dog instead. Also, if you are very small and your prospective dog is very big, think about how you'll physically take care of him if he gets tottery in old age. (Assistive devices do exist.)

quick to go into action ——————————— slow to go into action?

If you're proactive, you'll find your dog easier to train. For instance, if you're slow to get up when your puppy starts to sniff and circle, housetraining will be more laborious. There's no shame in being pokey, but you'll probably be happier with a dog whose behavior is low maintenance.

confident ——————————— not so confident?

Nope, this isn't about "alpha." It's about stigma. Certain breeds and types are stigmatized, and if you fall for a Pit Bull/Rottweiler/Doberman/Mastiff some folks will curl their lips at you no matter how nice he is. It can be tough to take.

Another question to ask yourself is what aspects of life with a dog might drive you crazy. Check out Chapter 11, "Stuff Dogs Do That Annoys People," for a whole range of normal dog behaviors that tend to get on human nerves. I stress, these are normal dog behaviors; if you can't stand even a little bit of barking, the "breed" you want is the one scientifically known as *Felis catus* (and its members have their own methods of making people tear their hair out*). I'll offer a few general suggestions, but please bear in mind the following:

1. Every individual trainer's experience is skewed—by whatever her specialty is, by what breeds are popular locally, because small samples are always skewed, by her own perceptions, by her development of a reputation as being "good with X problem or Z breed" (and hence being sent a lot of dogs with X problem or of Z breed).

2. Every individual dog is an individual (at least, behaviorally speaking; there's probably no such thing as a Poodle who needs no grooming). I know a woman who has had four or five Shelties over her lifetime

---

* If you don't know what I mean, go to YouTube and search for "Simon's Cat."

What Kind of Dog to Get If You Have Kids

Quick and Dirty Tip

You know what makes dog trainers want to bang our heads against the wall? Cute pictures of puppies and babies, or puppies and toddlers, nestled among the daisies, cuddling. Head, meet wall. Here's why.

How much supervision does your toddler need? How wrung out do you get in the course of a day, providing that supervision? Right. How much supervision do you think a puppy needs? *Every waking minute.* Just like your child. You can't always take good care of two species of infant simultaneously. Say you're bathing Babylini when Puppalini wakes from his nap. Puppalini needs to go out *right now,* but you can't leave Babylini. Puppalini pees on the floor. Now not only do you have an extra mess to clean up, but also every such accident will make housetraining harder.

Then there's the problem I mentioned in the questionnaire on p. 11—very young children don't clearly understand that other beings have feelings and needs. (Puppies obviously don't, either.) I was once called to a household where the 10-week-old puppy was growling at the children. They were very nice children, but they did not understand that a sleeping puppy needs his rest. The puppy wasn't a bad puppy; he was *exhausted*. And exhaustion had brought him to the point where now, at just 10 weeks, he had "aggression toward approaching children" in his behavioral repertoire.[*]

Please: Either don't get a dog till Junior's old enough to regulate much of his own behavior, or get a middle-aged dog who is housetrained, doesn't need an hour of off-leash aerobic exercise every morning before breakfast, and utterly adores children and also will go take a nap in the master bedroom instead of trying to grab their ankles when they play tag.

While I'm at it, get a medium-size or larger dog. Yes, yes, small person, small dog, very cute. A small, breakable dog combined with a small, active child can all too easily lead to a grouchy dog plus a child clutching his hand and crying, "He bit me!" or a dog with his leg in a cast plus a child crying, "Mommy, Daddy, I didn't mean to step on Scooter!" Or both. Sturdy, solid, adoring, unflappable: That's what you want in a children's dog. (P.S. "Adoring and unflappable" doesn't constitute a license for children to ride on the dog, pull his ears, or jump on his belly while he's sleeping.)

---

[*] The parents' failure to supervise and intervene was a problem here, obviously. But we might save a lip curl for the breeder who sold a puppy to a household with a four-year-old and a six-year-old where the parents had never had a dog before.

and who swears on her mother's grave that all except the current dog were non-barkers. Whenever I meet someone who has a Sheltie, I tell them about this woman, because I enjoy hearing their bitter laugh.

3. I mention all these breeds as points of reference, not because I believe you should focus your search on pedigreed dogs. Whether a dog's a mixed-breed or a registered Byelorussian Flapdoodle tells you absolutely nothing about her physical or behavioral health or whether you'd enjoy living with each other.*

WANT A QUIET DOG?

Get a Sheltie! (No, no, that was a joke. See a few paragraphs back.) Terriers generally bark a lot; so do Shetland Sheepdogs, Miniature Pinschers, Miniature Schnauzers, and German Shepherd Dogs. Northern-breed dogs (Malamutes, Huskies) yodel. Hounds and Beagles really do howl. It is hard to find a dog that doesn't bark some of the time, but Basenjis are reputedly "barkless." Excitable, playful dogs may bark more than average.

WANT A SUPER-BONDED, SUPER-INTERACTIVE, AFFECTIONATE DOG?

There is a T-shirt that says "Free Tongue Bath. See Pit Bull for Details." Akitas, Shiba Inus, and other Asian breeds are generally not so affectionate, although the other day I met a Tosa Inu who lives for the lap. Most of the Poodles I've met, of all sizes, seem strongly engaged with their people. Ditto a lot of the herding breeds (less so the Cattle Dogs).

Human-oriented dogs tend to be easier for most of us to train than dogs originally bred to work independently and at a distance. (But breed descriptions often need decoding—more about that below.)

If you picture yourself cuddling a small dog, remind yourself repeatedly that "small" and "cuddly" aren't equivalents (a lot of popular terriers are small; Lhasa Apsos were bred as guard dogs and are exactly as cuddly as you might expect a guard dog to be). Pugs are usually friendly, and Cavalier King Charles Spaniels have a rep as sweet-tempered dogs, borne out by the ones I've met. Small dogs in general seem to run to the snappish, but I suspect that's at least partly because people forget even cute dogs need personal space and downtime.

---

* Though, of course, the health records of an individual dog's parents and grandparents (etc.) will be revealing.

WANT TO RUN OR HIKE WITH YOUR DOG?

You can't run or hike with a brachycephalic (short-headed, short-nosed) dog or a dog with orthopedic or cardiac problems. Choose a young, lean, athletic dog with sound joints and a strong heart.

ARE GROOMING AND DROOL AN ISSUE FOR YOU?

Most dogs shed seasonally, but Northern breeds and other double-coated dogs shed like the dickens. You will be able to build entire new dogs out of what you find in your vacuum cleaner bag. Long or wiry coat = needs careful grooming: Poodles, Airedales, Rough Collies, Maltese, Shih Tzus . . . Short-coated dogs shed dirt more readily than heavy-coated dogs. Dogs with hairy ear canals, such as Cocker Spaniels, need special care as they are prone to infections (and infections hurt, and pain makes dogs crabby).

Mastiffs, St. Bernards, and other jowly dogs drool. A lot. *Really* a lot.

DO YOU HAVE PLENTY OF MONEY?

If not, stay away from breeds with long lists of pervasive health problems. See the discussion of pedigreed dogs' health, below.

DO YOU HAVE OTHER PETS?

If so, you need a dog who's animal friendly, or who can easily be taught to accept other nonhuman household members. Terriers were bred to chase and kill small furries; the various retrievers were bred to pick them (and birds!) up and bring them to you; Pit Bulls, Akitas, Chows, and terriers in general are often prone to fight with other dogs. Individuals vary, and plenty of people live with multiple dogs of these breeds and their mixes, as well as with cats and predatory dogs, but expect to have to do some work to keep everybody safe.

WHERE DO YOU LIVE?

Not just city versus country, but hot versus cold. If you live in a warm climate, be aware that to keep a brachycephalic dog comfortable, or in the hottest weather even alive, you may need to run the air conditioning 24/7, 365 days a year. Northern-breed dogs and Newfoundlands aren't crazy about hot summers, either.

At the other end of the spectrum, your Chihuahua or other tiny dog will not enjoy the great outdoors in Minneapolis in February. (Tiny dogs are not being wimps; they have a harder time maintaining body heat than big dogs.) Plan on housetraining to a litter box or pee pad as well as to the outside. Bigger dogs with short coats and no undercoat suffer in cold weather, too. Buy your Pit Bull a nice jacket.

REALIZE FANTASY IS JUST THAT: FANTASY

When you've got an idea of your dream dog's personality, activity level, and age, and how much you can or can't stand dealing with regular grooming, it's time to take a deep breath and step back. *You will not get your dream dog.* You will get a real dog. The real dog may be quite a lot like your dream dog, and with care and a bit of luck he or she won't come with any dealbreakers. What she also won't be is a perfect match for your fantasies. And a real dog can't get everything right every single minute of every day any more than our family and friends can. I know a woman who hired a trainer to teach her new dog to run to a certain chair and look out the window from it because that's what her old dog used to do. Try to avoid this trap: Your dog will be an individual. In some ways, she may be just what you expected; in others, she'll surprise you, for good and probably for ill.

PUNCH LINE
Once you know and love a dog, you often learn to enjoy qualities that weren't on your short list of "Gee, how fun." I'm just sayin'.

What If You're Looking for a Particular Breed?

Many people try to match their hopes with a specific breed of dog. As I mentioned earlier, this isn't a bad strategy: Breeds do differ behaviorally.

However, beware the official breed standard, which you can find on the Web site of the American Kennel Club.[1] Looking more or less at random through the descriptions offered for several breeds, I found words like "aristocrat," "fastidious," "free and merry." As applied to a dog, what do these terms mean? They don't even come from the "Temperament" section of the standard, which is supposed to describe the breed's personality and behavioral inclinations—and which is invariably shorter than the list of permissible color variations. There are breed standards that include no "Temperament" section at all.* This tells you something about the breed clubs' priorities.

Sometimes you can glean clues to breed-typical behavior from the "Meet the Breed" section at the top of each breed's page at the AKC site. The breed *standard* for the Lhasa Apso, for instance, has no "Temperament" section, but under "Meet the Breed" you learn that Lhasas, bred as "indoor watchdogs," "can be suspicious with strangers, so early socialization is critical." Oh, how true. But, like the breed standard, "Meet the Breed" sections don't always tell you all you need to know. For instance, English Springer Spaniels in the United States are plagued by aggression, apparently the heritage of a single popular sire.[2] You will not find this information on the AKC's breed page (or, for that matter, on most ESS Web sites).

Where else can you look for information? The national breed clubs maintain Web sites, and—surprise!—they too are a mixed bag informationally. Breed aficionados often seem to have a lot invested in thinking their breed is unique, and not only in its looks. The Dachshund Club of America, for instance, is pleased to inform you that Dachsies do something "peculiar": they like to "roll around in smelly things."[3] Remarkable! So my Juniper, who weighs 80 pounds and whose mama sure did look an awful lot like a Pit Bull, must be a Dachshund after all. (I don't mean to pick on the DCA, because, believe me, they aren't alone.) Do read what breed people have to say about their dogs, but take with a grain of salt any suggestion that X breed is like no other.

(Also oddly, as much as breed aficionados know about their breed, they often don't know much about modern training. Any number of clients have come to me about some training issue or behavior problem, having first consulted the breeder and gotten terrible advice of the "Show him who's boss" variety.)

Yet another possible source of information: breed rescue groups. For my money, the question to ask is "What are the most common reasons dogs of your breed lose their homes?" The answer you get will reflect someone's personal experience rather than a carefully conducted longitudinal survey, but it may be quite useful. "Because people get X breed and can't keep up with their energy" gives you a good strong hint about X breed's activity level.

---

* Kerry Blue Terrier, for one, on the AKC site.

Dog Labels to Watch Out For

Quick and Dirty Tip

Certain breeds are often characterized as "stubborn" or "willful." These terms reflect the sordid history of force-based dog training (for more about that, see Chapter 3, "Anything but 'Obedience'"). You can take them to signify that the dog isn't easily motivated by praise and may fight back when jerked by the neck. Many of the so-called stubborn breeds were historically intended for dangerous work such as going after rats in their dens. How astonishing that they came out tough and independent. You can train them, all right, but you'll do a lot better working with instead of against them, finding ways to reward them rather than being locked in a cycle of "disobedience" and "correction."

I need to put in a word here for German Shepherd Dogs, of whom it's said ad nauseam that they "need a firm hand." GSDs, in my experience, run to the sensitive and easily damaged. Nothing is easier than to make them spooky, and harshness only makes them spookier. Be gentle, consistent, and clear—good advice for any dog.

Finally, keep a sharp eye out for euphemism. In everyday life, "reserved" means "not effusive till she gets to know you," but when it's used in breed descriptions it can mean "will never make friends with anyone she didn't know before she was twelve weeks old." A dog like that makes it tough to have dinner guests.

Talk to people who actually have dogs of the breed you're interested in—not just breeders, not just people who compete avidly in dog sports, but ordinary people who have pets. As a template for your interview, you can use the questions I suggested asking yourself. What's life like with a dog of such-and-such a breed? And here's an info source you may never have thought of: a behaviorally knowledgeable vet or vet tech. My vet-tech friend Jessica has a list of breeds she will not handle unless they're muzzled.* As she's the first to say, it's not that every dog of that breed has a bite history, or even a history of aggression at the vet's. Plenty of those dogs live peacefully with their families, too. But in her (personal, limited, unscientific) experience, the breeds on her list

---

* Pit Bulls aren't on it.

are the ones likeliest to respond with aggression when restrained or handled invasively by strangers.

As for the many commercial Web sites that list a bajillion breeds and their "designer" crosses: Just. Please. Don't. Waste. Your. Time. If there is such a site that provides accurate information and isn't a vehicle for puppy-mill Web sales, I haven't found it. (And the training and behavior sections are usually dire.)

A Word of Caution About "Purebred" Dogs[4]

Many of us think about dogs automatically in terms of breed—even discussions of random-bred dogs and shelter dogs always refer to the breeds or breed groups they might be mixes of. The whole section you just read relates dogs' needs and behavior to the needs and behavior of dogs who belong to identifiable breeds. So what do we mean when we talk about "purebreds"? This hardly ever seems to be discussed, but it has huge implications for your choice of dog.

The modern dog breeds recognized by the American Kennel Club, which is most of the breeds you're likely to run into, have one thing in common: a closed stud book. That is, if Dogalini is to be considered a member of the breed, both her parents must also have been members of the breed; and if they were members of the breed, then their parents, Dogalini's grandparents, must also have been members of the breed; and so on. This is a big fat problem.

A closed stud book means a limited number of potential mates. When the circle of dogs with whom a given dog may mate is limited, the odds go up that animals bearing deleterious recessive traits will mate with others who bear the same gene and produce offspring. (This happens in humans, too, of course, which is why researchers who study rare genetic diseases gravitate toward the small, isolated groups where such illnesses crop up more often.) Look up any breed you can name, and you'll find a list of genetically linked disorders prevalent in that breed. This didn't just happen; it's the inevitable result of breeding in a closed population. In some breeds the list of disorders is dozens of items long.[5]

Conscientious dog breeders' answer to this problem has mostly been to support research into screening for genetic disorders and not to breed animals that bear "bad" genes. But although it's good to avoid perpetuating genetic disorders, cutting those animals out of the gene pool has a downside: You lose not only their problem genes but also all the rest of their genetic material. Remember, this is in a closed gene pool, so whenever you cut out *all* the genes of a given animal, you're also losing some of that gene pool's already limited diversity. And, thanks to sperm storage and artificial insemination, one male dog can sire any number of puppies, even years after his own death. All those puppies are at least half siblings—if they share any grandparents, they're more closely related still.

The result of all that is rapid shrinkage in effective population size, a measure of genetic diversity. A 2008 study in the UK reported that the effective population size among Chows, Rough Collies, English Bulldogs, Golden Retrievers, and several other breeds was *under 100* although the actual populations of these breeds ranged from 1,060 to 703,566.[6] The smaller the effective population size, the more genetically similar the breed's members are. With a small enough effective population, the members of the breed are nearly clones.[7] This is a dangerous state of affairs; here's why.

First, in some breeds the dogs are so close to identical that it's hard to find *any at all* who don't carry a dangerous gene. All registered Dalmatians in both the UK and the United States, for example, carry a mutation that puts them at risk for urate bladder stones, which cause abdominal pain and if uncontrollable will require euthanasia.

Second, suppose a dangerous pathogen comes along. It reaches two groups, each of which includes a thousand dogs. Group A has a lot of genetic variability; in Group B, the dogs are all genetically quite similar. The odds are that some dogs in Group A will be able to resist the pathogen and recover from the illness, because in all that variability there will be a gene that confers at least partial protection. As for Group B, the odds are that none of them will have any gene that's protective. Bye-bye, Group B.

Some breeders have begun outcrossing their dogs—breeding their dogs with others from related groups, to bring in some genetic diversity. This is the only scientifically credible response to the "clone problem," but breed clubs fight it tooth and nail because outcrossed dogs are no longer "pure."[8]

SINGLE-TRAIT BREEDING

Health problems in pedigreed dogs also arise from what's called "single-trait breeding." Suppose you have a town full of people whose reproduction you can control, and you really like redheads, so you allow only the redheads to have children. Hey presto, a couple of generations go by and you've got a town full of redheads. But your new redheaded population will also have another trait you weren't intentionally choosing for: Most will have very fair skin. As a result, they'll be more prone to sunburn and to skin cancer. So in selecting for one trait, you've also increased the odds that your redheads will get sick in a specific way (which may, or, like skin cancer, may not be directly genetic).

There are many analogies in dog breeding. For instance, if you breed dogs to have flat heads and short noses, the way English Bulldogs do, your dogs will also have deep wrinkles in their facial skin, and it turns out that those wrinkles harbor infection and get itchy and sore. (Shar-peis have similar problems.) If you breed dogs to have long floppy ears with thick hair on the inside, they'll be more prone to ear infections. Dachshunds, bred to be long and low, are technically congenital dwarfs, and many of them suffer from intervertebral disk disease, which can paralyze them permanently. Dachshunds account for 45 percent to 70 percent of cases of this disease.[9] Roughly speaking, the more a breed diverges from the size and shape of the basic dog body (a Dingo is a good example of a basic dog), the more physical problems it's likely to have. So what's the answer? It's unfortunately more complicated than you may think.

Breeds to Think Twice About

Quick and Dirty Tip

I would never "ban a breed." But I hope I can persuade you not to choose one of the brachycephalic types—English and French Bulldogs and Pugs are the most popular right now. Many of us find those flat faces and pop eyes cute, but the feeling lasts only as long as you're not aware of how much the dogs suffer for that look. Imagine spending your whole life short of breath or close to it; that's what many of these dogs experience. They may suffer from cleft palate, narrowed nostrils, and tracheal hypoplasia, a condition in which their windpipes are so narrow they struggle for every breath. This is to say nothing of their orthopedic, skin, and digestive problems, or how vulnerable they are to heatstroke because they can't cool themselves effectively by panting.[10]

Should You Just Get a Mixed-Breed Dog?

After reading about all the health problems of "purebred" dogs, you might think the obvious response is to get a mixed-breed. And there is evidence that, in general, mixed-breed dogs are healthier.[11] But general statistics can't predict the health of an individual dog. Mixed-breed dogs aren't immune to genetically linked disorders. And factors other than genetics are at work. Early malnutrition can damage the health of a dog with the strongest genetic makeup. Puppies whose mothers had a rough time during pregnancy (from life as a stray, for example) may suffer behaviorally from the stress-hormone bath they enjoyed in utero.[12]

So the answer isn't as simple as "Adopt a mixed-breed dog." (Though I certainly will support that decision!) Many factors contribute to the overall health of your prospective dog, and the more you educate yourself about them, the better your dog's chances of living a long and happy life. In considering what breed you want, remember that dogs live and suffer inside those exotic, aesthetically fascinating bodies that don't function so well. If you must have a pedigreed dog, please make a thoughtful choice, not only of what breed you want, but about where you get her.

Should You Get a Dog from a Breeder?

One option is to get a dog directly from a breeder. But which breeder? I'm sure it's abundantly clear from the foregoing that a dog's registration with the AKC (or the UKC, or any other body) is no guarantee of anything. Every last pet store puppy comes from a puppy mill—a breeder!—and every last one is registered.*

When choosing a breeder, I'd be wary of one whose dogs competed only in conformation shows, like Westminster and Crufts. Conformation is a beauty contest; breeding for narrow and exaggerated criteria is part and parcel of what got pedigreed dogs into so much trouble. It's a much better idea to look for a breeder whose dogs participate in activi-

---

* The pet store staff may try to tell you they don't source from puppy mills. Laugh in their faces. It's important to note, by the way, that many ethical pet-supply shops provide space to local rescue groups or host on-site adoption events. This is a good thing, although rescue groups also vary in quality.

ties, such as agility and herding, that require actual physical function-ality. Be aware, though, that if a breed is more or less divided into working lines and show lines, the working-line dogs are often more intense and energetic.

SIGNS OF A GOOD DOG BREEDER

As I mentioned earlier, a good breeder will perform available genetic and other health tests before breeding a dog. She knows her breed's history and health like the back of her hand; she won't breed dogs known to carry heritable disorders, nor will she breed shy or aggressive dogs. However, as I've explained, this alone won't get pedigreed dogs out of the genetic health trap they're in. So the breeder gets a gold star if she supports outcrossing to increase genetic diversity and reduce or eliminate heritable health problems.

It's not easy for one person to develop a deep expertise about many breeds, so a good breeder specializes in a single breed or maybe, *maybe* two. Run, run, run from the fellow who advertises six varieties of dog and all their mixes as well.*

Pregnancy, whelping, and nursing all tax the mother dog's body. A good breeder will limit the number of times he breeds a bitch—many will breed a female only two or three times over her whole life. The puppies will be raised in the breeder's home and he'll see to it that they are appropriately socialized. (Livestock guardians intended for work are an exception to this rule—they will grow up with their flock. But you're not getting a livestock guardian as a family pet, anyway.) A good breeder provides pleasant experiences of household life, various people and animals, and all kinds of sounds, sights, and textures. Even tiny puppies are learning machines, so the best breeders start reward-based training of manners behaviors by the time the puppies are a few weeks old.

The care and time involved in raising puppies, and the limits of what can be asked of a female dog's body, mean you'll probably have to

---

* Cockapoos, Labradoodles, Goldendoodles, Chorkies, and so on are simply mixed-breeds. The genetics are beyond my ability to explain, but, in a nutshell, the difference is this. If you breed, say, Border Collies for generation after generation, you get dogs that look and act like Border Collies. The various kinds of "designer dogs" don't breed true in this way (though some breeders are trying to produce a Labradoodle that does). To call these dogs "pure" breeds constitutes deceptive marketing. Okay, it's deceptive marketing of a concept ("breed purity") that's suspect to begin with, but still.

wait a while for a puppy. A good breeder probably won't plan a breeding until she has homes waiting for as many puppies as the litter is likely to include. And you will not get a puppy from her by sending her an e-mail and plugging your credit card information into PayPal. She'll want to meet you, and she'll want answers to many questions about your life, your house or apartment, your landlord if you have one, what exercise and training you plan to give the dog, how much experience you have with dogs, and what drew you to her breed. She'll make you agree in writing to return your dog if things don't work out. She may even choose a puppy for you, because she's the one who knows the litter best. I was once contacted by a breeder who refused to sell a perfectly nice but inexperienced woman a puppy unless the woman agreed to hire a reward-based trainer to work with her. Color me awestruck.

A good breeder will encourage you to visit the puppy in the weeks before he's ready to leave his litter. Which is fine, because you'll also want to visit the breeder, especially if you found her on the Internet. Probably most people know that all puppies sold in pet stores come from puppy mills, but many haven't caught on that anybody can put up a pretty Web site with stock photos of home-reared puppies. Go in person to make sure the reality matches. It's a red flag if the breeder will ship you a puppy without meeting you. Same goes if she asks all the right questions but discourages a visit and instead offers to rendezvous in a convenient parking lot halfway between your homes, where she'll hand over the puppy of your dreams.

It's often said that you should meet both parents of the puppy you want. Do it if you can, but you may not be able to: The sire may be owned by someone other than the breeder who has the dam. But if you're warned away from the mother dog, or she's mysteriously unavailable, go elsewhere. Temperament is to a large extent heritable.[13] An aggressive mother certainly *can* produce nice pups, but why lower your odds of getting a friendly companion? Besides, the person who has bred an aggressive dog is not someone whose work you want to support.

HOW TO FIND A GOOD BREEDER

Plug into a search engine the name of your breed, plus "breeders," and you will be brought to despair at the bajillion hits on obvious puppy brokerages and puppy mills. You can cut through the commercial noise a couple of ways. The American Kennel Club's Web site includes informational pages (of limited use, as I explained above) on all AKC breeds, with links to each breed's national club. In turn, the breed club's site will include a breeder referral page. The breed clubs have codes of ethics that members subscribe to, so this supplies an initial filter for your search.*

A second source of breeder referrals is word of mouth. This could mean your neighbor who has a nice dog, though nice dogs surprisingly often come from unpromising sources. But make it a point to talk to people who participate in formal obedience, agility, herding competitions, and the like.

Finally, there's my preferred route. Get in touch with breed rescue groups (search on your breed's name plus "rescue," or find rescue groups through the breed club's site). Ask to be put in touch with breeders who always take responsibility for relinquished dogs that turn out to have been bred by them. Better yet, talk to the breeders who participate actively in rescue work. And find out, if you can, which breeders *don't* take back their dogs. The ones who do are the ones who really care. You'll still have to verify the breeder's expertise, of course.

If you buy from a pet store, an Internet broker, or anybody who breeds to score beauty pageant prizes or to make a few bucks, you're supporting the suffering of animals exactly like the companion you love. Yes, it's a project to find a really good breeder. And the odds are high you won't get a puppy tomorrow or next week. Some legwork and patience are a small price to pay if you want a puppy from someone who genuinely cares about dogs' welfare.

---

* But the code of ethics may not be all that ethical. For example, the ridge is the most distinctive feature of the Rhodesian Ridgeback breed, but associated with it is a condition called dermoid sinus, itself related to spina bifida. Dermoid sinus is rare or nonexistent in Ridgeback puppies who are born without the ridge. In the UK, the breed club code of ethics used to call for ridgeless puppies to be culled— that is, killed. In the United States, the breed club code of ethics (http://www.rrcus.org/club/clubinfo/COE2010.pdf) doesn't require the killing of ridgeless puppies but leaves this decision up to the breeder: "When puppies with serious defects or faults (Dermoid Sinus, ridgelessness) are sold rather than culled, the breeder must take the extra responsibility to see that the dog is spayed or neutered." In other words, the U.S. breed club's ethical code *permits the killing of healthy puppies because they don't meet a cosmetic standard that is itself associated with a serious health condition.*

The Dalmatian Club of America takes the position that all deaf Dalmatian puppies should be euthanized. The club's statement claims (supplying no evidence) that deaf dogs are "hard to raise" and "often become snappish or overly aggressive" (http://www.thedca.org/deafi.html). If you have a deaf dog, visit this book's Web site, www.TheDogTrainerBook.com, for further resources.

Your Guiding Principle for Choosing a Breeder *Quick and Dirty Tip*

At every stage, ask yourself whether the breeder is behaving the way you would behave if you cared about the puppies you produced and you wanted them to enjoy healthy, happy lives. If the breeder's policies and actions don't reflect such loving-kindness, go elsewhere.

Should You Get a Dog from a Shelter or Rescue Group?

Adopting a rescue animal is a good deed—and, honestly, my preferred option. Do it with your eyes wide open. Petfinder lists hundreds and hundreds of groups; some are wonderful, some shockingly lax in their policies. Adopt from a careful, responsible organization that works to make good matches between people and pets.

Many people turn up their noses at "kill shelters" and prefer to adopt from facilities that call themselves "no-kill." Several million animals are euthanized in U.S. shelters every year.[14] That isn't because the staff of so-called kill shelters are bloodthirsty maniacs. Some animals are desperately sick or badly injured. Some present behavior problems; more about that below. And some die because the shelter is full and there aren't enough adopters. The municipal shelters and animal control authorities that must take every animal brought to them—call them full-service shelters—don't have the resources to keep animals indefinitely.

Besides, life in a shelter, even a modern, well-funded shelter, is stressful and lonely. An animal may start out friendly and calm but grow behaviorally disturbed as time goes by, even to the point where keeping her alive stops being kind. Euthanasia rates have declined in recent decades, but they remain the downstream result of animal-related problems too big for a single shelter to resolve.

"No-kill" isn't a very good descriptor, either. Resources are always finite, so a shelter or rescue can't be no-kill *and* accept every animal brought to it *and* provide adequate space and attention for all of them. A no-kill shelter has to limit the number of animals it takes in. Or it has to put an asterisk after "no-kill," with a footnote saying "except for sick animals and those with behavior problems." Or it has to adopt dogs out without worrying too much about whether the match is a good one and what will become of the dogs and humans a year down the line. Or it has to warehouse animals regardless of their mental health and whether it's possible to give good care. Some animal hoarders may get started this way. A rescue group may reasonably decide it can help only *x* number of animals. But somebody, somewhere, has to deal with the rest.

So you're not looking for a shelter or rescue group that wears any particular label. Instead, you want to see people doing their best to figure out which dogs can safely be adopted and which dogs and people will suit each other well. While the dog's in their care, they'll work to keep her behaviorally healthy and maybe teach her manners, to make her even more welcome in her future home.

DOG BEHAVIOR EVALUATIONS

Shelters and rescues should use formal behavior evaluations (sometimes called "temperament tests") to judge which dogs can't safely be adopted. Most groups that do this use one of several well-known procedures, or a variation on them.[15] Evaluators should be trained and the results of their assessments should periodically be compared against the results of other experienced evaluators. That helps prevent eccentric judgments.

Some aspects of an evaluation reflect normal human interaction with a dog. Others purposely try to push common dog buttons. For instance, an assessment might start with the evaluator just standing outside the dog's kennel, looking at the dog. It's worrisome if the dog reacts to such benign human behavior by throwing herself against the wire and snarling. Later steps involve various kinds of handling, such as wiping her paws and looking in her ears. How does she respond to a human who takes her by surprise? What happens if a human inflicts minor pain, such as a pinch on the flank? Evaluators also try to learn whether the dog gets unmanageably excited or starts biting hard when people play with her.

A biggie is the dog's response to people touching him while he eats, sticking a (fake) hand in his food bowl, and trying to take away a super-valuable chew such as a pig ear. For me, this is often the heartbreaker. A dog may behave affectionately and sociably right up until that fake hand touches her bowl, and then—Cujo.

Many skeptics about behavior evaluation point out that shelter dogs are under stress and that former street dogs may have been chronically hungry for a time. The hole in this argument is that any life includes stress. Certainly it's possible that the dog who leaps at the fake hand and bites it five times wouldn't so much as growl at a human messing with his food bowl if he were living in that human's home. So why not place such a dog in an experienced home with no young children and a rehabilitation plan? Because visitors happen, and kids running up to the dog on the street happen, and getting casual about prevention happens when weeks and months go by with no aggressive incidents. Also bear in mind that dogs with no behavior problems, or only mild ones, die every day for lack of homes.

Of course, evaluations can't guarantee that a dog won't bite. One study found that they can miss territorial aggression, predatory aggression, and dog-dog aggression, in particular.[16] But in another study that compared assessment results with the dogs' known histories, the two matched up pretty well.[17] The rate at which adopted dogs are returned for biting drops when evaluations are properly taught and used.[18] The cold fact is that using behavior as a yardstick, however imperfect, beats making life-and-death decisions on the basis of cuteness.

REMEMBER YOUR DEALBREAKERS

So you're at a shelter, or you're looking at the Web site of a rescue, and they do careful behavior evaluations. Sorry! Still not done! Not every dog adoptable by *someone* is adoptable by you. Remember your dream dog and know your dealbreakers. A super-energetic adolescent probably won't suit a couple with two-year-old human twins. That family already has enough to keep it busy. On the other hand, if you have a blast teaching tricks, you might loooooove a quick, clever dog who would drive most normal people nuts.

Extra points, then, to shelters and rescue groups that steer dogs and people together by personality. Is this dog barky or quiet? Is he focused mainly on people or on other dogs or on that squirrel down the block? Is she cuddly? Does she live for fetch? Many shelters use the ASPCA's Meet Your Match program, which puts each dog in one of three personality categories. A rescue group that cares for dogs in foster homes may be able to give all kinds of detail about your possible dog. Word to the wise, though: Not everyone who fosters dogs has a sophisticated understanding of their behavior. Every so often I hear a fosterer say, for instance, that a dog is "alpha" when what she means is that he barks and lunges at other dogs. Go for those nuggets of actual observed behavior.

Pet Stores: Just Say No

You'll find no section in this chapter on choosing a good pet store. That's because you should never buy a dog (or any other animal) from one. Ever. The pet store people have learned that their customers want to avoid supporting the detestable puppy-mill industry, so lots of them put up signs saying something like "The puppies in this store come from breeders." Well, yeah, they do. Puppy millers breed dogs. Puppy millers are breeders. So pet-store puppies come from breeders. They just don't come from good breeders.

If you think about this for five seconds, it becomes blindingly obvious. Would someone who gave a rat's patoot about his puppies sell them to a pet store, where they could then be sold on to anybody with a credit card? One more time: Just say no.

Still tempted? Visit Google Images and plug in "puppy mills" as your search term. That's the industry your purchase will help support.

When Should You Get a New Dog?

I would be remiss if I didn't include a section in this chapter on the best time to bring a new dog home. If you're tempted to give a puppy or dog as a holiday or surprise gift, don't. Regardless of a puppy's exact age, you must meet certain needs if he's to have the best chance of growing into a beloved and friendly companion. Housetraining, for one. Many young dogs lose their homes because they've never clearly learned where pee and poop should go.

Now, the key to housetraining success is to confine or diligently supervise your puppy in between frequent toilet breaks. (See Chapter 4, "Housetraining," for a detailed plan.) The ideal is that your puppy never has a chance to eliminate in the wrong place. For the youngest puppies, "frequent" may mean "hourly" whenever the puppy is awake.

Wait, there's more! Excitement and activity—you know, like what goes on during holidays?—get that puppy bladder and bowel zipping right along. Furthermore, up to the age of about four months, your puppy will likely need an overnight outing as well. That is all sounding so compatible with going to Grandma's house, and having the neighbors over for eggnog, and staying up late to assemble the . . . something or other. Isn't it?

And oh yes—did I mention that the more times your puppy eliminates where you don't want him to, the harder it will be for him to learn what you do want?

Additionally, puppy socialization is harder during the holidays. If I could get every adopter to do two things for their pup, careful housetraining would be second. Good socialization would be first. You can pretty much always repair a dog's bad manners, but when behavior problems—chiefly fearfulness and aggression—are caused by poor socialization, they cannot be undone. That's as close to an absolute statement as any behavior specialist is likely to make. But, you might object, the holidays are an ideal time to socialize a pup. All kinds of people come over. The puppy experiences varied sights and sounds. She'll just naturally be well socialized, right?

The catch is that appropriate socialization is pleasant and relaxed. (See the next chapter for a detailed discussion and how-to.) Holidays mean hustle and bustle and overexcited, overstressed people—I'm not just looking at the kiddies here! Many puppies, especially those who aren't the boldest in the bunch, can feel overwhelmed. Uncle Jack is feeling his eggnog and practicing the Scottish reel, you and your sister are having a screaming fight over who should have inherited Aunt Minerva's cameos, and while nobody's looking, the neighbor's four-year-old decides to experiment with lengthening Baby Dogalini's tail.

Yes, I know, I'm piling it on. But don't you sometimes feel a bit frayed by the time New Year's rolls around? Puppies need rest and quiet as well as play and engagement. They should meet the wide world enjoyably and be encouraged to explore—not be swamped by Grand Central Station in the living room.

So when's the best time to get a new dog? One aspect of a good time to get a dog is that it comes *after* you done plenty of preparation—read this book and others, found a vet, gotten your dog supplies ready, and agreed on who's got responsibility for what aspect of your new friend's care.

Assuming all the adults in the household have full-time jobs, a vacation week might be a good occasion to bring Dogalini home—you'll be well able to focus on housetraining, if necessary, and on early manners training. Just remember to incorporate some alone time into your new dog's early experiences of life (or of life with you). That way, your return to work won't come as a rude shock, which could precipitate separation anxiety.

Dogs As Holiday Gifts

Quick and Dirty Tip

Choose a dog bed, chew toys, bowls, leashes, and whatever other doggy paraphernalia suits your fancy. (See the checklist below.) And write your kids an IOU good for one grown-up, child-adoring dog. That's what goes under the tree. Choose and bring home the dog herself at a more appropriate time.

What Do You Need Before Picking Your Dog Up?

You've thought through what kind of dog will fit in well in your household, and you've amazingly been matched with just that dog at a reputable shelter. Before bringing him home, make sure you've got the following equipment:

- ❏ a flat buckle collar, a martingale collar, or a front-clip harness (or, hey, all three!)
- ❏ an ID tag with your phone number on it (if you haven't named your dog yet, use a temporary tag)
- ❏ a six-foot leash (cotton is more comfortable to hold than nylon, but less durable; leather is most comfortable and durable, so choose leather unless you have ethical objections)
- ❏ the best dog bed you can afford
- ❏ stainless steel or perhaps ceramic dog bowls. Don't waste your money on plastic bowls.
- ❏ an appropriate-size crate (see the crate-training section in Chapter 2, "Socialization").
- ❏ a starter supply of whatever food your dog's been eating, plus whatever food you plan to use

You may also want an ex-pen (essentially, a canine playpen) or baby gates, especially if you're bringing home a puppy.

How to Choose a Good Veterinarian

Just as you select a pediatrician before your child is born, select a vet before you bring your dog or puppy home. You and I are laypeople.

We don't know how to assess a veterinarian's breadth and depth of knowledge or her creativity or ability to do the detective work needed to diagnose illness in a patient who can't speak for himself. If you don't already have a connection with a vet you trust, here are some points to consider in choosing one.

Ask for a tour. Call in advance and explain that you're a prospective client. If they're too busy at the moment, set up a time that's convenient for them. If they won't give you a tour at all, forget it.

Your tour should include the surgical room or suite; this should be a separate space, it should be clean, the door should be closed, the space should not be used for storage, and you shouldn't find an office cat hanging out inside. If there's a surgery taking place, you can't go in, of course, but take the opportunity to get a sense of how careful the practice is about sterile procedure. Full gown, mask, and gloves, please, not just a scrub top. And there should be an assistant working with the surgeon.

Check credentials. It's nice if a facility billing itself as an animal hospital is, in fact, accredited by the American Animal Hospital Association. The office will probably post the certificate; if you don't see it, ask.

Diplomas are nice. A very suspicious person could get in touch with the vet school or specialty association, too.

Ask about pain management. Once upon a time, in the Dark Ages, vets used to not give pain meds because pain would supposedly keep the animal quiet after surgery. Notice I mention that was the Dark Ages. Good pain control speeds recovery and helps prevent certain complications, for animals both human and nonhuman.* If the practice you're considering isn't up to speed on this issue, run away screaming.

Is the whole place clean? This is so obvious I almost feel silly including it, but check anyway. Sick animals do have accidents, but the place shouldn't reek.

Is the staff courteous? Look for a pattern, since everybody has a bad day.

Ask for referrals from people you know. They're probably not experts any more than you are, but they can tell you about how gentle the

---

* For the benefits of pain control in humans, see "Pain Control After Surgery," on the Cleveland Clinic Web site: http://bit.ly/muTzxN. For veterinary pain management, see this page on the Cornell University College of Veterinary Medicine site: http://bit.ly/iRqj55.

vet and the techs are, whether the office returns calls promptly, how good the vet is at explaining things . . .

Is the vet a know-it-all? Nothing warms the cockles of my heart like a professional who sometimes says, "I'm not sure. Let me look that up and get back to you." If there's a vet school or specialty clinic nearby, you want to hear that your prospective vet may refer complex or specialized cases to them. (And you might ask that vet school or specialty practice for a referral to a general-practice vet.)

Online reviews may be helpful, but some angry people get very angry indeed, and not always for good reason. People can be unreasonably biased in favor of a professional, as well. And it's not easy to know the source of a review—who's behind that screen name?

Ask about options for overnight care of hospitalized animals. The hospital may have a tech on staff for this, or may pay one as needed. Leaving hospitalized animals alone overnight is a dealbreaker.

Bear in mind that vet school costs as much as med school does and that veterinary equipment and medications cost exactly what their human equivalents do. Surgery to repair your dog's anterior cruciate ligament tear takes the same time and expertise that the same surgery would take if performed on you. Et cetera. Some health conditions get very, very expensive to treat, to the point where money is an issue for most people. Please discuss money frankly with your vet; if she wants a test or a treatment whose cost makes you flinch, let her know, and have an honest discussion about the alternatives. But don't assume that that expensive test is an attempt to fleece you, please.

Having been put through the wringer of how to choose a dog, get ready for the Dog Guardian's First Commandment:

Thou Shalt Socialize Properly.

That's up next.

Socialization

THE ONE THING TO DO IF YOU DO
NOTHING ELSE AT ALL

See that chapter title? I mean it. If all puppies everywhere got appropriate socialization, most of us behavior specialists would have to look
for a new line of work. Sure, we'd get the occasional case of difficulty
housetraining or separation anxiety or inborn shyness or aggression.
It's true that many of my clients with fearful or aggressive dogs don't
know their companions' early history. But check this out: Of the aggressive and shy dogs I have seen in nearly a decade of behavior work, I
can think offhand of *two* whose known history included decent early
socialization. (In both cases, there was strong reason to think that the
aggression was inherited.)

The revenue stream from undersocialized dogs is one that I would
really, really like to lose. Socialization is the dead easy, dirt cheap, and
essential route to a behaviorally healthy dog. No, it's not infallible. Yes,
some undersocialized dogs do adjust well to normal life. But failing to
socialize a puppy is a bit like leaving your umbrella home when the
forecaster mentions a 90 percent chance of rain. You can't quite bet the
farm on getting drenched, but . . .

What Is Puppy Socialization?

During what's called the "sensitive period" of very early life, puppies
learn about what's normal in the world. They're not immune to fear or
even trauma, but in general they accept whatever they have a pleasant
encounter with. It's almost as if they develop a catalog of sights, sounds,
smells, and experiences that fall under the heading of "safe." As a special bonus, if the range of pleasant early experiences is wide and varied,
the puppy also seems to learn that "new" does not necessarily mean
"scary."

For example, when I adopted my dog Juniper as an eight-and-a-half-week-old puppy, I socialized him carefully. But I lived in a walk-up apartment at the time, and one thing I forgot to introduce him to was elevators. I never gave them a thought till the first time Juni and I stayed in a hotel. He had a moment of surprise when the sliding doors closed and the little room started to move. Then his broad experience of the world kicked in to reassure him that this novel situation was okay. The same went for that huge, potentially suspect metal cart with our luggage on it.

The catch about socialization is that it's a window of opportunity and when it shuts, it *slams* shut. Different experts will give you different closing dates, ranging from 12 to 16 weeks old. Individual puppies will vary, too. I urge you to play it safe—socialize diligently from the minute you get your puppy home.

I'm betting you don't want to know the details of the isolation experiments done in the middle decades of the last century. Let's just say that puppies reared in isolation grew into shy, anxious adolescents and adults. Various studies find them avoiding human touch, freezing up in new situations and when subjected to frustration and stress, and ignoring or avoiding other dogs.[1] A lot of the dogs did improve after their release from isolation, but it's not clear how much. Unfortunately, the experiments were not only cruel but badly done; many details are left vague and the researchers seem rarely to have done any long-term follow-up.

My own experience, as I've mentioned, suggests that poor early socialization has lasting effects.* Without good socialization, your puppy will likely be shy and skittish as he grows up. And as he gains experience, he may learn, usually when he hits adolescence, that going on the offensive can drive away the things that frighten him. Enter my many clients with their lunging, snapping young dogs. The ones who had those dogs in puppyhood are all singing the same song: "He was really shy right up until a few months ago."

Badly socialized dogs seem brittle rather than flexible—they respond to change and novelty with fear, taking nothing in stride. They may do well in a familiar context, then fall apart when their family moves to a new home. I have worked with dogs who could not go outdoors in the daytime, when the streets were busy with people and noise. Other dogs could stand to walk outside, but only just—they slunk along

---

* Admittedly, since I work mostly with behavior problems, I don't see a whole lot of happy, confident dogs, and that means I don't learn as much about the life histories of those dogs.

with their tails down and pulled frantically toward home. Some barked and lunged at everything. There are no guarantees in life, so I can't promise you that high-quality early socialization will prevent a hundred percent of behavior problems a hundred percent of the time. But the odds of trouble do go way, way down.

An aside here about physical health. Some veterinarians, understandably concerned about the risks of infectious disease, advise adopters to keep their pups indoors till all vaccinations are complete. If that's your vet, direct him or her to the position statement on this issue by the American Veterinary Society of Animal Behavior.* The statement points out that behavior problems are the chief cause of death for dogs under three years old and that "the risk of infection [is] relatively small compared to the chance of death from a behavior problem." Puppies are somewhat protected by antibodies they got from their mothers and by their first set of vaccinations. Besides, good socialization doesn't require you to plop your pup on the ground and expose her to every dog and garbage pile on the street.

How to Socialize Your Puppy

At the end of this chapter you'll find a socialization checklist. Copy it or tear it out and check off each kind of experience. In fact, make sure you check off each kind of experience more than once. Take your puppy places—by car, in your arms, or in a child's wagon if she's too heavy to carry. Take her to a mall, to a hardware store, to the bus station, to a train station, on a train if possible. Take her to a gas station, auto body shop, florist. Step into the vet's waiting room and out again. Visit a park, a farm, a construction site, a police station. Encourage her to scramble among rocks and logs. Let her experience many surfaces underfoot, from grass to concrete to leaves to metal gratings. Teach her to use stairs, starting from the lowest step and working your way up till she can navigate a whole staircase comfortably, up and down.

Introduce your puppy to all the kinds of people in the world. Our country is still racially and culturally segregated. Many a client has confessed to me with embarrassment that his dog reacts strongly to people of races other than the client's own.[2] So make a special point of being multicultural. Carry some high-quality dry dog food. Encourage po-

---

* It's available at http://www.avsabonline.org, under "Position Statements."

lite children to stroke your puppy and feed him a treat. People who use wheelchairs and walkers, delivery truck drivers, bearded men with deep voices, nuns, homeless people collecting bottles from the street— none of these ordinary folks should be extraordinary to your dog.

The same goes for animals. A puppy who grows up knowing cats is less likely to treat them as prey when he grows up. If you live in the country, exposure to other domestic species may come easily; if you live in the city, work with what you've got—police horses can be viewed from a distance and paired with treats if your puppy is skittish about them. As for other dogs, screen them! Your puppy should meet dogs and puppies who you know *for a fact* are friendly and healthy. A well-run puppy manners class or play group will help. Avoid even well-managed dog parks until vaccinations are complete. (See the discussion of dog parks, coming up.)

Many dogs are afraid of unfamiliar sounds. Make sure your pup hears police sirens, fire trucks, the repetitive beep a truck makes when it's backing up. Birdsong, music, rolling steel gates, obnoxious ring-tones. Banging pots and pans, doorbells, intercoms. Gunfire and similar sharp, cracking sounds are often culprits in dog phobias; download free recordings from the Internet and play them as background music one day.

WHAT TO DO IF YOUR DOG GETS SCARED

Say you're introducing your puppy to a friend with dark glasses and a headdress, and your puppy shies away. Take a deep breath, relax, and let your puppy retreat. Ask your friend to sit down and ignore the puppy. Let your pup approach at his own pace, while your friend pays him no mind. Praise your puppy softly and warmly when he explores. You can click and treat (see Chapter 3, "Anything but 'Obedience,'" to learn how clicker training works) for looking at the Scary Person and for moving toward her, even a little bit. You can also encourage your puppy to play with you around the Scary Person, to help him associate her presence with fun. But avoid luring your puppy forward with food—it's important that he stay within his comfort zone. If he relaxes completely near your friend, she can offer him a treat; if that goes well, a scritch comes next. If your puppy remains a bit skittish, don't push. Instead, repeat the meeting later or another day.

Follow the same pattern for anything or anyone your puppy doesn't take in stride: Let him retreat to a distance where he feels safe, then

venture forward in his own good time. Praise and click/treat his brav-
ery, but do not lure.

If you find that your puppy is easily spooked in many circumstances
or by many kinds of people, speak with a behavior specialist right away.
Early behavior is often highly malleable, and the quicker you intervene
in any potential problems, the higher your odds of fixing them.

Are you cringing as you read because you just brought home a
puppy who's at the end of the normal socialization period and you suspect or know he's had limited exposure to the world? Or did you follow
advice to keep your puppy home till all her vaccinations were complete? Roll up your sleeves, cross your fingers, and start making up for
lost time. If you have a resilient puppy, you may well be able to socialize
her adequately even though you're running late. Watch closely for signs
of fear and shyness and get professional help pronto if you see them, or

Dog Case Study: Hattie

I had a client who adopted a five-year-old dog from a facility one cut
above a puppy mill, where she'd been used for breeding. Hattie started
out somewhat withdrawn in my client's apartment, and wary of strollers,
mail carriers, and cats (among other commonplaces of city life). She
jumped whenever she heard the beep-beep-beep of a truck backing
up. Yet nothing actually panicked her, and although she wasn't entirely
comfortable with physical contact, she did choose to remain close to
my client and any other people who were present. After meeting and
evaluating Hattie, I felt cautious optimism about her chances of suc-
ceeding as a family pet. Other trainers I talked to about her pointed to
her history of life in a kennel and disagreed. Hattie surprised us all—
given a consistent routine, reward-based training, and time and space
to get accustomed to the phenomena that worried her, she didn't just
turn out okay, she blossomed into an outgoing, relaxed companion.

I have mixed feelings about including Hattie's story here; she was an
exceptionally resilient personality, and maybe her very early history was
better than we knew. More often, clients with seriously undersocialized
dogs struggle to provide them anything like a normal life. Still, Hattie is a
shining example of how some dogs can make one hell of a comeback
from a not-very-promising start.

if your pup doesn't seem to be relaxing and growing comfortable with new sights and sounds.

For more about shy dogs in general, see "Shyness," in Chapter 12, "Stuff Dogs Do That Worries People."

Since it's so difficult to make up for lack of early socialization, you might hope that the results of proper socialization would be equally difficult to undo. No such luck; if your adult dog lives the life of a hermit, rarely or never leaving your home and backyard, his social skills and aplomb can deteriorate. (Humans, too, get into a rut when we do the same thing all the time.) So take your grown dog places, introduce him to new people, and generally keep him up to speed with goings-on in the world.

SOCIALIZATION WITH OTHER DOGS

Unexamined Idea Floating Around in the Ether Warning! An awful lot of people seem to think that the way to teach a puppy to get along well with other dogs is to bring her to the dog park and let 'er rip. It's like bringing your toddler to the playground, right?

Well, no, starting with the fact that at the playground your toddler isn't mixing with a crowd of adults with what we might call disparate social skills. Also, even if you think that other kid's parent is an idiot, you probably have to concede that he knows more about the normal behavior and appropriate upbringing of human children than most people know about the normal behavior and appropriate upbringing of dogs.

For a puppy, your best dog-socialization bet is dates with known, friendly, healthy grown dogs and pups. Many dog trainers offer supervised puppy play groups (see the section on how to choose a trainer in Chapter 3, "Anything but 'Obedience'").

As for adult dogs, surprisingly many trainers flatly warn their clients off dog parks. As I hinted earlier, a big drawback of public dog parks is that not all the dogs will be socially skilled and friendly. Some pick fights; some are a bit timid about other dogs and snap when a bouncy puppy comes too close; some have learned that it can be fun to bowl over small dogs and make them squeal. Not all dogs' play styles mesh well. Some dogs do well meeting other dogs one-on-one in an open area, but get touchy in a confined space with a bunch of strangers.

Encouragingly, though, a 2003 study of dog-dog aggression at one dog park found that of 177 dogs observed over 8 months and 72 hours, only 12 behaved in ways the researchers classed as aggressive toward other dogs. None of the aggressive encounters lasted as long as a minute. Once the dogs themselves, or their guardians, ended the encounter, none of the dogs went back for more. And nobody got hurt.[3] Take note: There was an annual fee to use this locked park, and users had to submit proof of current vaccinations. So presumably the people who brought their dogs were self-selected for a degree of organization and responsibleness.

My view is that a confident, behaviorally healthy adult dog can take an *occasional* difficult encounter in stride. If you have few other opportunities for off-leash exercise, and access to a clean, well-equipped, reasonably large dog park, then go. But choose uncrowded times and check out the party carefully before you enter. Watch for tension, posturing, or ganging up, and if you see them or other undesirable behavior, come back later.

If you have a small dog, stick to areas designated for them. Large dogs can easily intimidate or hurt smaller dogs without even trying. And sometimes, play tips over into predatory behavior, as if the large dog stops recognizing the smaller animal as a dog. I haven't found any solid information about the prevalence of such "predatory drift," but the potential for tragedy is obvious.

Because many dogs guard toys and treats, it's generally best to leave these at home. I say that with a wince, though—in urban areas, the dog park may be the only place available for a game of fetch. If you do bring a toy, be careful and sensitive. If your dog will argue over his ball, then don't bring his ball. Bear in mind that even a dog who appropriately delivers polite warnings to pushy dogs, such as a brief freeze or a lip curl, may eventually meet a dog who escalates in response.

If your dog doesn't pick fights but tends to pester dogs who have toys, teach him a rock-solid recall and "Leave it" (see Chapter 5, "Total Recall," and Chapter 7, "Leaving Stuff Alone . . .") and use them. And if yours is the dog who steps up the argument when another dog mildly warns him away, he shouldn't visit the dog park. His behavior won't improve if he keeps practicing it, and it's not fair to subject the other dogs to his problems. The reverse is also true. If your dog is afraid of other dogs, dumping her into the deep end of the dog run isn't going to help her feel better about them, any more than dumping me into a vat full of cockroaches would make me feel all cheery and entomological.

Fear and aggression aside, somehow many of us have gotten the idea that all normal dogs enjoy meeting and greeting and playing in dog parks. It's not true, any more than it's true that all socially healthy people enjoy big, loud parties where they know hardly anybody. Although many puppies and adolescents happily play with any willing dog, in general, socially mature dogs play less with other dogs and even seem less eager to interact with them.

An adult dog who has a few dog buddies and who politely greets new dogs but then minds her own business is perfectly normal and has no particular social need for the dog park. She'll have at least as much fun taking a long off-leash hike with some canine and human friends, or just playing fetch or tug with you in the backyard.

SPECIAL CONSIDERATIONS FOR SMALL DOGS

In my experience, little dogs seem scared and defensive more often than big dogs do. People often assume this is because there's something basically wrong with them. It's possible that miniaturization affects the expression of other genes that in turn inflect behavior; I don't know of any research on this subject, whether about dogs or any other species. But even if the genetics of smallness affect a dog's tendency to behave one way or another, we're still left with plenty of controllable factors to address.

Look at it this way. My dog Juniper loves every person he has ever met. He also weighs in at 80 pounds of muscle and bone, and he has a big grin with a lot of teeth in it. Here is one experience Juni doesn't often have: A total stranger swoops down on him, cooing, "Oh, how cute!" and draping herself over his entire body. Without exception, my small-dog clients tell me this has happened to their dogs. More than once. Sometimes the stranger actually grabs the dog and picks him up.

Doesn't that sound like fun? You're walking along, minding your business, when a much larger animal that you have never met before grabs you and sweeps you into the air. Perhaps it's not surprising that many of those same small-dog clients tell me that their dog shrinks down, growls, or snaps when people reach for them.

Here's another common scene: A small child trots up to a small dog and wants to pet him. The small dog runs behind his owner's legs. The owner feels bad for everybody—for the disappointed child and for her scared dog. So she picks up her dog and holds him in place for the child to pet. People tell me that when they do this, they're hoping their dog will confront his fear and learn that the child is no threat. This happens with adults, too, but children are a particular problem for

A True Dog Story: Jimmy

Jimmy the Bichon lived on Fifth Avenue in Manhattan, along the especially posh stretch called Museum Mile. His immense, white-carpeted flat was chock-full of works by contemporary artists from Jeff Koons to Jennifer Bartlett to Jean-Michel Basquiat. Jimmy's guardian, Mrs. Waterston, looked startled when I asked her husband's given name—clearly, she'd expected me to know it without being told. When I Googled the family later, I understood why. (Nope, they're not really called Waterston.)

Several times a day, one or another member of the household staff took Jimmy outside for a short walk, but he also had a playpen in the kitchen, with a bed and many toys. Mrs. Waterston held Jimmy in her lap and stroked him as we talked about a typical day in his life. He often visited Bergdorf Goodman and Barneys, where Mrs. Waterston carried him through the crowds and where many, many people wanted to pet him. It was easy to see why they'd be attracted to this bright-eyed fluff-ball. The problem was, Jimmy wasn't attracted back; lately, he'd been growling and snapping when people reached for him.

I asked Mrs. Waterston to let Jimmy walk freely on the couch where we sat; I made a kissy noise and wiggled my fingers in his direction. He sniffed tentatively and then retreated, tucking himself between Mrs. Waterston and the back of the couch. When she reached to pick him up again, he pinned back his ears and shrank away. Not such an outgoing little dog! And no big fan of handling. Mrs. Waterston described his interactions with the staff and with various family friends. It sounded as though, given time and space, Jimmy warmed up to people just fine.

I could have recommended a carefully planned course of counter-conditioning and desensitization for Jimmy, hoping to put him at ease with handling. But Mrs. Waterston didn't even take him on his potty walks herself—no way was serious behavior modification in the cards. Besides, the truth is I don't think little Jimmy's behavior was what needed to change. He was small even for a Bichon, and he had never drawn any blood. He was a quiet, retiring little dog who spent hours every day in overheated, crowded places where strangers handled him constantly. He got tired and fed up. And he never had a chance to just do doggy things: sniff, mark, poke around, and (gasp!) roll in the grass.

In my follow-up letter to Mrs. Waterston, I recommended that she stop taking Jimmy on her shopping trips. Instead, I suggested, have one of the staff—well, what do you expect? *she* wasn't going to do it—take him for a half-hour walk every day in Central Park, just across the street.

I never heard back.

many dogs. They move so fast. They flail. They are *loud*. They can be rough even when they don't mean to be. Whether the stranger is a child or an adult, though, the dog's experience is this: A stranger is handling him and he can't get away. It's not a setup for teaching a calm and confident view of the world.

And the third strike for many little dogs is undersocialization. I suspect this problem is more common among small dogs, maybe because small puppies seem frail, or because it seems easy to paper-train a Chihuahua rather than go outside at six a.m. People generally take bigger puppies outdoors to pee and poop no matter what, and housetraining has the side effect of getting the puppy (you guessed it) outside in the world.

If you've got a small dog, then, you've probably already figured out what to do. I tell my clients, "Be rude so your dog doesn't have to be." No dog, big or small, exists to make up for any perceived shortage of petting zoos. Don't let random people swoop down on your dog. If he retreats from someone or something, let him. Encourage him to explore. Tell him how great he is and slip him a treat when he checks out the person or object. (For more, see the section on shy dogs in Chapter 12, "Stuff Dogs Do That Worries People.") Socialize him as you would any other dog, while taking extra care to protect him from being swamped and overwhelmed.

See Chapter 3, "Anything but 'Obedience,'" for tips on training small dogs.

Part of socialization is preparing your dog—large or small—for certain experiences you know he will have. People will groom him, he'll have to be crated or otherwise confined, and there's no such thing as never in your life seeing a vet. For many dogs, these experiences are a source of stress. They don't have to be.

Teach Your Dog to Accept (and Enjoy) Human Handling

We subject our dogs to many indignities. We hold their feet while we clip their nails. We pull burs out of their tangled coats. *Ouch.* We hold their mouths open while we examine their teeth. The more at ease your dog is with grooming and general being-poked-at, the better.

Make handling practice part of your socialization program. As you cuddle your puppy, gently manipulate body parts. Stretch out his legs; press his paw pads to extend his toes. Take hold of his upper and lower jaws, open his mouth gently, and pop in a tiny piece of chicken. Practice that a few times, then hold his mouth open a little longer and play dentist—inspect those bright white teeth. Clip a toenail every day; every time you clip a toenail, give your puppy a treat. (Oh, and just barely clip the tip: If you cut into the quick, it will bleed like an abattoir and also hurt, so your puppy may suddenly get much less happy about you messing with his feet.)

Hold his head steady and look into his ears. Lift up his tail and touch his anus with a gloved finger or the tip of a cotton swab—he'll be getting his temperature taken at the vet's for the rest of his life. (More about vet visits below.)

With a tissue or a moistened towel, clean sleepy gunk from the corners of your puppy's eyes. Even if he has a short coat, give him a few strokes with a soft brush every day. Wipe his legs and feet with a towel. You've seen video of monkeys picking through each other's coats looking for fleas? Pick through your puppy's coat just like that. Unless you're one of those rare people who never ever forget the preventative, you will probably find yourself plucking ticks someday.

The trick is to keep these exercises light and pleasant, and—this is crucial—to pair them with fun, affection, and treats. No need for marathon handling sessions. Just include bits of all kinds of touch in your usual affectionate interactions with your pup. The message is that there's nothing special or out of the ordinary about, say, a nail being clipped; it's just another weird thing people do, and by the way sometimes a dog gets a little piece of chicken, or a ball toss, or a butt scritch out of it.

By the way, many people whose rescue dogs have difficulty with handling take this to mean their dog was abused. That's certainly possible, but more likely your dog just didn't get a lot of human handling in early life and so never learned to feel comfortable with it. Whatever the cause, you can probably make a big dent in the problem with patience and the right professional help. And you may be able to resolve mild problems on your own.

TROUBLESHOOTING HANDLING ISSUES

Let's say you didn't get around to nail-clipping practice with your puppy, and now that he's all grown up he'll hold still while you clip one nail but pull away when you go for a second. Or maybe you've got a newly adopted adult dog who responds the same way. Here's how a do-it-yourself fix might work.

Check out what's deluxe in your fridge—leftover roast chicken, a sardine, the rind of an especially stinky cheese. Pick something that your dog adores and that, ideally, she never gets at any other time. Have it ready well in advance and give your dog time to become distracted from its presence. (This is crucial. If you want to teach your dog to enjoy nail clipping, then nail clipping needs to become a reliable signal that a special treat is on its way. If you get it backward—if your getting out a special treat becomes a signal that nail clipping is about to happen— your dog may get nervous about the treat. Yes, really.)

Trick Alert: Teach Your Dog to File His Own Nails

An end run around the oh-no-I-hate-it-when-you-touch-my-feet problem is to teach your dog to file his own nails. Believe it or not, this is *easy*, especially if you've already taught your dog to target with his feet. (See Chapter 10, "Play? Training? Tricks?," for instructions.)

To make a nail file, choose a sturdy board big enough for your dog to scrape his feet along. Too big is better than too small. Cover one side with glued-on sandpaper or that stick-on stair tread material. How coarse a grain you use depends on how large and hard your dog's nails are.

Have your clicker and treats ready and sit on a chair or on the ground holding the nail file. (If it's big, brace it against your legs as well.) Click/ treat as soon as your dog paws at the nail file with either foot. As he paws more confidently and vigorously, he'll be scraping his nails on the sandpaper; begin to click/treat for only the strongest scraping, and if he starts pawing mostly with one foot, wait to click/treat until he paws with the other as well. When he's confidently scratching away with both his right and left forepaws (he'll take turns), click and treat just occasionally, for vigorous scratches.

A YouTube search on "dog nail file" or "doggy nail file" will bring you to helpful videos. Some people find their dog enjoys nail filing so much they have to put the board away when they're not actively working on it; otherwise, the dog files his own nails right down to the quick. That hasn't been an issue for me, but just in case, you might want to keep your nail file in a closet.

Okay, so the deluxe treat has been hanging around for long enough that your dog isn't thinking about it anymore. You've also made sure to pick a time when she's tired, relaxed, and kind of hungry. Now clip *one* nail, and immediately deliver that special treat. That's it—you're done for the day. Tomorrow, or the day after, you can clip another nail. Just one.

You'll know your dog is ready for you to clip two nails in a row when she starts looking relaxed and happy about the first nail. It might take a couple of weeks or more to get to this point; be patient and trust the process. As long as your dog's body language is changing for the better, you're on the right track. There's a saying in behavior modification: "If you think you're going too slowly, slow down." Patient groundwork is always faster and more successful in the long run. Always wait for your dog to tell you she's ready before you add another nail. In fact, who says you *ever* have to clip all her nails at once? Better Dogalini should be relaxed and at ease while you clip two or three nails every week or so than that she should be tense and freaked out and just about able to stand it while you go through all four feet at once.

To desensitize your dog to brushing, apply the same rules as for mild nail-clipping anxiety. Combine a tired, relaxed, hungry dog with just a brushstroke or two, followed by a deluxe meaty or cheesy treat. Over the course of days or weeks, depending on how quickly your dog grows comfortable, add more brushstrokes and keep the treats coming. The same principles always apply: Go slow. Use super-special treats. Make sure the handling predicts the treat, not the other way around. Work when your dog is relaxed and hungry. Go slow. Go slow. Go slower.

SERIOUS HANDLING PROBLEMS

If your dog spooks easily, or resists several kinds of handling, or responds to handling by stiffening, curling his lip, growling, or any other display of aggression, you'll need to work in person with a trainer who's competent in behavior modification and can design an individualized program. See Chapter 12, "Stuff Dogs Do That Worries People," for information on how to find a competent specialist.

WHEN CAN YOU STOP GIVING TREATS?

People often want to know when they can stop giving treats. You can thin out the treat frequency as your dog becomes more and more comfortable with handling. But really, what is the problem with giving

Teach Your Dog a Warning Cue

Granted that ideally we've taught our dogs to accept and even enjoy all kinds of handling, sometimes we have to do things to them (eardrops, daily shots) that they don't like and that won't wait until we can help the dog feel more comfortable with them. A hot trend in Doggy Training World is the "warning cue."

The warning cue is a word or phrase you use to tell your dog that something unpleasant is on the way. Use a different cue for each unpleasantness—"Eardrops"; "Shot": You get the idea. At a recent seminar, the Swedish trainers Eva Bertilsson and Emelie Johnson Vegh described a dog who had to get eardrops five times daily and who had started to avoid her guardian for the entire day. Once the dog learned that eardrops came when she got a warning cue, *and only when she got a warning cue,* the all-day avoidance ended even though the dog didn't like eardrops any better than she had before.

The warning cue helps because it introduces predictability: Dogalini now knows when the bad stuff is on the way, so she doesn't brace against it anxiously every time you go near her.

Dogalini a tiny piece of cheese or chicken every 15 or 30 seconds while you groom her? Especially if you start with a dog who's twitchy about some aspect of handling, there's no harm in constantly refreshing that new, positive association.

Teach Your Dog to Accept Restraint

Dogs not only need to accept handling but also sometimes must be restrained—at the vet's, for instance, when blood is being drawn. Many trainers advise that you teach your puppy to accept restraint by cradling her on her back and, if she struggles, not letting her go till she gives up. That approach does work with many or most pups, but a significant minority struggle frantically; I would even call them panicked. Some frantic puppies just keep trying to escape; some will experiment with a growl or a nip. And, of course, you can't know whether your puppy falls into the "Eh, I'm being held" group or the "Lemme go lemme go lemme go!" group till you've made the experiment. Guess wrong and it gets mighty hard to convince Baby Dogalini that restraint is really okay after all. Not to mention that she trusts you a little less than she did before.

So, instead of holding your puppy while she struggles and letting her go when she gives up, do this: Pick a time when she's relaxed and sleepy to begin with, then hug her and hold her still for a nanosecond. Release her before she has time to do more than notice that she's being held. Over a couple of weeks, gradually prolong the time for which you hold her still, but take care to stay within her comfort zone. Hold her close to your body rather than letting her hang, which seems to be less comfortable and feel less safe.

If you hit a point where she begins to struggle, let her go *immediately*. If you hang on, and her struggles escalate to the point where you must let her go, she will have learned to struggle frantically. Bad lesson. Next time you do the exercise, go back to a much shorter period of restraint and work your way back up, slowly, over time. If you keep running into trouble, get competent professional help. You can probably muscle your way around a puppy, but pound for pound even a small dog is stronger and faster than a person, and of course she has pointier teeth. The road of confrontation leads nowhere good.

Make the Vet's Office an Un-scary Place for Your Dog

Think about vet visits from a dog's point of view. You have no idea why you're there. The place is crowded and smells weird. You can hear someone yelping in pain a few rooms over. Someone you haven't had a chance to get to know is all over you, poking and prodding. If you're not feeling well to begin with—say, you're working on a little ear infection— then some of those pokes and prods may hurt. The stranger may stick needles in your rump. If you try to escape, another someone you don't know will hold you still. And what does your best friend do? Stand there sweating bullets and telling you it's okay. News flash, Two-Legged Friend! It is not okay!

If you have a young puppy, it's easy to counter many of the factors that make vet visits not-okay. Think about the handling a vet would do, and get your puppy comfortable with it in a relaxed way at home. Open her mouth, inspect her teeth, then pop her a tiny piece of chicken. Look in her ears, then toss a ball for her. To simulate taking her temperature, lift up her tail and touch her anus with a Q-tip. Then give her a treat. Feel your way gently along her abdomen, then pick up her leash and take her outside. Press a pencil point slightly into her thigh, as if giving her a shot. Follow that up with, you guessed it, a treat. In short, teach your puppy that things a vet might do are not only safe, but are even pretty decent predictors that fun and treats are on the way. Ask your friends to practice handling your puppy, too. That helps her learn that it's safe to be touched by people she doesn't know as well as she knows you.

Unfamiliarity is often part of what makes vet visits problematic, so include the vet's office among the varied pleasant experiences you give your puppy while socializing him. No exam, no shots; just go to the office with a pocketful of treats that the vet staff can give him while they cuddle him and coo over him and in general make friends. A couple of fun visits will turn the background sounds and smells of the office into old news for your sophisticated puppy. And a history of pleasant experiences with strangers will help him grow into a friendly adult dog.

After these dress rehearsals, your puppy will probably take his first real vet exam in stride. If you know *you'll* be anxious, it might help to ask the vet to narrate each step of the exam to you, so you always know what's coming next. Distract your puppy with chest scritches and treats during the vaccinations, and keep your own demeanor quietly upbeat.

HELP ADULT DOGS FEEL BETTER ABOUT THE VET

Say you have a newly adopted dog and you don't know how he feels about the vet. I suggest holding off on any handling practice till you've gotten to know your dog a bit. Ideally, of course, he comfortably accepts handling. Good shelters and rescue groups perform behavior evaluations on the dogs they take in; a dog who responds aggressively to normal human handling shouldn't be placed in a nonspecialist home, if at all. However, behavior evaluations are imperfect, and as you'll remember from Chapter 1, "So Many Dogs, So Little Time," not all rescue groups are conscientious about what dogs they'll place.

Whether your dog is newly adopted or not, if he does growl, snap, or bite during a vet exam, get professional help. The same goes for significant skittishness or outright fear. But suppose your adult dog is just a bit timid about the vet—you don't have to drag him in the door, but his tail droops and he hasn't got his happy on. In that case, you can give a more informal approach a try. Just remember that it's always harder work to undo a problem than to prevent it. Frequently walk or drive your dog on the route to the vet's office without going in, so that route stops being a good predictor of distress. Then take him to the office to pay lots of treat-heavy social calls. Teach your dog fun tricks that he can do in the waiting room. Can you get a playful mood going? Fun is incompatible with fear.

TEACH YOUR DOG TO WEAR A MUZZLE

Why, you ask, should you need to teach your dog to wear a muzzle when you're teaching her that being handled is pleasant? Muzzle conditioning is a failsafe. There may come a time when a vet has to do something painful to your dog without anesthetic, for instance. Also, behavior is not a hundred percent predictable or controllable; even if you do your best to accustom your puppy to handling, she may grow up touchy. (Though probably less touchy than she would have been without your help.) Finally, you may have an adult dog who's already uneasy to the point of aggression about particular kinds of handling that can't be avoided.

A wire basket muzzle is safest for your dog (it allows panting) and easiest to work with. Have several practice sessions in which you gradually work up to having your dog wear the muzzle for several minutes. Start by smearing the inside with peanut butter or cream cheese and letting your dog lick it out. Next, combine that with feeding tiny treats through the basket as you draw the straps around her head. (You may need to clip out a little of the basket near her mouth to fit the treats through. Use wire cutters.) Continue feeding treats while you fasten the straps. With your dog wearing the muzzle, play a game and feed treats.

At each step, practice till your dog is relaxed and comfortable. Try to keep her from ever hitting a point where she wants to paw at the muzzle or otherwise struggle with it—it's best if the experience is always pleasant and upbeat for her. If you make a mistake, take the muzzle off right away so that she doesn't learn to paw persistently or wind up getting frantic. Then go back a couple of steps in your practice and work your way up again.

PAY ATTENTION TO YOUR VET'S BEHAVIOR

In considering your dog's behavior at the vet's, also consider your vet's behavior toward your dog. Vets who rush animals or handle them, let's say, briskly aren't ideal, but they are acceptable for many confident, relaxed dogs. However, if your dog dislikes visiting a vet who comes on strong, ask the vet to be gentle himself. You are your dog's advocate! If the vet can't or won't be gentle, then switch vets. A vet with a light touch may be able to examine an anxious dog more thoroughly, so the change may even have a positive effect on your dog's health.

Teach Your Dog to Love His Crate

Ah, the dog crate. It makes housetraining easier. It provides your shy dog a refuge during your six-year-old's birthday party. It provides your traveling dog a measure of protection in a car accident. Some hotels require that doggy guests be crated when their humans leave the room. And all of that goes out the window if your dog hates his crate.

As always, you're at an advantage with a puppy or dog who's had no unpleasant experiences to undo. Set yourself and your dog up for success by planning ahead. If you brought your new puppy home on Friday afternoon, don't introduce him to his crate right before you leave for work on Monday morning. And don't let your grown dog's first experience of crating be the first time you leave him on his own in a hotel.

Choose a crate big enough for your dog to stand up and turn around in, and also to stretch out comfortably when he lies down. Make it inviting with a cushy bed. If your dog's inclined to chew his bed, get a chew-resistant bed, give it some competition from safe, chewable toys, or use rags and old sheets that your dog can destroy without giving you an aneurysm. (Actual ingestion of cloth or other inedibles is a whole 'nother problem, called pica, and you should get help PDQ. See Chapter 12, "Stuff Dogs Do That Worries People," for information on how to find someone competent.)

Set up the crate near where you hang out—in your home office, in front of the sofa where you watch TV, or by your bed. You can move it from place to place, or for that matter have multiple crates if your house is all that big. Once your dog loves his crate, it can be his remote hideout when he needs one, but his first lesson shouldn't be that crate = social isolation.

The easiest and most relaxed way to crate train starts with keeping the crate open and available in a spot where your dog likes to rest anyway, or in your puppy's safe enclosure if you've got a young thing. Every so often, toss a treat inside. When your dog enters her crate to get the treat, click or say, "Yes!" and deliver another treat to her while she's still inside. If you happen to catch your dog resting on that supercomfy bed you put in the crate, tell her what a good dog she is and drop a treat in with her. You can also feed your dog his meals in the crate. All this sends a simple, clear message: Good things happen to dogs inside their crates.

A sneaky but effective tactic is to smear peanut butter or cream cheese on the crate wall, or put a food-stuffed toy inside the crate, then close the crate door—without your dog inside. When he notices those good smells floating out of the crate, he'll likely try to reach the source. Let him get just a tiny bit frustrated—you don't want to drive him out of his mind—then open the crate door and let him in.

Once your dog is entering the crate happily and you've caught her resting inside a couple of times, start closing the door for a few seconds at a time. Some dogs settle right in, but for others the transition to a closed door can be a big deal.

You can help make the process easy by choosing a time when your dog is relaxed after vigorous exercise and has a reason to stay in the crate for a few minutes anyway. For instance, she might be enjoying an edible chew or excavating a food-dispensing toy. While she's thus occupied, open and close the crate door a few times, leaving it closed for gradually longer periods.

How long should you keep the door closed at first, and how quickly should you progress? The only hard-and-fast rule I can give you is to let your dog be your guide. Is he completely absorbed in his stuffed chew toy, so he doesn't even notice that you've closed the door? Is she a four-month-old who's just enjoyed half an hour of play and training in the backyard and who eliminated right before you brought her indoors, so when you put her in her crate she said yip yip yip and promptly collapsed into puppy sleep? Then odds are you can work fast.

On the other hand, maybe your dog took her sweet time getting to the point where she'd enter the crate at all. And then it took her a few days to learn to linger there instead of grabbing your tossed treats and dashing out again. If that's your dog, don't even think about closing that crate door for the first time till she's lost all trace of anxiety about hanging out inside with the door wide open. And when you start, start small, with the door closed partway and then shut but not latched. Slow and steady will always win the skittish-dog crate-training race.

For many dogs, though, crate training goes 1-2-3. I confess that with my own puppy, I got lucky with a super-fast approach. We set up his crate, we brought him home, we tired him out, and then we popped him in to sleep. His first few nights away from his mother and litter, we took turns sleeping next to the crate with one hand resting just inside the door. That is about as brisk as any intro to crate should be, and notice that we didn't ask our puppy to get used to his crate *and* to sleeping alone all in one swell foop.

TEACH YOUR DOG TO ENTER HIS CRATE ON CUE

Once your dog is at ease in the crate, you can easily teach him to enter it on cue. You'll say the cue just before your dog enters the crate, and only at that time. After some individually variable number of reps, your dog learns that those particular sounds coming out of your mouth predict that he might just get a reward for entering his crate. Suppose your cue is "Crate time!" Say it, then toss a treat in the crate so your dog goes in. After a few reps, say the cue and move your empty hand as if tossing a treat. Then deliver a treat from your other hand. Once your dog has associated the cue "Crate time!" with going into his crate, you can begin to give treats occasionally instead of every time. (By the way, the gesture with your empty hand may also be a go-in-your-crate cue.)

HOW TO DEAL WITH BARKING AND WHINING IN THE CRATE

What if your dog or puppy vocalizes while in his crate? As usual, the answer is "It depends." If your young pup wakes you at three a.m., odds are he needs a toilet break. Take him on leash to his pee and poop spot and then immediately put him back to bed. The idea is to meet his needs but not turn the wee hours into puppy funtime.

As a general rule, you don't want to reinforce demand barking or demand whining—"I want out, and I want it now!" The same goes if what you're hearing is your dog's usual response to the mailman or some other everyday stimulus. Remember, even a reprimand constitutes attention and may strengthen the behavior you're trying to quell. Instead, ignore it. Let your dog out when he's calm and quiet.

But all bets are off if your dog is in distress. Puppies aren't the only ones who sometimes have urgent toilet needs. And a thunder-phobic dog may panic when he senses an approaching storm; feeling trapped in the crate won't do him any good. Finally, separation anxiety doesn't mix with crates. Dogs with this disorder may bloody their paws and break their teeth trying to escape.

A WORD ON CRATE ABUSE

Crates look like cages, which is because, well, they are. But accepting confinement comfortably is a useful skill for any animal living in the human world.

On the other hand, crates can easily be abused. The rambunctious, pushy, destructive dog who's spending twenty-two hours crated out of every twenty-four needs exercise, training, and company. And while a well-exercised dog will likely snooze most of the day while you're at work, she needs at least one break to relieve herself and stretch her legs.

Those cautions aside, your dog's crate may surprise you with its popularity. When my Juniper stops dead at the door of his crate instead of going in at bedtime, it's because our smallest and snarkiest cat has parked herself smack in the middle, glaring at him to keep out.

A SOCIALIZATION CHECKLIST

People (singly and in groups)
- [ ] men
- [ ] women
- [ ] children: playgrounds, schoolyards, running, shrieking, skate-boarding, bicycling; babies in strollers
- [ ] black, white, East Asian, South Asian
- [ ] people coming over to your house/apartment
- [ ] delivery people
- [ ] homeless people
- [ ] can-collectors
- [ ] wheelchairs (motorized and manual)
- [ ] canes
- [ ] walkers
- [ ] collapsible grocery carts ("granny carts")
- [ ] shopping carts
- [ ] hats
- [ ] beards
- [ ] dark glasses
- [ ] heavy coats
- [ ] uniforms: police, fire department, UPS, FedEx, USPS
- [ ] shouting
- [ ] spasmodic movement

- ❑ slow, cautious movement
- ❑ rapid movement

Places
- ❑ apartments of friends
- ❑ subway/subway station/commuter train
- ❑ vet's office
- ❑ car, car rides
- ❑ dog-friendly stores
- ❑ farm
- ❑ woods
- ❑ beach
- ❑ street
- ❑ stairs
- ❑ elevator
- ❑ escalator (take care your puppy's feet don't get caught)
- ❑ parking lot
- ❑ highway overpass
- ❑ city park (but please see the section on dog parks before going)
- ❑ skating rink

Noises
- ❑ cars backfiring
- ❑ rattling metal
- ❑ banging pots and pans
- ❑ doorbell/buzzer/intercom
- ❑ metal street plates banging as cars go over them
- ❑ garbage trucks
- ❑ construction and utility trucks
- ❑ trucks backing up
- ❑ construction zones

Animals
- ❑ *friendly* puppies and adult dogs
- ❑ cats
- ❑ birds
- ❑ horses
- ❑ deer

❑ chickens, cows, sheep
❑ any others as the opportunity arises

Of course, take the puppy with you to as many indoor places as you can. Playgroups with screened puppies are appropriate, as are visits to and from friendly, immunized adult dogs.

For outdoor socialization before vaccinations are complete:

1. Carry the puppy to a busy street corner or a mall entrance and hold her in your arms. Have part of the pup's meal available for people to feed the puppy. Encourage them to handle her (gently!); they or you can give a treat.
2. Tote the pup around in a collapsible grocery cart ("granny cart") with a comfy bed at the bottom: This way he can see the world from near ground level.
3. At the point when you feel comfortable with the balance between vaccination and socialization needs, take the puppy for walks. (Caution: no meetings with unknown dogs, even if their guardians say they're healthy, vaccinated, and friendly!)

Anything but "Obedience"
THE WHYS AND HOWS OF BUILDING
A *COOPERATIVE* DOG

Troll the Internet or the "Dogs" shelf at your local megabookstore, and, as you probably know already, you'll find a bunch of people selling secrets of dog training, a bunch of people selling their years of experience, a bunch of people telling you not to bribe your dog with cookies, a bunch of people telling you you'd better make yourself the alpha dog before Zippy takes on that role for himself. Some will explain how properly to fit a choke collar and deliver a collar correction—a sharp jerk on the leash. How sharp? One well-known book says that if your dog doesn't cry out, you haven't yanked her hard enough. Some will explain how to fill a plastic bottle with pennies and shake it at your dog whenever he misbehaves. Some will tell you to stare your dog down because that shows him who's boss. Some will tell you to grab your dog and force her to the ground (an "alpha roll") every day, because "that's what alpha wolves do." Lately, shock collars seem to be all the rage (what is it with human beings and remotes, anyway?). Many of these trainers use food rewards and tell you that "corrections" should be "fair" and that you should never deliver them in anger. Still, there always seems to be a reason to hurt or frighten your dog in the name of teaching her . . . something.

You'll also find some crackpots, like me, grinning away and telling you that you don't need the choke chain, you don't need the collar correction, the alpha roll is bogus, and Zippy is not plotting against you while you sleep. Instead, we claim, what you need is this: access to the things Zippy wants in life. What does Zippy want? Food, walks, ball throws, scritches, attention, the chance to sniff a fire hydrant or to say hi to a person he likes. Set Zippy up to do things you like, deliver the goods in return, and you'll find Zippy getting in the habit of doing what you like. It's nonconfrontational and fun (okay, okay, there's always a certain amount of repetitive practice involved). As for whether

Zippy thinks he rules the world: I seriously doubt it. But so what if he does, as long as he gets off the couch happily when we ask him to, and has a welcoming manner toward guests?

So you're standing there in the conglomegabookstore or sitting at your desk staring at half a dozen browser windows, and how do you know which trainer's program to follow and which method to choose? To help you out, here comes some background to explain why we reward-based, non-"correcting" crackpots aren't really crackpots after all. I've supplied more info here than most basic dog books will give you, and you're welcome to skip ahead to the nuts and bolts of clicker training (beginning on p. 69) if you prefer. But if you take a few minutes to learn why so many modern trainers have abandoned forceful methods, and why reward-based training works so well, you'll be like the cook who knows how to make soup—not just a particular soup, but soup in general. She wants a recipe sometimes, but she doesn't need one every time; the ingredients she's got are enough to inspire her. Like the cook who knows the principles of soup, you'll be able to figure out how to teach your dog much of what you want with what you've got on hand. Okay? Here goes.

Why Reward-Based Training?

Force-based training works for a lot of dogs. If it's done well, many or most dogs learn how to avoid the collar jerks and electric shocks, and behave accordingly. But there are some catches.

One: You caught that "if it's done well," right? Doing it well calls for impeccable timing; if you "correct" too late or too early, you wind up punishing something other than what you meant to punish, which is unfair and confusing to your dog.* Doing it well also requires a high degree of consistency. If you want to drive an animal out of its mind, deliver aversives (those collar jerks and electric shocks) unpredictably. At best, you teach nothing. At worst, you produce "learned helplessness," a condition in which the animal basically stops doing anything at all.[1]

Two: Some dogs (and you can't always tell in advance which ones)

---

* Of course you can mistime rewards. But even a mistimed reward contributes to creating safe, pleasant associations in your dog's mind—pleasant associations to training and to you. In consequence, the downside of mistimed reward is rarely as serious as the downside of mistimed punishment.

react to force by fighting back or shutting down. The alpha roll, for instance, is notorious for resulting in bites to people's faces. (I'll offer some speculation later about why.) Just recently, I worked with someone whose dog snapped at him under only one circumstance: When my client caught him raiding the garbage, he grabbed the dog's collar and shouted at him. "Softer" dogs may simply avoid training or avoid you.

Three: Even if the trainer's timing is perfect, the dog may not necessarily associate the punishment with her own behavior. Instead, she may link it with something else in the environment. I have had any number of clients whose dogs bark and lunge at other dogs on leash. Most of those clients had heard somewhere or other that the appropriate response to such behavior was to hiss at their dog or force her to the ground or shout no or jerk on her collar. So that's what they did, and the dog's behavior got worse. Correlation doesn't prove causation, but for my money these dogs had learned that when other dogs appeared, their guardian hurt them. And what happened when the other dog left? The leash jerks stopped, the yelling stopped, they were let up off the ground. No surprise that their motivation to drive other dogs away ratcheted up and up and up.

Four: What about our ethics? Force-free training is relatively new in the dog world, but has shown itself successful not only in pet-dog manners training but also in competitive dog sports, in commercial and movie work, in service-dog work, and in search and rescue, police work, and bomb detection (even though only a minority of trainers in the latter fields have eliminated force entirely). It's hard to justify the use of force when nonviolent methods work at least as well.

Five: Correction-based trainers often assert that their dogs work "for praise" or out of "respect." I'm sure many of these trainers believe it, too. The cold truth is that praise does indeed develop a very high value for a dog who has learned that "Good dog!" means he's not about to get hurt. For "respect" under these conditions, read "fear." I am not a perfect human being and sometimes I lose my temper, with my dog as well as with the people in my life. But I will not deliberately introduce threats into my relationships.

The reward-based, no-corrections approach usually elicits several questions, and they're good ones. First, "But what if my dog does something wrong?" Second, "But what about rank—shouldn't I be the pack leader?" Third, "Don't dogs want to please us?"

"WHAT IF MY DOG DOES SOMETHING WRONG?"

"Something wrong" covers a lot of ground, from jumping up to greet a person to tipping over the garbage can to biting.

A good reward-based trainer will suggest safe, effective ways to prevent undesirable behaviors and/or prevent the dog from getting what he wants from them, meanwhile making sure that behaviors you do like work well for the dog. For instance, it's usually easy to raise a puppy who has no interest in chewing table legs: You crate or pen the puppy when you can't supervise; you supervise the puppy closely when he's at large; and you provide the puppy plenty of acceptable outlets (chew toys; controlled games of tug) for using his teeth.

As for behaviors that are "wrong" because they frighten and hurt other animals and people, we can deal most productively with them if we set human moral ideas aside. If a dog aggresses, you can be confident that he perceives a threat (the same is usually true of us, isn't it?). The threat may not be "real," but from the dog's perspective it's a threat nonetheless. If you want to change the dog's behavior, you need to remove that perception of threat and replace it with more positive associations. This is how all scientifically sound behavior modification works. You can punish a dog for aggressing till the cows come home, but in doing so you've done nothing to improve his opinion of whatever blew his gaskets in the first place—or, for that matter, to improve his opinion of you. And, as I explained earlier, you run the risk that the dog will fight back.

Neither I nor any other reward-based trainer will tell you not to protect yourself against physical attack, okay? Just bear in mind that "self-defense" and "behavior modification" are not synonyms.

"BUT WHAT ABOUT RANK? SHOULDN'T I BE THE PACK LEADER?"

Lay that burden down! Kick back, relax, and enjoy a little history of the "pack leader" and why you don't have to pay this idea no nevermind.

The pack leader idea is predicated, in the first place, on the assumption that wolf behavior is equivalent to dog behavior, so let's take a look at wolf behavior. For a long time, much of what we perceived about wolf behavior relied on observations of captive wolves. Wolves in the wild are shy and elusive, whereas captive wolves are, obviously, captive, and therefore easier to watch. Unfortunately, captive wolves aren't typical of wolves. In the wild, wolves seem most often to live in family groups—Mom,

Dad, the adolescents, the new pups.* Captive wolves are generally un-related to one another. Wild wolves generally disperse as they mature, to form new family groups. Captive wolves can't disperse. The behavior of unrelated animals who haven't chosen their own social partners and cannot leave to form new groups might strike you as not the best pos-sible guide to normal behavior for that species.

As a rule, in a group of free-living wolves—that is to say, a family group—the "alphas" are the parent wolves and (big surprise here) they lead the group *because* they're the parents. There isn't a whole lot of bloody conflict, which makes sense because social predators can't afford to waste energy on bloody conflict with their packmates. (How you gonna bring down those moose, even elderly moose, if you're limping and your leg is infected?) Where fights do get savage is *between* packs.† Lone wolves, too, face deadly attack.

To make a long story short, it's not that wolves don't have hierar-chies; it's that rank generally arises out of family relationships and isn't maintained through harsh conflict. Nor is it obvious that interactions are always about rank. Here's one of my favorite descriptions, ever, of a wolf-wolf interaction. The protagonists are Mama Wolf and Papa Wolf:

> Often the breeding female awoke first and tried to awaken the male.... [She] sometimes seemed to urge the male to become active and go foraging. She would lead the male away only to have him lie down again, and the two would then begin howling. After that, the two would arise and go off again, but sometimes they would repeat this behavior a few times. Eventually the pair would leave the area, and after 5 to 30 minutes the female often returned alone ... apparently having sufficiently motivated the male well enough to trust that he was actually continuing on.[2]

---

* I've made my little sketch of wolf behavior as accurate as I can. However, wolf researchers say "seems" and "usually" a lot. The size and organization of wolf packs can vary substantially, depending on local environmental conditions. Also, when resources are scarce, within-pack conflicts may escalate; it's not all happy families all the time. Remember two things. One: Wolf behavior is flexible and incom-pletely understood, so flat statements about "what wolves do" have low odds of being true. Two (repeat after me): Dogs are not wolves anyway.

† This leads to my hypothesis, which is also a lot of other people's hypothesis, about why alpha-rolling your dog can be so dangerous to your face. Neither among wolves nor among dogs would one animal forcibly roll another over except in the context of a serious fight. I suspect that a dog whose human is alpha-rolling him perceives not a mere assertion of rank but real physical danger. Some dogs up the appeasement level and some go limp, but some fight back.

It's not all alpha rolls out there, people. In fact, it seems never to be alpha rolls: When what looks like an alpha roll is captured on video, it's clear that the "rolled" wolf has dropped to the ground and voluntarily displayed his or her belly and groin.[3] The "displaying" wolf *offers* deference, and the interaction is ritualized, not damaging. That rough, tough, no-nonsense alpha? Not, perhaps, the Wolf Most Likely to Succeed:

> We had . . . a female wolf, [designated number] 40, who ruled her group, the Druid Peak pack, really above the male. . . . 40 ruled her pack with an iron fist. She was killed in 2000 by her pack mates, her female mates, some of whom were her daughters.
>
> In another pack, the Leopolds, it was hard to tell if the alpha male, 2, or the alpha female, 7, led it. In fact, 7 led with a very unassuming, almost hidden style. You knew she was the leader because the other wolves deferred to her.[4]

So much for the wolf pack as a venue of constant jostling for power and control. And—as I mentioned earlier, and as you might happen to have noticed anyway—dogs are not wolves.* Free-living dogs are mostly scavengers, not hunters; they hang around garbage dumps and other food sources, which is what they evolved to do. Because they're not social hunters like wolves, they generally seem to form loose, temporary associations, not permanent family groups. When a group of dogs does form, the evidence suggests that more than one dog at a time may lead it, and furthermore that the likeliest leaders are those who get the most "affiliative" (basically, friendly) submission from other dogs, not those who get the most "agonistic" (basically, conflictual) submission.[5]

While in any given interaction between two dogs, one may dominate and the other may defer, it doesn't follow that if Dog A dominates Dog B in one situation, and Dog B dominates Dog C in a similar situation, Dog A will dominate Dog C.[6] Nor does it follow that if Dogalini guards the comfiest bed from Zippy, she will also get to take away his chewy or push him away when he seeks attention from you. Nor is it

---

* It's true that dogs are sometimes designated *Canis familiaris,* sometimes *Canis lupus familiaris,* and that scientists who use the latter designation consider the dog a subspecies of the wolf. Either way, though, dogs and wolves differ behaviorally and in the ecological niches they inhabit. Wolves raised with humans don't grow up to act like dogs, as the researcher Ádám Miklósi points out (*Dog Behaviour, Evolution, and Cognition* [Oxford University Press, 2007], Box 2.2 and *passim*).

clear that control over a particular resource (bed, chewy, human attention) is necessarily rank-related to begin with. Maybe it is; but maybe
it's just a function of how much each of the dogs involved values that
resource at the moment. Maybe Zippy is "really" Dogalini's Exalted
Leader but just doesn't care as much as she does about the comfy bed,
because his bones don't ache that day and hers do. And odds are that
your dog barges out the front door ahead of you because he likes to go
out and you've never taught him to wait at the door, not because he's
staging a palace coup.

Much aggression, both against people and against other dogs, is
ascribed to dominance—*but not by trainers and behavior consultants
who keep up with the science*. Stress appears much more often the culprit. The anxious, undersocialized dog repeatedly approaches and retreats from unfamiliar human visitors, barking, snarling, with pinned
ears. The confident dog with lots of early experience of friendly guests
trots out to meet them with wiggling butt and smiling face. The socially inept dog greets other dogs tensely, with tail high, ready to erupt;
the confident dog greets with soft body language and no fuss.

Or an aggressive behavior may result from successful experimenta-
tion. Your newly adopted Dogalini feels somewhat uneasy when people
approach her food bowl, so she stiffens up when she sees you coming.
You note her response and back off; her stiff-bodied warning worked,
so next time she does it again. Alternatively, you grab Dogalini by the
scruff of her neck and shake her to punish her for guarding her food
from you; she may quit aggressing (but she still doesn't like it when you
come near her bowl, and the first time a little kid comes close, she bites
him in the face). Or she may fight back, scaring you enough to make
you withdraw (and now she's learned what a hardass she has to be
when she needs to defend herself).

Is it obvious that Dogalini guarded her food because she thinks
you're lower than dirt and she's the Queen of the Jungle? Nah. An animal who gave up her food to anyone who approached wouldn't live
long enough to reproduce; food guarding is an adaptive response, and
it shows up to various extents in many dogs.[7] It becomes a problem
when dogs live with people, so preventative exercises are part of basic
puppy rearing and adult-dog care. And there are well-accepted procedures for defusing it when you do see it. In the example of Dogalini,
backing off was the best damage control you could do; the next step is
to use one of a couple of nonconfrontational protocols to change her

emotional response to human approach when she has food. (See Chapter 12, "Stuff Dogs Do That Worries People.")

How do you know what's going on inside your dog's head, what motivates her? When my clients ask me this question, I shrug and say, more or less, this: I've been living with the same person for more than twenty years. We're the same species and the same sex, and we're of fairly similar ethnic ancestry. We have similar educational backgrounds. We are both native speakers of English. *I frequently have no idea what she is thinking,* and I do not expect that I can know what goes on in the mind of someone belonging to a different species, with radically different cognitive and sensory capacities.*

What I can do is observe behavior. Does my dog move over when he's lying on the sofa and I want to sit down too? Good. Does my dog's body remain relaxed if I stroke his back while he eats supper? Good. Does my dog come when I call him? Good. Do I end our walks with my shoulders unwrenched and my arms the same length as when we began? Peachy keen.

Do I have any idea whether my dog thinks he's the lord of the universe and I'm his lowly servant? I don't think he does, but I don't really know, and anyway we get along just fine.

"DON'T DOGS WANT TO PLEASE US?"

Those of us who use food and other rewards in training have had a standard reply to this, something like "How would you feel if your boss never paid you money but just said, 'Thanks! Nice job!' every other Friday?" This makes a good point—thanks can get to seem pretty thin when nothing tangible ever accompanies them. Plus, many of the things we want to teach our dogs make no particular sense from a dog's point of view, so, sure, the dog ought to get something she values in return.

Yet, the "salary" answer doesn't quite satisfy: It doesn't account for why praise and affection aren't enough, given that we have such close relationships with our dogs. Even trainers who are invested in a rank-based view of those relationships tend to see them as more intimate, less commercial, than our relationships with our bosses usually are.

---

* And when I say "radically different," I mean it. Just for starters, we have about 12 million to 40 million olfactory neurons; dogs have between 220 million and 326 million. Hmm, I wonder why our dogs often act distracted when "nothing's going on."

In her book *Dogs Are from Neptune,* the trainer and behaviorist Jean Donaldson points out that for those of us who "merrily food train," our "bond with the dog is separate from the technical task of manipulating his behavior."[8] On the one hand, I have adored all my dogs. On the other hand, I need to teach them manners, and the most efficient, pleasantest way to do that is to elicit the behavior I want and then reward the heck out of it with food and experiences that the dog wants, thereby turning the behavior into established habit.

Donaldson's right, but I still think we need to say something about how the training and the emotional relationship interact. It's not as simple as "A good relationship makes training better," because that isn't always true. I am far from being the most polished clicker trainer in the world, but my skills are decent, and I can often demonstrate the efficiency and fun of clicker training by shaping a new client's dog to perform some behavior that the client has never been able to teach.* "I can't get him to lie down," the client says, but given a few minutes with a clicker and some treats I can have their dog flinging himself to the ground as fast as his little body will let him. Look, I have no mojo, and *obviously,* the client's dog does not love me more than he loves the client. Many of my client dogs become my client dogs because they have one or more behavior problems, usually including some suspicion of strangers, so they don't start out liking me even a little bit. Often, by the time we're ready for the here's-how-to-teach-your-dog part of an initial session, I've at best established myself as somewhat less worrisome than the average unfamiliar human. You don't need much of any relationship at all with most dogs to start training.† But.

But then you start training, and the relationship changes. Clients often remark on how much their dogs like me. My behavior is clear and predictable. I avoid doing things (staring, looming, invading space) that behaviorally troubled dogs may respond to fearfully or aggressively. And many of my interactions with a client dog involve clicker training in one form or another, which is to say that I present the dog with opportunities to get hold of things the dog likes in the context of

---

* Assuming here that the dog isn't afraid of the clicker (some are) or so suspicious of strangers that he won't even work with me.

† With very worried, spooky, fearful dogs, you need to build up some trust—but (surprise!) consistent reward-based interactions and training do just that.

a puzzle ("What did I just do to make her click and give me roast chicken? . . . Was it this? That? Oh, *yeah*") that the dog enjoys.*

That's it, really: I'm safe, I'm fun, and it's easy for dogs to figure out how I work. I think the connection between relationship and training may be as simple as that. Deliver rewards—food, attention, play, walks, scritches, anything your dog likes—in exchange for the behavior you want, and your dog learns not only the behavior but also that you're fun, safe, reliable, and worth paying attention to.

I recently read a post to an e-mail discussion group mentioning "pets who have their own agendas for what they want to go after, and must be taught to behave." Give me a break. Of course dogs have their own agendas. They want to eat, run, play, get butt scritches, roll in smelly things, chase squirrels, sniff the fire hydrant. The point of pet-dog manners isn't to wipe out the dog's reasonable agenda and replace it with our own (heel, dammit!); the point is to *teach our dogs to get what they want by behaving in ways that make it easy for us to live with them.* Do you want dinner? Lie down quietly a few feet away instead of getting underfoot. Do you want to go for a long walk? Keep the leash slack rather than pull me hither and yon, because I won't enjoy walking you if you sprain my shoulder every time. Do you want my attention? Sit down next to me and rest your head on my thigh rather than barking in my face. Do you want to greet visitors? Sit or stand or wiggle pleasantly around them when they come in, instead of jumping up and tearing their clothes.

I admire the precise, dedicated training that results in Attila Szku-kalek's freestyle performances with his amazing Border Collie, Fly. (Check out their "Gladiator" video; you can easily find it on YouTube. And yes, Attila's a reward-based trainer.) Heaven knows I appreciate the reliable, complex work done by bomb-sniffing dogs and search-and-rescue dogs. And this book is, after all, devoted to explaining how to teach your dog to attend to you and take your cues promptly and happily.

But let's set aside the notion that we are our dogs' "masters"—that, by gum, we have a right to command them, and they have an obligation to obey. Instead, think of training as a way to translate, from Hu-

---

* Dogs with exceptionally poor frustration tolerance need the criteria for success set very low at first, while they gradually learn to keep trying without lashing out if they make a mistake and don't earn a reward. Even they can enjoy the training game, though, if you play at a level where they can succeed.

man to Dog and (when we attend to our dogs' communications and respond to them in turn) back again. The Human-to-Dog equivalent of Babelfish is a child's toy: a clicker.

How Clicker Training Works (and Works for You)

Clicker training isn't magic. It isn't mysterious. And although the most sophisticated clicker trainers will spend days discussing its finer points, we ordinary mortals can use it with great success.

The clicker is a little plastic doohickey that makes a clicking noise. It's also a ridiculously simple means of taking advantage of how animals learn and of bridging the annoying gap caused by the fact that nonhumans don't have spoken language, while most of us humans rely on words to communicate. The sound of the click signals the dog that a reward—a "reinforcer"—is on the way.* As a result of this association with a pleasant consequence, she becomes more likely to do whatever she was doing when she heard the click. Like all animals, including us, dogs will do more of whatever behavior gets them something they want.†

GETTING STARTED

We used to tell clients to "charge the clicker" before they started training. You'd take a small stash of treats and a clicker, and you'd click, then treat, ten or twenty times in a row. The point was to teach your dog the specific lesson that a click means a treat is coming.

This step turns out to be unnecessary. All you have to do is get a clicker, get some treats, and start training. Dogs figure out the click's significance PDQ. I *do* recommend (strongly!) that you read the rest of this chapter first. Also, if you are clumsy or have trouble with timing, like me, do yourself a favor and have a couple of short, dogless practice sessions in which you visualize your dog doing something you like; you click at that very moment, and you immediately fake-deliver a real treat. You can use a human partner as your test subject. (They don't

---

* Reinforcer" is the correct scientific term for any consequence of a behavior that strengthens (reinforces) that behavior. Many people who study learning use the term "reward" for a consequence that might be pleasant enough but isn't actually reinforcing. I don't think this distinction exists in everyday speech and writing, and for the sake of accessibility I've chosen to ignore it in this book. If you want to dig deeper into the literature of animal training, be aware of it.

† That's true whether or not a clicker is involved; for instance, if pulling on leash gets a dog over to the tree she wants to sniff, and then gets her to the park faster, and then gets her within grabbing range of a chicken bone, she will associate pulling with goodies. Pulling works for her. She will pull more. .

actually have to eat the dog treats.) Another good way to reduce performance anxiety is to make your first real lesson with your dog a simple behavior. I like to start off my clients with targeting (see Chapter 10, "Play? Training? Tricks?"), because it's easy to teach and a good basis for many manners behaviors as well as for entertaining tricks.

Two common and very reasonable questions: Why a clicker instead of a word or some other sound? And why can't the reward itself be the marker—why introduce the extra complication?

WHY USE A CLICKER?

As I've said, there's nothing magic about the clicker. But it offers advantages. The bright, staccato click stands out, carries well, and is always the same; also, it doesn't sound like anything else. I encourage my clients to teach their dog a marker word as well as the click, because there will be those moments when your hands are full, or you forgot to bring the clicker on a walk and your dog does something superlatively

---

Why "Cue" and Not "Command"?

Quick and Dirty Tip

I use the word "cue," not the word "command." That isn't only because I dislike the traditional view that humans order dogs around and they are obliged to obey us for whatever reason. It's also because the word "command" leads us into a conceptual error: It implies that our words are what *make* dogs do certain behaviors. Your dog sits *because* you command him to sit.

Unfortunately for the human ego, this is flat-out wrong. The truth of behavior is that *it is driven by its consequences, not by our authority to give orders.* Your dog doesn't sit because you said "Sit"; he sits because he's learned that when you make that sound, he's got an opportunity. If you're a modern, reward-based trainer, he might get a treat, or permission to go out the door, or a scritch under the chin, or any one of a hundred other Good Consequences for Dogs, none of which would happen if he didn't sit when he heard "Sit." If you're an old-school, coercion-based trainer, your dog has learned that when you say "Sit," sitting will enable him to avoid a yank on the neck or a push on the rump or an electric shock. In other words, sitting when he hears "Sit" prevents Bad Consequences for Dogs.

great such as turn away from a chicken bone. But a clicker's better than a marker word because we human beings yammer yammer yammer all day long and most of what comes out of our mouths is meaningless and irrelevant to our dogs. This makes words a weaker means of communication. (We'll see more implications of that later, when I explain how to effectively teach word cues.)*

You can use the clicker in formal training sessions for particular behaviors—not only manners behaviors, such as walking politely on leash, but also tricks, such as taking a bow on cue. You can also use the clicker throughout the day to mark behaviors the dog just happens to do and that you like. For instance, suppose you and your dog are hanging out in your living room and a dog begins barking outside. Your dog looks up but is quiet. Click! and then give your dog a food treat. Every time you do this, you make it a little likelier that when your dog hears barking outside, he'll keep quiet instead of barking back.

WHAT IF YOUR DOG IS AFRAID OF THE CLICKER?

Some small dogs, sound-sensitive dogs, and undersocialized dogs are frightened by the short, sharp click. If you suspect your dog is one of them, try a pen that clicks, or use a tongue click. If even that's too much for your dog, stick with a spoken word as your click. Choose a short word that you habitually speak in a pleasant, bright tone and that you can say in more or less the same way every time. (I use "Yes.") These qualities will help your click word stand out and make it easier for your dog to recognize its significance for her.

Fear is sneaky, by the way. Many dogs who turn out to be afraid of the clicker pick up right away that it predicts a treat, so for the first few reps of training they look just fine. The next minute, you realize that they're becoming *slower* to perform the behavior you're clicking, or they're offering the behavior but from a distance, or their ears are pinned, or they take the treat from as far away as they can and stretch their necks to reach it.

Such fear isn't all that common even among the behaviorally troubled dogs who make up most of my students. But watch out for it. The last thing you want is to make training sessions scary to your dog.

---

* If your dog is deaf, your marker can be the flash of a penlight or a distinctive hand signal. See this book's Web site, www.TheDogTrainerBook.com, for more resources.

ADDING THE CUE

So you've been clicking and treating your dog for performing a given behavior, but, wait: Problem! How do you tell the dog when you want her to do that behavior?

If you happened to read the box about cues versus commands, above, you might have noticed that I characterized a cue as a signal to the dog that he now has a chance to earn a reinforcer for a given behavior. To put it less technically, once you teach the cue "Down," hearing it tells your dog that if he now lies down, he might just get something he wants. At the same time, you teach him that nothing in particular is forthcoming if he lies down when you haven't asked him to, or if he lies down when you've asked him to do something else. Once the dog has gotten these points into his little doggy brain, we say that the behavior's "on cue."

To put a behavior on cue, you need to anticipate when your dog is about to do it. I'll stick with "Down" as an example. Suppose you and your Puppalini have been having a practice session: Puppalini lies down, you click and deliver a treat, you toss a treat to get him up and moving so he can do another rep, he grabs the treat, returns to you and lies down, click/treat/toss, etc., etc., etc. Puppalini is performing like clockwork, coming back to you and dropping into a down as fast as he can get his little puppy legs out from under him. You know exactly when he's going to lie down again. Puppalini is ready for you to add the cue.

Do this by saying the cue *just before* Puppalini would lie down anyway, then click/treat/toss. Repeat, repeat, repeat. After some number of reps like this, Puppalini will associate the sound of you saying "Puppalini, down" with the sequence of events that follows—he lies down, you click/treat. Practice in several different contexts. Also, no click/treat for Puppalini now if he lies down without being asked, or if he lies down in response to some other cue you have already taught. Click/treat every time he lies down after you say, "Down," and not otherwise.*

In my example, you the trainer give a spoken-word cue. But you can also use a gesture, and you can teach both a gesture and a word. (Teach one at a time, please, or your dog will not understand either of them when given alone.) Pick cues that come naturally to you and that

---

* However, if your dog spontaneously does something terrific, such as lie down when a guest enters your house even though you haven't given your "Down" cue, you should absolutely reward that choice.

How Long Should Each Session Last?

Quick and Dirty Tip

How long should each training session last? Let your dog tell you! As a general rule, puppies and beginner dogs have shorter attention spans and will tire more quickly; a ten-treat or fifteen-treat session is probably plenty long enough. But surprisingly often I find client dogs, meeting the clicker for the very first time, turn into instant Einsteins—they start learning rapidly right off the bat and don't seem to tire or show any signs of stress. On the other hand, even an experienced, clicker-savvy, training-junkie dog can have an off day. If your dog's yawning, sniffing, turning away, missing cues you're sure he knows, cut him a break. Tell him, "All done," and come back to training later or another day.

For a good example, check out "Knowing When to Abort a Training Session," a YouTube video by thistlemiss, aka Sarah Owings of Bridges Dog Training, http://bit.ly/dYMB3p.

you can reproduce pretty consistently so that your dog will recognize them.

You'll notice I said "some number of reps." I can't predict how many! The answer depends on many factors. How much practice has Puppalini already had in learning from you? The more learning he has under his belt, the easier new learning becomes. How much do you talk during training sessions? The more you talk, the harder it will be for your dog to figure out which of the sounds coming out of your mouth is relevant to him.* How meticulous are you as a trainer? You don't have to be a superstar to teach your dog pleasant manners and entertaining tricks, and you don't have to be a superstar to have a blast training your dog, but of course the more polished your skills, the easier your dog will find it to learn from you.

You won't click and treat forever for every behavior your dog learns. Click and treat (tiny treats!) generously when you're teaching your dog good behaviors, especially new behaviors. Remember that you are building up habits for a lifetime and teaching your dog that paying attention to you and doing as you ask are fun, rewarding activities. As

---

* This is one of the many reasons clicker training is so fabulous. It forces humans to shut up, which in turn means that when we *do* speak, our dogs are more likely to take an interest.

your dog's new, good behaviors become established habits, you can phase out the clicker and give food treats only occasionally, for especially good performances. Also, you can use other things your dog values, such as access to the outdoors and opportunities to sniff and play, as rewards for good behavior.

TIPS FOR CLICKER TRAINING

In this book, I'll give instructions for teaching dogs specific skills such as paying attention to you and coming when called. Here are some important points that always apply.

- Click first, *then* treat.
- Click *once*. If your dog does something extra special, you can give an extra-good treat, or give more than one treat, or give a treat and then praise warmly, or give six extra-good treats and then praise warmly.* But just one click!
- Always deliver a food treat after the click. Though clicker-trained dogs learn to love the sound of the click, that's only because they associate it with a goody. The clicker isn't important to them for its own sake. If the association between the click and the treat is weakened, the click will become less useful as a marker for good behavior. In fact, dogs whose expectations are violated in this way often check out of the training process and behave as if they have lost trust in their trainer.
- Try to deliver the food treat about half a second or a second after the click.
- Some things the clicker isn't: a remote control (don't point it at your dog!); an attention-getting device; a substitute for praise; a way to give "commands." *The sound of the click points out to the dog what she just did to earn a reward—that's it.*
- As much as you can, avoid using food to lure your dog into a behavior. Of course, your dog will know that you have food in your pocket or treat pouch, or in that bowl on the table. But if she often sees the food up front, or if you always lure her into position with a treat, then the presence of food becomes *part of the cue* for

---

* Controlled studies find that jackpots are ineffective. But they don't do any harm, either, and, hey, it's fun to give your dog a jackpot sometimes.

Get Your Dog's Focus Off Food

Quick and Dirty Tip

A good way to get your dog's focus off the food is to have it around constantly. Carry treats in your pocket all the time. Stash covered treat containers out of reach in several places around your home. Your dog will learn that the mere presence of treats means nothing much. Your cues and the click are what she needs to attend to if she wants to know when goodies are coming her way.

the behavior, and she may not learn what to do when she doesn't see food. On pages 77–78, I explain how to use lure-and-reward effectively. And in later chapters, where I describe how to teach specific behaviors, I explain how to get your dog to offer those behaviors without being lured.

- Clicker training is very forgiving of beginners' mistakes! If you click too late or too early or forget to click or sometimes give the treat before you click, it will take your dog a bit longer to learn the specific behavior you're teaching her. But she will still be learning that good things come from working for you, and that's the most important lesson of all.

HOW TO END A CLICKER-TRAINING SESSION

Dogs enjoy reward-based training. Why wouldn't they? It's fun to figure out how to get you to click and treat, and then, of course, there's the treat. Clicker-trained dogs often turn into junkies for training; my Juniper, whom I started training the day I brought him home at eight and a half weeks of age, doesn't seem to ever want to quit at all, though in the evenings when we've attended all-day training camps he conks out approximately one minute after dinner and it's all I can do to wake him for his late-night pee break.

This joy in training has two pitfalls. The first is that your dog may experience the end of a training session as aversive—unpleasant. The result can be that whatever behavior he did last has been punished, in the technical learning-theory sense. In other words, because (from your dog's point of view) that last behavior produced an unpleasant consequence (the end of the training session), it becomes less likely to occur in future.* So when you pick some absolutely brilliant, letter-perfect response as the moment to quit, you might be punishing that letter-perfect response. Oy.

Get around this problem by ending the session with a pleasant coda. Give your dog a belly-rub, or hand him a small chewy, or scatter a dozen treats on the ground for him to forage, or play a quick game. Go for a walk if it's time to go for a walk. Training is done, but the aftermath is pleasant, too.

The second pitfall, closely related to the first, is that some dogs get to be pests about training. The session's over? No it's not no it's not no it's not! They nose you, they offer every behavior you've ever taught them, they jump on you, they bark at you, they find the clicker and bring it to you.

Pestiness persists *if it works*. Give in to the dog who's nagging you for attention of any kind, including a training session, and you've rewarded nagging. (By the way, does your Training Nag dog make an attention-seeking pest of himself in other circumstances as well?) If you don't mind being nagged, fine! But if you would prefer that your dog accept the session's end without pestering, then consistently apply the rule that when a training session is over, it's over. Dogalini can't make it resume by noodging.

You can help your dog learn "Training's over for now" by giving him a consistent signal at session's end (right before you deliver a sweetener, as I described above). I say, "All done!" and show my dog my empty hands. What signal you use doesn't matter, as long as it's pleasant, clear, and distinctive, and as long as you present it consistently. Of course, your dog won't understand your signal the first time you use it; the meaning will become clear to her over time because the signal will always mark the same event.

By the way, here's a bit of perspective on "clicker training pitfalls." I have a small collection of old dog-training books, written before trainers began to assimilate the science of animal learning and instead relied on

---

* Note for technically inclined readers: If you're scratching your head here and thinking, "But I clicked and treated that last brilliant behavior. Didn't that reinforce it?" you're right. Also, the potential punisher (ending the training session) is somewhat delayed; delaying a punisher, like delaying a reinforcer, diminishes its effectiveness. However, the punisher here isn't delayed *much*. If a training session ends abruptly, the sequence (behavior → click/treat → loss of your attention and of the opportunity to earn further reinforcers) takes place within just a couple of seconds. This is a brief enough interval that the aversive effect of ending the session may wash back onto the final click/treat and the behavior that earned it.

anecdote, folklore, and, to a greater or lesser extent, force. Some of these books are almost unreadable because their authors appear actually to relish using violence to get dogs to comply.

But other writers clearly loved dogs and don't seem to have been so happy with their own methods. Willy Necker, the author of a 1953 booklet called "Train Your Dog with Kindness," describes teaching dogs to "down" like this: The dog's leashed and wearing a choke collar. The trainer stands next to the dog, passes the leash under his foot, says, "Down," and then delivers multiple short sharp jerks on the leash so that the dog is forced to the ground. Eventually, the dog learns to lie down in order to avoid being dragged down. (If this strikes you as a ham-handed approach to teaching—well, it is.) After explaining this method, Mr. Necker writes: "This exercise has a depressing effect on most dogs. It is well not to keep at it very long at a time." And, he says, you might want to play with your dog a bit after a session of teaching "down," to cheer him up.*

Most dogs taught to lie down with a clicker and treats will fling themselves onto the ground wearing doggy smiles. They'll do it as fast as they're physically able, as often as they're physically able. There's no need to cheer them up afterward. A dog who looks forward eagerly to training and doesn't want to quit? Some pitfall.

LURE-AND-REWARD TRAINING

One popular form of dog-friendly training is called lure-and-reward. You've used lure-and-reward if you've taught your dog to lie down by putting a treat in front of his nose while he's sitting, and then bringing the treat down to the ground. He follows the treat, winds up lying down, you say, "Yes!" and instantly give him the treat, and that's lure-and-reward.

You're probably already wondering: Will you wind up with a dog who'll lie down only when he's following the treat in your hand? Many people call this situation "bribery"; it's probably more accurate to say that the dog has learned to perceive the treat as part of the cue, or has learned that he never gets a reward of any kind unless he sees a treat up

---

* If you think 1953 was a long time ago, let me assure you that in this century I have seen an "obedience club" class demonstrate a similar method for teaching sit. Choke chain on the dog, jerk upward with the leash to force the dog's head up and the hindquarters down, release the pressure when the dog's butt hits the ground. I imagine they use thumbscrews on their children as well.

front. (Parenthetically, this problem doesn't generally arise with the clicker training techniques that I'll describe in this book.)

To avoid having the treat be part of the cue, we do what's called "fading the lure." When you teach a behavior by lure-and-reward, use the treat to lure your dog only the first few times. The next time, make the luring gesture, but with your hand empty—then say, "Yes!" and deliver the treat with your *other* hand. Ideally, you're keeping the treats on a counter or elsewhere off your person.

When you fade the lure this way, you can gradually morph your luring movement into whatever hand cue you'd like to use. Or you can choose to lure a few times, then stay still and just wait to see what your dog does. Let's stick with the example of teaching him to lie down. Since he's just done that behavior several times and gotten rewarded, he's likely to try it again. Give him a few moments to think. If he lies down all the way, immediately say, "Yes," and deliver the treat. If he starts to go down hesitantly, catch the beginning of his downward movement, say, "Yes," and deliver the treat relatively low, so that he has to drop a little further to eat it. Then wait to see what he does next. Chances are good he'll get the point this time.

How to Use Food Rewards Effectively

You can use anything a dog likes—play, butt scritches, kicked-up leaves, permission to go outside, a chance to sniff the new kitten—as a reward for behavior you like, but in clicker training sessions it's almost always best to use food. Food is what's called a "primary reinforcer," meaning something animals don't need to learn to like. A rule of clicker training is that the click should always be followed by a primary reinforcer. Besides food, some of the other primary reinforcers are water, air, and sex, but you can see how using these might present logistical and ethical problems.*

Food is Number 1 on most dogs' hit parade, and because you can give a food reward quickly and your dog can eat it even more quickly, it

---

* Though the behaviorist Patricia McConnell wrote a blog post (www.theotherendoftheleash.com, July 20, 2010) about using a drink of water to reward a dog for coming when called on a hot day. That was good training and perfectly humane. But it's one thing to capitalize on circumstances or to choose that peckish pre-dinner hour for training, it's another thing to *deliberately* let a dog get thirsty enough to work for water.

lends itself to training with multiple repetitions. But even food can be used more or less effectively, so you might as well use it effectively.

Here's the most important point: *Be generous.* To us, what we're trying to teach our dogs seems simple and reasonable. To our dogs, it's not so simple and it's often weird. Dogs have brains the size of lemons and they like to roll in dead animals.* They are not us! It's hard for them to learn that the sounds coming out of our mouth in one context mean the same thing in a completely different context that offers many distractions. We make our lessons even more confusing when we're not consistent in our choice of words for a cue, when we use different tones of voice, and when our body language varies from situation to situation. Rewarding generously is part of clear communication with them.

Because you'll be giving many, many food rewards, each one should be minute. Use bits of food—for my eighty-pound Pit Bull mix, I use dry dog food and pieces of cheese and meat smaller than my pinky nail. For tiny dogs, use the smallest pieces of food you can handle. Or try offering a lick of canned food.

DELIVER THE TREAT WHERE YOU WANT YOUR DOG TO BE

When you're teaching your dog a certain position, she should be in that position, or on her way to it, when she gets the food. That's because whatever position she's in when she's rewarded is the position she's being rewarded *for.* If you're teaching your dog to walk next to you on leash without pulling, deliver the food at your side where you'd like her to be. If you're teaching her to lie down, deliver the food low and right to her mouth or between her forepaws, so she doesn't so much as have to stretch up to get it. If she does start to get up, lure her back down with the food, then deliver it. For a more advanced learner, you can pull the food away and wait for her to lie back down on her own, then redeliver the food.

WHAT TO DO IF YOUR DOG ISN'T MOTIVATED BY FOOD

Fairly often, we trainers hear from a client that his or her dog isn't motivated by food. Assuming the dog is healthy, four common reasons account for most of these situations.

---

* Jean Donaldson famously titled a chapter of her book *The Culture Clash* "Lemon Brains but We Still Love Them."

1. **The dog has food in her bowl all day long.** If that's your dog, feed separate meals instead. Pick up any uneaten food after 15 minutes. Training with food isn't about keeping your dog hungry, but food does lose value if she never feels even a little bit peckish.

2. **The dog is anxious.** This often comes up with undersocialized dogs working outdoors—when I meet them, I find they pull frantically on leash, their tails are tucked, their ears are down, and when their person offers food they eat it mechanically or let it fall out of their mouth. Training needs to happen in an environment that doesn't scare the dog; as for the great outdoors, we have to alleviate the dog's anxiety before she can learn.

3. **The dog is too distracted to eat in the training situation.** Dog sees squirrel, dog fixates on squirrel, owner tries to distract dog with a food treat, dog appears completely unaware of food treat. This dog needs more practice in non-distracting situations. And we may need to find a way to use the distractor itself as a reward.

4. **The dog doesn't like the treat.** There seems to be a lot of wishful thinking out there regarding what dogs like. "He loves sliced apple," for instance. Well, yes, some do. For most dogs, though, break out the meaty-cheesy-fishy-smelly if you want their full attention. That goes double if you're teaching them to leave the pot roast alone. Who are you kidding with the dry biscuits, there?

WHEN CAN YOU STOP USING FOOD?

Clients often ask: "When can I stop using food?" When your dog responds to a given cue at least 90 percent of the time in different contexts, you can start making your food rewards random and less frequent. But *stay generous*. Reward sometimes with food, sometimes with play, sometimes with the chance to go back and do more of whatever he was doing when you called him, sometimes with butt scritches. These are all ways of thanking your dog. People often fetishize this idea that dogs should do our bidding just because. That's a trap. In any good relationship, reciprocity's the name of the game. The same goes for good training.

WHEN NOT TO USE FOOD

At times, your dog may want something else more than he wants food. When you teach polite leash walking, for instance, the chance to move faster or move forward or sniff a tree or hydrant may constitute a more valuable reward than a food treat. In teaching an eager dog to wait for permission to go out an open door, that permission is a more important reward than food. A behavior-modification procedure called the Constructional Aggression Treatment is based on the insight that the usual reward for an aggressive display is removal of the offending stimulus—your aggressive dog snarls at another dog, for instance, and the other dog moves away. CAT leverages this knowledge by giving the learner dog the distance he wants in exchange for nonaggressive (and, eventually, pro-social) behavior. In this work, food is very much beside the point.

Some dogs become agitated and overaroused, even aggressive, in the presence of food. Sometimes the fix is to hold very short training sessions and use low-value treats (dry kibble, for instance, rather than chicken), but sometimes the dog needs to learn frustration tolerance in other contexts before you can safely use food in training.

People who want to help a shy or ambivalent dog often try having a stranger feed the dog treats. This can work but has pitfalls; fearful dogs may push themselves past their own limits, for example, snatching the food and then snapping at the hand that held it. Food can be useful in behavior modification, but get a behavior specialist to help.

SPECIAL TIPS FOR SMALL DOGS

Vets often advise that small dogs not skip any meals, and some may need to be "free fed," that is, have food available at all times. Additionally, it's hard to handle treats tiny enough to enable you to deliver two or three dozen without throwing a very small dog's digestion or nutritional balance out of whack (Malteses, I'm looking at you).

Workarounds: Use single licks of a high-quality, super-tasty canned dog food as rewards. Figure out what nonfoods your small dog especially likes (chasing her ball, maybe?) and leverage those as much as you can. If your dog must be free fed, notice what times of day she chooses to eat, and set training sessions just before those times. Otherwise, train right before mealtime—in fact, use your small dog's whole meal in training, and you don't have to worry about her nutrition at all.

Small dogs spend a lot of time being loomed over, and most of them don't like it. Many of them *do* appreciate being up off the ground for training, so you don't loom over them when you deliver a treat. A big coffee table, with you sitting on the couch, maybe?

Also see "What If Your Dog Is Afraid of the Clicker?" on page 71.

How to Choose a Dog Trainer

It's entirely possible to teach pet-dog manners with help from books and videos—I never attended a class with my first dog, Izzy, but she easily earned her Canine Good Citizen certificate, a basic manners evaluation offered by the American Kennel Club. As I've said before, I have no mojo; I just read carefully and practiced.

But in-person coaching helps a lot of people; besides, classes can be fun. (And at the end you usually get a little certificate of which you'll be ridiculously, absurdly, eye-wateringly proud.) The trouble is that anyone can legally call himself a trainer, and often does, because there is no governmental licensing or mandatory certification of any kind. There exist proprietary schools, which issue designations such as "master trainer," but, again, no generally accepted definition exists. Some private trainer-training programs are excellent; the best are probably those offered by Pat Miller (http://www.peaceablepaws.com), Dogs of Course (http://dogsofcourse.com), and the Karen Pryor Academy (http://www.karenpryoracademy.com). Jean Donaldson, who used to run a highly regarded program at the San Francisco SPCA, has launched a new distance learning site (http://www.academyfordogtrainers.com). Pick a graduate of one of these programs, and the odds of competency go way up. However, costs of attending are high, and many good trainers have educated themselves by the more economical route of reading, watching videos, and serving informal apprenticeships.

There is one independent national certification program, the Certification Council for Professional Dog Trainers (http://www.ccpdt .org). The Web site has a search function to enable you to find a nearby trainer.

For manners training, the council offers a single level of certification, "Certified Professional Dog Trainer–Knowledge Assessed" (CPDT-KA).* The holder of a CPDT-KA must have completed 300 hours as the lead or sole trainer in classes and/or in private work, must submit references from a veterinarian, a client, and another CPDT-KA, and must pass a 250-question exam. Trainers are required to sign a code of ethics and to recertify every three years, either by submitting proof of continuing education or by retaking the exam.

---

* The council added a behavior certification in 2011. For more information, see "How to Find a Behavior Specialist," p. 216.

This is a good start, but it's a floor, not a ceiling. Those 300 hours may or may not mean much, since the quality of the teaching isn't assessed. The written test is not difficult and someone can give the right answers while still defaulting to coercive methods in real life.

So, once you find a CPDT-KA (or a graduate of one of the programs I mentioned) near you, screen him. He should use clicker training or lure-and-reward training, or a combination. He should not recommend choke ("correction" or "training") collars, prong collars, or collars that deliver electric shock (sometimes euphemistically called "remote training collars"). If he uses the language of dominance ("alpha," "pack"), he's not keeping up with the science of dog behavior. "Punishment" is not necessarily a bad word; technically, it applies to time-outs, for example, which may disappoint dogs but rarely distress them. But look for a trainer who focuses on setting dogs up for success and on managing behavior to prevent problems.

A good trainer will attend professional seminars offered by modern trainers and behaviorists or, if none are offered locally, will take telecourses such as those offered by Raising Canine (http://www.raising canine.com) and Animal Behavior Associates (http://www.animal behaviorassociates.com). She may go to meetings such as Clicker Expo and the annual meeting of the Association of Pet Dog Trainers. She probably belongs to at least one professional association, such as the APDT or the International Association of Animal Behavior Consultants. These two groups espouse noncoercive training and behavior modification; others, such as the International Association of Canine Professionals and the National Association of Dog Obedience Instructors, explicitly allow all forms of training. If your prospective trainer belongs to one of them, interview carefully concerning what methods he uses.

Classes should be fairly small; five or six students per instructor is a good maximum. Ask to observe. Positive reinforcement matters to people as much as it does to dogs, so the teacher should welcome questions, encourage the humans, and build on what students do right, rather than focus on mistakes. Look for clear demonstrations and explanations. Although a class may include shy dogs, in general you want to see happy wags and bright eyes; the dogs should be having a good time and act eager to learn. If the class includes playtime (puppy classes, especially, often do), any bullying should be *gently* interrupted. Puppies may be separated by size and play style, too, though this isn't always necessary.

It's difficult to say what classes should cost. Overhead, such as rent, varies hugely depending on location; all other things being equal, smaller classes with more instructors will be more expensive.

In Chapter 12, "Stuff Dogs Do That Worries People," I explain how to choose a behavior specialist. But "regular" trainers specialize too. The emphasis and skill sets (canine and human) needed for pet-dog manners, agility, competitive obedience, tracking, Schutzhund (and on and on) are all different, even when trainers are committed to reward-based, noncoercive techniques. I'm very good at teaching people how to teach their pets, and at designing and carrying out behavior modification programs for difficult dogs. The skills of formal obedience competition, such as the retrieve at a distance and over obstacles—well, they're not so much my thing. On the other hand, I have the impression that those who train dogs and handlers for canine sports don't always have a good picture of what kinds of help ordinary mortals tend to need. There'll always be exceptions, of course, but on the whole I'd say that if you're looking for help to teach your pet dog nice manners, you should look for someone who works mostly on, yes, pet-dog manners.

Housetraining

4

Here's the good news about housetraining: It's pretty much cookbook. Start with a healthy puppy, follow two rules (just two!), and you'll wind up with a housetrained dog. (Yes, you can housetrain an adult dog, but more about that later.) You spotted the catch there, no doubt: "Follow the rules." The more vigilant and regimented you are about the process, the easier it is, and the sooner you can go back to evenings spent in sweet communion with your laptop, and nights of unbroken sleep. Let yourself fall into a routine of a little puppy accident here, another little puppy accident there, and before you know it you have an adolescent dog who doesn't know where the toilet is. By "adolescent" I mean "much larger, and therefore depositing much larger volumes of urine and feces in your living room."

The Rules of Housetraining

1. Bend over backward to make sure your pupil has plenty of appropriately timed opportunities to eliminate in the right place.
2. Supervise and/or confine your pupil in between toilet outings, so that she doesn't have a chance to eliminate in the wrong place.

Let me spell these out in detail. Very young puppies have no real control over their bladder and bowels; they feel the urge to go, and next thing both of you know, they've gone. This means you need to get your puppy to the toilet area fast and often. For a nine-week-old, that can be every waking hour, *plus* the following:

- immediately on waking in the morning or after a nap
- after a few minutes of playing or getting excited for any reason
- after he's been chewing for a while and then stops

- a few minutes after eating or drinking
  (Take careful note of the difference between those last two items.
  It's "a few minutes after eating," but if you wait to take your puppy
  out until "a few minutes after playing," the odds are good you'll
  find yourself cleaning the floor.)
- whenever you catch them circling, sniffing the floor, or generally
  acting restless

WHAT ABOUT HOUSETRAINING AN ADULT DOG?

The same rules apply to a grown dog who's being housetrained (or re-
housetrained). Two differences apply, and they cut against each other.
To your advantage in housetraining an adult dog, he has the ability to
control the muscles that govern elimination, though he hasn't learned
to use them. To your disadvantage, it's harder to replace one habit
(eliminating wherever) with another (eliminating only outdoors) than
it is to teach a habit from scratch.

How to Housetrain Your Dog

There's nothing quite so frustrating as seeing that squat-and-pee
happen just as you're half a step from the front door. Here's how to
get that puppy outside before she eliminates. Oddly enough, a puppy
or small dog in arms will usually hang on to her bladder while you
carry her outdoors—provided, of course, that you're taking her out
promptly and moving fast. With a larger dog or puppy, you can take
a second leash (i.e., besides the leash clipped to her harness or collar),
make a U with it around the dog's groin, and *gently gently gently* hold
the ends of the U with just enough tension to prevent a squat as you
walk to the door. The sole purpose of this move is to prevent that
squat; if it distresses your dog in any way, forget it. By around five
months, your puppy will probably have pretty good control over his
bladder and bowels. He won't be able to hold it as long as an adult dog
can, but he will be able to get out the door without eliminating on the
way.

Bring your puppy/dog outside on leash to a place where you'd like
her to eliminate, and stand there quietly. Give her three minutes to
eliminate. If she does eliminate, praise calmly and warmly, give a treat,
and take her for a walk. *The walk is a reward for eliminating.* By rewarding elimination with a walk, you encourage your dog to eliminate

as soon as she reaches the designated spot. If she urinates right away, and later defecates during your walk, you can reward the outdoor defecation; no need to reward any urinations after the first one.

If after three minutes she doesn't eliminate, take her back inside, but keep her on leash with you, or tethered to a piece of furniture with a comfy bed to lie on, or in her crate, or in a small confined area like a playpen. Wait fifteen minutes to thirty minutes and take her outside again. Repeat this process until she eliminates outside, then praise, treat, and reward with a walk.

If you have reason to believe that your dog needs to defecate (maybe it's first thing in the morning, or she hasn't defecated all day), but when you go out she only urinates, go ahead and take her for a walk. The exercise may stimulate her bowels; if not, then, when you come in, keep her confined (either on leash, tethered, in a crate, or in a small area such as a puppy pen) and try again 15 to 30 minutes later. Keep a close eye on her in the meantime.

When you know your puppy or dog has an empty bladder and bowels, he can spend a few minutes unconfined (remember rule number 2: you're supervising your housetrainee or keeping him confined when he's indoors). But you'll need to supervise carefully, watching for any sign that he needs to eliminate again. "Supervise carefully" is code for "keep your eyes on him every single second." As this implies, you and your puppy should be in the same room.

Ten minutes at large is a good starting point; when time's up, either bring your puppy to his elimination spot again (Has he eaten, drunk, played, chewed? Does he just kinda sorta seem to need to go?) or confine him in his crate or pen. Yes, puppies need exercise and attention; like other babies, they also need plenty of rest and sleep.

Even when your puppy/dog is completely empty, give him access to only the room you are in for now. When you and he have been 100 percent successful for one week, you can begin expanding his "empty time" freedom room by room. Spend time with him in each room, feeding him and cuddling him there, to help him perceive this new space as part of the den.

WHAT IF YOUR PUPPY "CAN'T GO OUTSIDE" YET?

Many vets advise that puppies who haven't had all their vaccinations should stay indoors. As I explain in Chapter 2, "Socialization," veterinarians familiar with dogs' behavioral development agree that it's imperative to get young puppies out in the world and give them pleasant experience of its many sights, sounds, and smells. However, you may indeed expose an unvaccinated puppy to disease *if you put him on the ground.* What you decide about this depends on local circumstances and your own perception of risk. Is "the ground" your fenced backyard or a rubbish-strewn street? Do you live in an area where most dogs have homes and regular veterinary care, or someplace with lots of strays?

If you need to keep your puppy off the ground outside until she has some or all of her vaxes on board, set up an indoor elimination area and use that: Proceed as with normal housetraining, but go to the indoor elimination area instead.

Although newspapers and "pee pads" are pretty standard, they may not be the best choice. Dogs develop strong preferences for particular surfaces on which to eliminate, and neither papers nor pads much resemble sidewalk, dirt, or turf. (Also, the odds that your dog will find newspaper lying around on your floor at some point during her life are fairly high.)

One alternative is a couple of large cat litter pans filled with dirt and sod and/or pieces of stone. There's no getting around the difficulty of keeping these clean, but they may help your puppy adjust when the big day comes and you hit the sidewalk. Commercial products for indoor elimination are also available; you can find them with a Web search (try "dogs" + "indoor elimination" + "box," for example).

If you use pee pads, try bringing a used one outside and setting it on the ground when it's time to make that transition. I hear mixed reports about whether this helps, but it won't hurt. Treat and praise warmly the first few times your puppy uses the big outdoors; it's a big change, and some dogs don't find it easy.

WHAT IF YOUR DOG ELIMINATES IN HIS CRATE OR CONFINEMENT AREA?

This is fairly common among pet-store puppies, who may lose their inhibition against soiling their dens because they have no choice. Sometimes dogs from shelters where the animals aren't walked regularly have the same problem. If the dog was housetrained before entering the shelter, he often recovers his cleanliness as soon as he's given the opportunity to, and so is not difficult to re-housetrain.

If your puppy soils her crate or confinement area, you'll need to whisk her outside more often than a "clean" pup, keep her confinement area scrupulously clean, and supervise her even when she's confined.

SPECIAL CONSIDERATIONS FOR ADULT DOGS

If you're housetraining an adult dog, start as you would with a baby puppy, but you can expect to stretch the intervals between elimination opportunities a little more quickly if the dog is confined and/or supervised between times. Like a puppy, an adult dog needs something to do while she's confined. Food-dispensing toys are usually a hit. The idea is "teenager in the bedroom with Xbox and iPod," not "convict in solitary at Sing Sing." (For more about crate training, see Chapter 2, "Socialization.")

If you're working against a long-established habit of eliminating indoors, however, plan for reliable housetraining to take at least a month or three—the older the dog, the longer reliability is likely to take.

How Long Will Housetraining Take?

The amount of time it takes to housetrain your dog depends on the individual dog's propensities and history, as well as on your diligence and consistency. Some puppies get the idea pronto and start signaling a need to go out even though they're still incapable of holding on till they get there. Others aren't reliable for a long time. Some small breeds have a reputation for being difficult to housetrain; it's an open question whether this is a real breed characteristic or a function of the fact that a small dog starting to squat is less conspicuous than a large dog doing so, so that people don't prevent as many mistakes.

WHAT ABOUT MISTAKES?

A few mistakes are inevitable and won't ruin your housetraining program. If you have more than two or three in the first week, or if you can't seem to get the number of accidents down over time, your puppy/dog is not being housetrained. Consider whether you need to give your trainee more potty opportunities, less house freedom, or both. Also consider the possibility of a urinary tract infection or other medical problem that may be interfering with housetraining (see below).

If your puppy eliminates indoors, the right way to react is by cleaning up the mess calmly and cheerfully. Scolding, spanking, and other punishments are pointless—as far we we can tell, dogs don't see urine and feces as disgusting. Your dog isn't likely to understand what you're so upset about, and punishment may even make her afraid to eliminate in

How to Clean Up Accidents

Quick and Dirty Tip

Use enzymatic cleanser for soiled spots. Petastic, Urine-Off, Get Serious!, and Anti-Icky-Poo are some good brands. I hate to say this, but in my experience if it's not sold in a pet supply store, it doesn't work, even if the label says it does. As for ordinary cleansers, they may eliminate the smell by human standards, but not by the standards of a dog nose. And if it smells like urine and feces, it's a toilet.

front of you. The result can be a dog who doesn't pee or poop on walks and instead leaves surprises behind the sofa.

Many trainers suggest a clap or other sharp noise to interrupt a puppy who's just getting ready to go. The idea is that then you bring her outside to finish up, and reward her when she does. I'm not wild about this tactic. For a sensitive pup, interruption may bump right up against startlement and fear. It's not always so easy to gauge what's loud and sharp enough to interrupt but not loud and sharp enough to scare. Don't try this tactic at all with a puppy or dog whom you already know to be timid. And if you do use it and your puppy seems at all scared, abandon the experiment.

Anyway, housetraining goes faster if you keep mistakes to a minimum. Grit your teeth, drag yourself out of bed, don't tell yourself it's just a few minutes till the commercial break, and watch that pup!

How Long Can Your Puppy Hold It?

It's commonly said that a puppy can hold her urine for a number of hours equal to her age in months, plus 1. By this rule, a four-month-old puppy could hold her urine for five hours while she's awake. That's pretty unrealistic for most puppies, even if we assume the clock starts running with her bladder completely empty.

Definitive general information on how long puppies can hold their urine (and feces) at different ages is surprisingly hard to come by. Puppies, being individuals, develop at individual rates, so some variation is built in. It seems to be a fact of life that small dogs need more toilet breaks than large dogs do, even though their equipment should be proportionately the same size. More variation comes from human housetraining chops; all other things being equal, a puppy being housetrained by someone who prevents almost all accidents is likely to develop control more quickly.

So the best answer to "How long can he hold it?" is probably "It depends." In the first week of housetraining, your puppy may need to go out every hour or hour and a half while awake. After a few accident-free days, stretch the interval a bit. Maybe Puppaloo can play for 10 minutes instead of 5 before you take him out to pee; maybe he can work on his food-dispensing toy for 15 minutes instead of 10. Perhaps, after a couple of successful weeks, he can walk to the door on leash rather than be carried out as fast as your legs will move.

WHAT ABOUT DURING THE NIGHT?

Overnights are a special case, because the metabolism slows down during sleep, so urine and feces aren't produced as quickly. However, you should expect to get up at least once overnight for your puppy's first few weeks. Try setting the alarm for halfway through the night. Each week push the time back an hour—say you started with the alarm set for two a.m. in Week 1; in Week 2, set the alarm for three a.m.; in Week 3, for four a.m. Once the overnight pee break reaches a point just a couple of hours before the time you regularly get up, you can probably expect your puppy to sleep through the night.

An adult housetrainee may sleep through the night from the get-go, but individual dogs have individual needs, and if she needs to go out . . . well, you'll need to take her.

WHAT SHOULD YOU DO IF PUPPALOO WAKES YOU IN THE MIDDLE OF THE NIGHT?

Many people wonder what to do if their puppy wakes them in the middle of the night. It seems like a dilemma: You don't want to force her to eliminate in her crate or pen, because that's unkind and also undermines housetraining. On the other hand, what if she's just awake and bored and looking for attention?

The answer is that you give your puppy a toilet break, but keep it dull. Take her out of her crate or pen without comment, bring her to her toilet area, give her a few minutes to eliminate, then put her back and go to sleep. You don't have to be Mr. Block of Ice—I won't fault you if you give her puppy belly just one kiss—but don't play with her or croon over her or engage with her any more than you can help. The idea is that waking you up in the middle of the night will get her a toilet break but not any kind of party.

WHEN WILL YOUR PUPPY MAKE IT THROUGH THE NIGHT?

Most puppies can sleep through the night without any toilet breaks within a couple of weeks—sooner, if you're starting with an adolescent or adult. If your puppy continues to wake and cry at night, take her out, but don't play with her or fuss over her; just put her back to bed, as described above.

WHAT IF YOU CAN'T BE THERE TO LET YOUR PUPPY OUT?

During housetraining, dogs need lots of breaks. If you must leave your trainee at home for longer than she can reasonably hold it, the best bet is to have a walker in. As an alternative, set up a puppy playpen with your elimination box or absorbent material in one area. Or you can leave the puppy in a puppy-proofed room (hard floor, no access to items the puppy can destroy by chewing on them, nothing dangerous accessible). There's no guarantee that the puppy will eliminate in the designated area, remember.

How Often Should You Give Your Dog a Toilet Break?

How many toilet breaks does a housetrained dog need? This is a common question, and I'll supply an answer, but first take a moment to think about what it means to ask how long a dog can contain her pee and poo. It's as if the goal of housetraining is to supply the absolute minimum number of toilet breaks. Granted that housetraining a dog is a chore; granted that walking a dog can be a chore, too, when you're tired or in nasty weather. Housetraining is nevertheless not meant to be the Olympics of pelvic and rectal muscle clenching. I still flinch when I recall the man who told me proudly that his dog got just two walks a day.

I recommend a *minimum* of four elimination opportunities daily, five or six for small-breed dogs. The first walk after waking should be a longish one, because, like humans, dogs wake up especially full and often need to eliminate more than once before they're really done. (Also, and especially if your dog is alone all day while you work, it's nice to get some solid aerobic exercise on board first thing.)

Over time, you'll get a sense of how fast your dog's digestive system moves and at what times of day she needs to go.

Expect your dog to need more outings as she gets older. My healthy but frail elderly dog got a minimum of six toilet opportunities a day in the year before she died. With advancing age, some dogs lose their housetraining because of dementia, or become incontinent because of lost muscle tone. Some spayed females leak urine in their sleep (there is a safe medication to help with this problem; ask your vet). Absorbent pads on the dog's bedding or on the floor of the room where a demented dog spends his time can make life much easier.

Needless to say, take your dog out when you suspect stomach upset. And if your dog's first pee on every walk is a deluge, increase the number of outings (see "housetraining, not Olympics of muscle clenching," above). Certain medications and medical conditions may increase input and output (more on that below).

SHOULD YOU USE DOG DOORS?

Probably not. Because a dog door enables your dog to relieve himself whenever he feels the urge, he may not strongly develop the ability to hold it. As I've emphasized, I'm no fan of forcing dogs to develop Olympics-grade bladder and bowel control, but life does have a way of bringing us situations in which we've got to hang on for a while. For a dog, this might be a road trip, a hotel stay, a hospitalization, a temporary or permanent move to an apartment . . .

If you're confident that this will never be a consideration for you and your dog, there's still wildlife to consider—even an entrance a small dog can fit through will also admit squirrels and stray cats, to say nothing of . . . other small dogs. Pet doors exist that open only when they get a signal from a transmitter worn around your dog's neck, but I have to say I would worry about the transmitter falling off or breaking down.

Last, I just don't like the whole idea of dogs going outdoors unsupervised. Dogs left in yards dig under fences, bark at passersby (and then the neighbors complain), get teased by kids, sometimes have rocks thrown at them or get stolen.*

---

* On the unsupervised-outside point, I'll make an exception for your old dog who likes to snooze on the sunny porch, as long as your yard is fenced and you're at home.

Three Ways to Undermine Housetraining

Housetraining is a lot of work. Here's how to undo it:

1. Don't follow the rules.

The easiest way to undermine housetraining is just not to follow the rules. Tell yourself your puppy can hold it just a little bit longer, until the next commercial break; decide that your (sleepy, empty, just-got-plenty-of-affection) puppy looks like a Guantánamo prisoner in his crate, and stop confining him between outings. But you can screw up housetraining in other ways, too.

2. End the walk when your dog pees or poops.

One common pitfall is to *walk* your puppy or dog when she needs to pee or poop. And walk her, and walk her, and then turn right around and go home as soon as she delivers. The lesson is, "My little outing ends the minute I pee and poop, so I'm hanging on as long as I can." Pretty soon "as long as I can" means "until my person gives up and takes me home." Behold the puppy who goes on lockdown during walks but drops a bomb in the living room two seconds after the front door closes.

It's easy to avoid teaching this lesson and, as usual, a bit more work to undo it. Either way, the trick is to make your puppy's walk a reward for eliminating. Bring the puppy on leash to your chosen elimination spot and just stand there. Do nothing, say nothing. Give the puppy two or three minutes to eliminate. If she does, praise her warmly and take her for a walk. If she doesn't, just bring her back inside without comment, and crate her or keep her on leash next to you. Fifteen to thirty minutes later, bring her outside and try again. Sooner or later she'll pee and/or poop and earn her walk reward. Result: She learns to empty her bladder and bowels as soon as she's outside, because that's how she gets walks. By the way, prompt elimination is a convenient habit for rainy days.

3. Punish your dog for accidents.

Punishment is usually a day late, a dollar short, mean, and a waste of time. In the first place, forget punishing *any* behavior that happened more than two seconds ago. It's history. Your dog won't get the point. But let's say you scold your puppy because you've caught him in the act of peeing on the rug. No way is he going to understand that your objections involve the textile. "IKEA"? What is this "IKEA"? As I suggested earlier, he's just going to figure that you get weird and scary when he pees or poops in front of you.

When the Problem Might Not Be Housetraining (and What to Do)

Let's face it, usually when people say, "But he's housetrained!," he really, really isn't. But there are exceptions.

EXCITEMENT URINATION AND SUBMISSIVE URINATION

Most of us have had the pleasure of meeting a puppy who's ecstatically happy to greet humans. Sometimes the pleasure is a mixed one, as when said puppy excitedly pees all over our shoes. Other puppies, a bit shy and submissive, roll on their backs and squirt, especially when a person bends over them, and double especially if the person is big and/or male and/or a little assertive in demeanor.

This may be my favorite dog problem, because unlike every other dog problem it will usually go away if you leave it alone. All by himself, the puppy will grow up and develop adequate muscular control. In the case of shy, submissive puppies, "leaving it alone" includes avoiding the Giant Human Loom-Over and whatever other behaviors set the puppy off. Teaching a pup to sit for greetings, or ignoring her till she relaxes, will often help her hold her stuff. Generally, submissive and excitement urination will resolve by the time doggy adolescence strikes.

You do have it in your power to make this problem worse, of course. Get your excited pee-er amped on purpose when you greet her, or shout at the shy pup when he dribbles, and watch that stream grow.

SIGNS OF MEDICAL PROBLEMS

A host of medical problems can lead your dog to eliminate indoors. I'll mention a few examples, but many more exist. And those I do describe may have symptoms I don't mention here. The short version is, suspect a medical problem if your dog's behavior has changed suddenly, if she's old, or if you're sticking to a regular, careful housetraining schedule and your puppy is having frequent accidents anyway.

Sudden, urgent digestive upset may come on too strong for even the best-housetrained dog. Possible causes include rich or spoiled food and certain parasites. A dog with a urinary tract infection may need to go much more often than usual and may dribble small amounts of urine. If you have a spayed female dog who leaks urine in her sleep, a possible cause is estrogen incontinence, which is usually treatable with inexpensive medication. Elderly dogs who develop canine cognitive disorder, a doggy analogue of Alzheimer's disease, may lose their housetraining as the condition progresses. Pain from arthritis, an injury, or illness can leave a dog reluctant to take a walk or make it hard for her to get into position to pee or poop. The bladder and bowels may wind up overfull and impossible to control.

Increased water intake accompanies some illnesses, diabetes and Cushing's disease among them; if you don't happen to notice that your dog is filling up more than normal and supply extra toilet breaks to compensate, he may be unable to hold his urine until his next walk. Certain medications may make animals feel thirsty, too—steroids are famous for this. If your dog's indoor pees coincide with a new medication or an increased dose of an old one, it's well worth asking your vet whether thirst or incontinence is a possible side effect. The same goes for any change in the bladder or bowel habits of a previously housetrained dog.

Malformations of the rectum and sphincter or of the urinary tract can make it impossible for a dog to control eliminations. So can age-related changes. My Izzy's anal sphincter lost muscle tone late in her life. The result was that when she sprang up with joy at going for a walk, she occasionally dropped a few little items from behind.

BEHAVIORAL CAUSES OF INDOOR ELIMINATION

Inappropriate elimination can signal certain behavior problems. The commonest might be separation anxiety, which in its more intense forms could be called separation panic.* One sign of true separation anxiety is that the dog may chew and claw at doors and windows, apparently trying to escape; another is that he may let go of urine and stool when alone, and only when alone.

Thunderstorm phobia can produce the same result, as can terror in other contexts. It's not unheard of for a dog to let loose during severe punishment. I'm tempted to say that in that case the behavior problem isn't in the dog, but harsh, ill-informed advice is everywhere and even the best and kindest people can be misled into following it.

Dogs too afraid to go outside will obviously sooner or later eliminate indoors. Sometimes the fear arises after a specific terrifying event. More commonly, dogs who fear going outdoors didn't get appropriate

---

* Some trainers distinguish between separation anxiety (having to do with the absence of a particular person or people) and isolation anxiety (having to do with being alone). See the discussion in Chapter 12 "Stuff Dogs Do That Worries People." For wieldiness' sake, I'll call both "separation anxiety."

Trick Alert: How to Teach Dogs to Signal the Need to Go Out

My experience with my own dogs has been that they're quite good at signaling without being taught—they get a little restless, or hang around near the front door, or come and rest their head on my leg at a time that's near one of their usual toilet breaks. Juniper, who is easily rattled, sleeps in his crate to protect him from cats jumping on him; he'll bang on the metal door if his stomach is upset and diarrhea is imminent. Izzy would stand by the bed and stare us awake (though unfortunately this tactic didn't always work for her, to judge by the rare unpleasant morning surprise).

But if you'd like a more distinct signal, it's reasonably easy to teach most dogs to ring a bell to go out. It helps if your dog knows how to target items first (see Chapter 10, "Play? Training? Tricks?" for how to teach targeting).

Hang a bell on a ribbon by the door you use to take your dog out for a toilet break (whether or not that normally includes a walk). Take your dog to the door and ask her to target the bell; as soon as it rings, leash up and take your dog to her toilet spot. Repeat over the next half-dozen or more outings; then, the next time, take your dog to the door and wait. Give her five or ten seconds to think. If she rings the bell on her own, take her out. If she does nothing, or if she seems to be getting frustrated and checking out of the process, give her a hint by touching the bell yourself. If she still doesn't ring the bell, give her the cue to target it. Then ask her to target it the next several times you take her out; after that, try letting her think again.

Some dogs who learn this trick start using it many times a day, even if they don't need a toilet break. (Kind of like the way I used to ask for a hall pass when I got bored in grade school.) To prevent this, handle bell ringing the same way you would a puppy's crying in his crate in the middle of the night: Take your dog to his toilet spot, then bring him directly indoors again. And if your dog persistently seeks entertainment in this way, consider whether he needs more attention or more mental and physical exercise. Remember that these are legitimate dog needs, which—since we're the ones who chose to get a dog in the first place—it's up to us to satisfy. A little boredom from time to time is one thing; playing stuffed animal is quite another.

socialization in early puppyhood; completely normal life experiences strike them as strange and alarming. That is among the saddest behavior problems any consultant sees—crucial parts of early development have been missed, and the resulting fear of the wide world can sometimes be ameliorated but can't be undone. Some dogs can learn to feel reasonably comfortable in a few outdoor contexts or at certain times. For others, the best we can do is teach them to use a designated spot indoors so there isn't any pressure to go out.

When Your Dog Pees in His New Home

Some dogs, especially male dogs, start life in a new adoptive home by marking every vertical surface they can find, indoors as well as out. It's best to treat this as a housetraining problem, just in case it turns out to be one, but often it seems to be a result of stress. As the dog settles into a clear and consistent routine and becomes comfortable, the indoor marking fades away.

For persistent markers and the seemingly un-housetrainable, you can try a diaper or a belly band, a cloth band that fastens around the dog's waist and covers the penis. Fortunately, most inappropriate elimination can be . . . eliminated, either through remedial housetraining or through treatment of the underlying physical or emotional problem. See your vet and consult a competent behavior professional for help.

Total Recall

GETTING YOUR DOG TO COME
WHEN CALLED

"Recall" is what trainers say when they mean "the behavior of coming when called." I'll usually say "recall," because (a) it's required by the dog trainer guild rules, and (b) the need to fit "the behavior of coming when called" into sentence after sentence produces some not-in-a-good-way-amazing syntax. Okay? Okay. Now, on to the oh-so-important canine skill of coming when called.

If you have a young puppy, you may be feeling smug right now, and you may be tempted to skip this chapter, because your Puppalini comes to you like a rocket when you call him, and never has to come from very far away on account of he sticks to you like glue in the first place. Feel as smug as you want—I like it when people are pleased with their dogs—but I must warn you that the reason Puppalini comes to you like a rocket and sticks to you like glue in the first place is that *he's a puppy.* Following the big dog is what puppies do. Quite soon, Puppalini will become an adolescent dog. This is the point at which old-school trainers will tell you he's "blowing you off" and "challenging your leadership." Piffle. He's growing up, exploring, and moving around more. He will still come when called, as long as you recognize his puppy glom-on-ality for what it is and take steps to turn it into a trained behavior.

"Official" training and practice are part of the recipe for a sharp recall. The other part is establishing yourself as fun and rewarding to be around. The two parts of the recipe overlap considerably, because much of your practice can come in the form of games, and of course games establish you as fun to be around.

Teach Your Dog to Orient to You

I lay the groundwork for recall (and lots of other things) with a simple attention exercise in which you repeatedly reward your dog for orienting toward you.

Have your clicker and treats ready.

1. Get Your Dog to Look at You

The first step in teaching your dog to orient to you is to go to a quiet room in your home and stand or sit with your dog. Don't speak to your dog or otherwise try to attract his attention; instead, just wait. Sooner or later, your dog will look at you. At that instant, click and treat. Then toss a second treat on the floor so that your dog looks away from you to get it.

Wait for your dog to look at you again; click/treat and toss a second treat on the floor. Repeat five to ten times. That's plenty for one training session.

Over a few days, repeat this training in every room of your house or apartment. Once you've done that, move your practice outside. If you live in an apartment building, move on to your hallway and then the building lobby. (Here you'll need to have your dog on leash, of course, for safety's sake.) If you have access to a small, safely fenced area (other than a dog park or dog run), go on to that. If you live in a house with a yard, practice in your yard. You can practice on leash at first. If your yard is safely fenced, even better is to practice off leash. Expect your puppy or dog to take some time to poke around or romp before she's ready to pay attention to you. That's fine; volunteered attention is golden and you will find that with additional practice your dog offers you her attention more and more quickly.

Practice in as many locations as you can manage. Have a couple of practice sessions in each location, say a dozen reps per session. Laying the groundwork in this diligent way will really pay off for you in the long run.

2. Introduce Your Recall Cue

As you practice, you'll find that you can tell exactly when your dog is about to turn toward you.

Pick a word or two that will mean "Please come to me now"—it could be "Come," "Here," "By me," or "Banana"; your dog won't mind. Choose a cue that comes naturally to you.

Just before your dog turns to you during the attention exercise, say your "Come" cue. Click and treat when she turns to you. Do five or six repetitions; then, on the next rep, back away a step so that your dog moves toward you to get the treat. Feed the treat as soon as she arrives.

Continue practicing with your dog moving toward you to get the treat. Practice in different places and at different times. All those locations you practiced in before? Go back to them for Round 2. Work in the calmest, least distracting locations first.

When you've had half a dozen practice sessions (each ten to fifteen treats "long") in each of half a dozen locations (so we're talking about six sessions, six locations, fifteen reps in each session, or 540 reps—yes, I mean it!), you can begin using your "Come" cue at random times *in a non-distracting environment.* Your apartment or a room in your house is the best place to start. Have treats stashed around your home for this purpose, so that you don't have to get set up and thereby tip your dog off.

Again, practice in various locations in your home, then outdoors during leash walks. Different dogs get excited to different degrees about different things. Observe your dog and get a sense of how to rank various situations for distractingness; then practice in them, working from easiest to hardest. The first couple of times you practice in any new environment, give your dog a few minutes to poke around before you get to work training; once the novelty has worn off a bit, she'll be better able to focus on you.

What to Do After You've Taught Your Dog to Orient to You

You've taught your dog that checking in with you is rewarding and fun, and she's begun to learn that your "Come" cue also signals an opportunity to get something good from you. She's also begun to learn that this is true in several different contexts. But she's not yet prepared to recall from deep in a game with another dog or from jumping up the tree where that squirrel just was. To get a response as reliable as that, the key is practice, practice, practice. Keep the following in mind: (1) Very few professional trainers believe there's such a thing as 100 percent perfection, even after a thousand successful reps. Some dogs get pretty darn

Quick and Dirty Tips for Recall Success

- Use a happy, high-pitched voice to encourage quick movement toward you.[1]
- Corollary: Avoid the "commanding" tone, and double-plus avoid sounding angry. Are you reluctant to approach someone who sounds belligerent? So is your dog.
- Treat coming when called as a game for the sharpest, happiest response. See "Recall Games," p. 105, for more.
- Angle your body sideways; polite dogs don't rush at each other head-on, so your sideways position may elicit faster movement.
- If you can squat, squat. If you're bent at the waist, you wind up looming over the dog when he has nearly reached you.
- Run away to encourage your dog to chase after you.
- Choose your moment! If your dog's deep in play with another dog, look for a break in the play and call him then. If he's sniffing something fascinating, wait for him to lift his head and look around. As your training progresses, your dog will be able to respond to you despite greater and greater distractions, but as long as there's no emergency you might as well call him when his attention isn't absorbed.

reliable pretty darn fast; others will always be more distractible, more focused on What's Out There. (2) You know your dog best. If she comes when called reliably in some contexts (out hiking, say), less reliably in others (when playing with other dogs, say), behave accordingly (go collect her from play instead of calling her repeatedly, and plan to practice more).

For practice indoors or in a securely enclosed yard or field, you can let your dog off leash, as in the orientation exercises you worked on earlier. And you should, because working without a leash makes your training more like the situation you're ultimately training for—that is, after however much practice, your dog can be let off leash freely (assuming it's legal!), with you secure in the knowledge that she will come to you when you ask her to do so. But there will be times when you want to give Dogalini some freedom even though her recall isn't polished yet. Or maybe the practice locations available to you aren't enclosed.

Or you've just begun to practice in a situation where the distractions are especially strong.

In these situations, you might like to let Dogalini trail her leash, or work with her on a long line (see the next section). If you need to leave the area, call her *once*, when her attention isn't completely focused on something else. If she doesn't respond, then just go get her. Remember, you're not arresting her! Pick up her leash or long line and give her exactly the kind of delighted praise you'd give her if you had called her and she'd come to you like a bullet. Give her a treat if there's no chance of its starting an argument with another dog, and make walking away with you a happy game.

Why and How to Use a Long Line

A long line is just what it sounds like—a light, strong rope or cord, or a leash, usually from 20 to 50 feet long. Long lines are not only handy for many practice situations, they can also supply a failsafe for dogs with behavior problems—for instance, a dog-aggressive dog who might charge if another dog suddenly appeared. Long lines aren't quite no-brainer tools, so I encourage you to practice in your backyard or another relatively small, secure area before you break out the line "for real."

Here's what you *don't* do with a long line: You don't clip one end to your dog's collar or harness and then hold the other. Even a small dog can work up quite a head of steam in 40-odd feet, send both of you ass-over-teakettle, and get both of you badly hurt.

To use a long line effectively and safely, follow these rules:

1. Decide whether to have your dog wear a collar or a harness with the long line. A harness is probably safer if your dog is liable to bolt hard, but in many situations dogs will spend most of their time poking around and sniffing, and a collar may be fine.

2. Once you've attached the long line, pay out only about eight or ten feet of it and then loop the line around your hand. (You can wear a glove to further protect your skin.) If your dog takes off, the loop will tighten and form a brake so you don't get rope burn and your dog doesn't either knock herself flat hitting the end of the line or head for the next county trailing forty feet of rope.

3. Be careful not to let the trailing line get between your legs or wrap around an ankle. Again, rope burn.

4. Try to keep the rope to your dog's side rather than between his legs, and if it ever loops around one of his legs *immediately* unwrap it.

As you walk with your dog, pay out and take up enough line to let her meander among the local attractions. Supervise her just as you would if she were completely at liberty. If she alerts to something out of sight, go closer to her, taking up some of the rope as you go so that neither of you can get hurt. If she's trotting toward an obvious goal that's within the rope's length, pay out enough line to let her reach it, then walk up to her, taking up the line as you go so that you're generally giving her no more than that original eight or ten feet of slack.

If you're going to let your dog drag the line, tie a knot in it every few feet; when you're walking up the line to collect your dog, the knots can serve as a brake if she starts to wander away and pull the line with her.

Practice your recall with the long line just as you would if you were in a securely enclosed place and had your dog off leash. As your dog's recall becomes fluent, you can stop using the long line completely. A more cautious approach is to shorten the line by a few feet at each practice session and stop holding on to it—let your dog drag the gradually shorter line instead. Take the gradual approach if your dog is one of those highly distractible "What's out *there?*" types. It isn't exactly that these dogs think they "don't have to listen" without the line attached; rather, the feeling of the line's weight may help to keep them oriented to you, and an abrupt change can leave that training more vulnerable to breaking down than it would for a dog who's more you-focused to begin with.

How will you know when your dog's recall is polished enough? If you'll be letting her off leash only in safe, enclosed areas, a pretty good recall might be good enough, as long as you don't weaken it by calling her repeatedly if she doesn't respond the first time. (Just go get her, instead.) If you expect to include wilderness hikes in your life with your dog, or if she's especially keen on chasing chipmunks and deer, or even if you just want to hang out with her in your unfenced suburban front yard, I'd like to see her executing pretty much an instant U-turn pretty much every time you call. And there are situations I'd never take a chance on at all: a city sidewalk or a highway rest stop, for instance.

"Gotcha!"

Quick and Dirty Tip

Lots of dogs come when called but then duck away when their guardian reaches for their collar. It's also not a bad bet that at some point in your dog's life, she'll be recalling in an emergency, when you absolutely positively have got to get hold of her and get the leash on, and also you're upset.

To teach your dog to love having her collar grabbed, pick a quiet time when she's relaxed and a little hungry. Be ready with about half a dozen small, delicious somethings. Touch her collar and give her one. Repeat till you're out of somethings. Over the course of a few days or weeks, repeat the whole scenario, about half a dozen reps at a time. First work up to gently taking hold of her collar. Then start moving your grabby hand toward her collar more and more quickly, but take her collar gently. Then practice grabbing her collar.

Remember, your dog should be enjoying each step of the process. If she starts ducking away, go back to a much earlier step and work forward again, more slowly this time.

Recall Games

As I mentioned at the start of this chapter, part of teaching your dog to come when called is teaching him that you're enjoyable to be around. It becomes much easier to teach dogs to come when called if being with us is fun and satisfying. Plus, training does require a certain amount of drill ("Do a dozen reps in a dozen locations . . ."). Train with play, and lighten things up for yourself as well as your dog.

ROUND ROBIN RECALL

One of my favorite recall games is the Round Robin Recall—a doggy party game, fun for the whole family (unless this is *Big Love* and there are 46 of you, in which case your dog's likely to get confused). You could also hold a small dinner party and rope in your guests. Let's say a max of seven players, counting your dog.

Here's how it works: Each person gets a clicker and some treats. One person calls the dog—*once*. Happy voice, please! As soon as the dog turns to the caller and starts to head her way, click; treat when the dog arrives. Another person calls the dog, same deal. And so on.

If Dogalini heads for the wrong person, give her a few seconds to figure it out before the correct caller tries again. Mix up the order in which people call her and the places where they stand, so that she attends to the actual cues she's getting instead of learning to travel in a fixed pattern.

When Dogalini's gotten so good at the game that she never, or almost never, makes a mistake, up the ante. Have some of the human players call the dog from different rooms. Or have everybody hold biscuits in front of them as temptations, then have the person who actually called the dog deliver roast beef when she shows up. (It goes without saying that Dogalini doesn't get the dry biscuit if she goes for it, I hope!) Or Person A calls the dog away from a game of tug she's playing with Person B. Or if you have two dogs, and they won't argue over food, have one person call Dogalini while another person calls Zippy. Move the game outdoors and hide behind bushes.

TREAT AND RUN AWAY

This game is dead simple. It's to be played anywhere your dog is safe off leash and you have enough room to run. Let's assume you're in a large fenced yard.

Throw a treat just behind your dog, so he turns to get it. As soon as he turns away from you, run away from him. As he turns back from getting the treat, call him with your recall cue. When he reaches you, deliver a food reward, then throw another treat and run away again.

This also makes for a fun variation on fetch: throw your dog's ball or other toy instead of a treat. Run like hell in the other direction when he goes after the toy, then happy-voice as he turns and comes tearing after you. Repeat till all concerned are laughing and out of breath.

"LOOKING FOR A BETTER DOG"

This game is courtesy of Nancy Abplanalp, CPDT-KA,[2] who posted it to a trainers' e-mail list and kindly gave me permission to quote her:

> "Looking for a better dog" is a technique I use where I remove my constant attention on my dog and begin to search an area that does not include my dog. Dogs are in tune enough with us that they will come over to see what we're looking for. When they do, I "find" a better dog

(my dog who just realized that I was there) and we have a party and some fun together. I teach this on a six-foot leash and expand from there. My dogs will come "look for a better dog" from a great distance away. My clients love playing this game with their dogs and think it's magical the first time I play it with a dog.

MORE GAMES FOR OFF-LEASH DOGS

When there's no chance of starting a doggy food fight, you can play the world's stupidest game, Find It!, which you teach like this:

Say, "Find it!" and toss a piece of kibble or chicken or cheese on the ground right in front of your dog. Voilà, the dog will find the food. Dogs with good noses will learn quickly to find the food as you toss it farther and farther away; dogs with less good noses will take a little longer, so increase the length of your toss gradually for them and use smelly items such as fish-flavored cat kibble or tiny bits of cheese. When your dog gets really good, ask her to down-stay while you hide the food under a stick, reward her lavishly for holding her stay, then release her to go for the hidden treasure. "What a lot of fun it is to practice stays!" says your dog.

Look for stuff your dog would be interested in, or plant it, and then make a huge big excited deal over the great thing you just found. When your dog shows up, give him custody. "Wow!" says your dog. "I better stick close to my person—she is terrific at finding used take-out containers with peanut butter smeared inside!" (The food-fight caution applies here too, obviously.)

Orthopedics permitting, jump around with your dog and encourage her to jump around with you. Roll in the grass. Run at your dog like the bogeyman (if this doesn't scare her), then run away again.

When you've called your dog and leashed him, give him a treat. Ask him to do a trick he enjoys, and give him a treat for that, too. Walk lively and talk to your dog happily on your way home or to the car. If he has found a prize stick and wants to carry it, for heaven's sake let him. Trade him the stick for a piece of cheese and then give it back. What a good dog!

MAKE BEING WITH YOU A GAME

Many trainers and training books advise that you shouldn't call your dog and then leash him at the end of an outing to the dog park, for example. The idea is that by leashing your dog and taking him home you're, in effect, punishing him for coming to you. Some people suggest calling your dog and leashing her a couple of times during any given off-leash outing, then rewarding her by unclipping her lead again.

Now, it is absolutely correct that you shouldn't call your dog to you for unpleasant purposes. If your dog hates having her nails clipped, don't call her and then clip her nails when she arrives. (If she *loves* having her nails clipped, go to town!) Nor, obviously, should you ever call your dog to you and then hit him or yell at him when he shows up. And, last but not least, when you have called your dog away from something swell, it can constitute a huge reward to let her have another off-leash go.

But where, I ask you, is it written that being with you is *necessarily* less enjoyable than playing with other dogs? Where is it written that walking home with you on leash *should* be tedious and unpleasant? This is the unspoken assumption behind the advice never to call your dog at the end of an off-leash play session. Don't buy it. The more Dogalini enjoys being with you, the less her little heart will break when it's time to stop wrestling with Zippy. Playing with your dog, even if the games aren't specifically geared toward recall, encourages her to hang around with you rather than always be looking elsewhere for fun.

It's sad to see a person trudging home from the dog park, looking as hangdog as his dog, disengaged and uninterested and if he had a tail it would be straight-down limp. Engage with your dog joyfully, and you'll both have a grand time whether there's a leash involved or not.

6

How to Park a Dog, or at Least Keep Her from Becoming Airborne

Healthy dogs like to move around a lot, which is convenient when you want to walk them, not so much when they jump up on visitors and bolt out the front door. In this chapter: how to come to a meeting of the minds with your dog about greeting styles; how to teach a stay; and how to teach a dog that an open(ing) door is a cue to stay put, *not* to run right out.

Teaching Your Dog Polite Greetings

The first skill we'll tackle in this chapter is how to how to teach dogs to keep their feet on the floor while greeting people.

Before you get started, it's useful to understand why dogs jump up in the first place (if only because it encourages you to be patient!). Part of the reason is probably plain old exuberance, especially if you've got a young and energetic dog. But a plausible explanation for why they jump up *at us*—rather than, say, five feet away—arises from their ways of communicating with each other. A puppy greeting an adult dog often licks the adult's muzzle—a polite, deferential behavior. Dogs, of course, descend from wolves, among whom muzzle-licking is how pups get the grownups to regurgitate food for them. Domestic dogs rarely nourish puppies this way, but muzzle-licking has survived, maybe because deferential behaviors are handy for a social animal. Think of humans saying, "No, after you." Muzzle-licking is also an appeasement behavior—something you trot out to deescalate a fight. A human might lift up his hands, palms toward the person he's arguing with.

Puppies in human households try to lick the weird, flat, usually bald body part we have instead of a muzzle. When a cute little puppy jumps up to lick face, many people can only say, "Awwww!" Hey presto! Jumping up has been rewarded. The puppy's natural inclination is now a learned behavior. Too bad for the dog when he's nine months old, bigger and less cute, muddying the pinstripes and knocking Granny to the ground.

Paying attention to a dog only when all four paws are on the floor can work well, *if* jumping isn't well entrenched and *if* everybody who deals with the dog follows the rules. Unfortunately, much of humanity will get busy undermining you. "I don't mind your puppy jumping up," they say, while you tear your hair out. Or they get all disciplinarian, maybe kneeing the dog in the chest. That is not only mean but counterproductive, because dogs often respond to aggression by trying to appease. Since humans are usually taller than dogs, reaching our muzzles to lick them appeasingly involves . . . yes, jumping up.

Fortunately, polite greetings are easily taught—most easily, of course, if you start out early so you aren't trying to undo a well-practiced habit. For simplicity I'll just speak of dogs, but of course the training tips here apply to puppies too.

THE HOW-TO

When you're teaching your dog to greet politely and stop jumping up, it's easiest to work with two people. One of the people will hold the dog on leash. The dog should have plenty of room to sit, stand, or lie down comfortably, and to move within a radius of a couple of feet. The second person can be anyone your dog likes. If you don't have a practice partner, tether your dog securely instead, so you can be the "approaching friend" in the steps below.

Step 1: With the dog's human friend about a dozen feet away, the person holding the leash asks the dog to sit.

Step 2: As soon as the dog does so, the dog's friend starts to approach. Because the dog likes this person, the approach will reward the sit. And, because the dog likes this person, he'll probably get up and move toward her.

Step 3: The moment the dog gets up, the approaching person stops dead, turns away from the dog, and retreats.

Step 4: The person holding the leash cues the dog to sit.

Step 5: As soon as the dog sits, the friend again approaches.

Step 6: If the dog gets up, the friend stops and retreats again.

Usually, after two or three tries, the leash holder can stop giving the cue to sit. Instead, count to five slowly, in your head. Given a few moments to think, most dogs will experiment—what was it that got my friend to come closer? Eureka! This is the first step toward a dog who sits spontaneously in order to get people to approach.

The self-control problem isn't solved yet—the bouncier the dog, the more tries you'll need. Once the dog holds his sit till his human friend has reached him, have a love party. The leash holder can tell the dog it's okay to get up at this point. But if the dog begins to jump, the friend should instantly back away. Notice how simple and clear the communication is. The consequence of sitting politely is that someone you like comes closer. The consequence of jumping up is that she goes away.

Here's a hot tip for bouncy dogs: Keep the love party low-key, and drop a few treats on the ground—the dog can't troll for smorgasbord and jump at the same time. Speaking of treats, the main reward for your dog in this training scenario is the chance to say hello. Feel free, though, to slip him treats as he holds his sit. You can phase out the treats over time. Finally, if your dog's really having trouble, work on a sit-stay without the greeting component first.

Another tip: Any dog will find it easier to stay put if he's not climbing out of his skin in the first place. Before you practice, make sure he's had a good long walk or a game of fetch—enough exercise so he can relax.

PRACTICE, PRACTICE, PRACTICE

Practice polite greetings with as many people as you can rustle up. Choose several locations where real greetings might happen. The more practice, the better. If visitors are the most frequent jump targets, your approaching person can enter the house as any guest would do. Again, you encourage the dog to stay in a sit by having the visitor immediately stop and retreat each time your dog gets up. To up the ante, have the faux visitor make with the big "Hello! Haven't seen you in aaaaaaaaaaaages!"

When your dog's heinie is glued to the ground till you okay him to get up, start the whole process over again minus the leash. If the dog breaks his sit more than once or twice and goes over to the approaching person, go back and practice some more with the dog leashed.

Finally, while your dog is learning to sit patiently as *fake* guests come in, don't set him up to practice jumping on *real* guests. Having company? Crate your dog, leash him, or put him behind a baby gate till everyone's settled and he's calmed down. Then bring him out, on leash, to say polite hellos.

Teaching Your Dog to Wait for Permission to Go Out the Door

Many trainers will tell you to go through doors ahead of your dog so as to assert your rank. There is exactly zero science behind this advice. Doors lead to the outside, dogs love to go outside, and dogs don't come with impulse control factory-installed. If they have a thought in their heads when they bolt out the door, it's "Whee! Squirrels!" Orderly exits are safer for both of you, but Zippy is not staging a palace coup every time he acts rude and doggy.

To teach your dog to wait for permission before going out an open door, you'll also need to teach her that bolting will no longer work. Never open a door that leads outside unless you have first made it impossible for her to exit by that door. Leash her, crate her, or put her in a closed room before you answer the doorbell or pick up the mail. If you're leaving the house for a while but don't want to confine your dog in your absence, then be ready to gently block her from dashing out as you go.

Strive for 100 percent prevention—so that your dog never makes it through that door—not only for safety reasons, but also because it makes training easier. Behaviors that are rewarded occasionally and randomly will hang on much longer than behaviors that aren't rewarded at all. If bolting completely stops working for your dog, it'll be easier for her to give it up in favor of the new strategy you teach her.

From now on, your dog will cunningly manipulate you into giving her permission to go out the door. She'll do it by sitting quietly until you say, "Okay," or "Go," or whatever word you've chosen to mean "You may exit now." Here's how to teach her this new trick.

THE HOW-TO

Choose a time when you're not in a hurry, your dog doesn't need a toilet break, and you're feeling cool and patient. Leash your dog and ask her to sit. As soon as her rear touches the ground, reach for the doorknob. Odds are, she'll instantly get up. "Oops!" you say pleasantly, and take your hand away from the door. Again ask her to sit, then reach for the door. Once again, she'll probably get up; once again, you'll say, "Oops!" and take your hand away from the door.

After a few tries, though, your dog will start to get the idea—you may see her put herself back into the sit after getting up. Now she's on her way to sitting automatically *in order to get you to open the door.*

For this first training session, count it as good progress if your dog learns to hold her sit while you turn the doorknob and just barely open the door. At that point, say your permission word and invite her to go out the door; then take her for a short walk, so the training doesn't end in frustration. You can do another quick session as soon as you get back, again rewarding your dog with permission to go through the door, plus a quick walk.

From now on, each time you take your dog for a walk, raise the bar a little. Put on her leash and wait; give her the chance to figure out that sitting makes you reach for the knob. Once she learns to sit automatically, you won't need to give the cue. Next time, open the door a couple of inches farther before you give permission to go through. When your dog is able to hold her sit while you open the door completely, wait a second longer before you give the okay. If she breaks her sit, mark her mistake with an "Oops!" and start over. Make the next try a little easier so she can succeed.

MAKE YOUR PRACTICE MORE CHALLENGING

Once your dog reliably waits for your okay even with the door wide open, you're ready to practice without the leash. Start over from scratch, with the door closed and your dog in a sit. Position yourself so you can block her and shut the door if she makes a break for it. As you did when your dog was on leash, work gradually to develop her skills. Throw in some practice while she's eating dinner or lounging on the couch. In real life, you'll be opening the door lots of times—not only when going out with your dog. She'll learn that no matter what she's doing when the door opens, making a break gets the door to close, whereas staying put earns her something good. At this point, an opening door is like a wordless stay cue; you don't need to say a thing.

USE THE RIGHT REWARDS

Which "something good" you choose when working off leash depends on what's outside your door. If it opens onto a fenced yard or a forty-acre spread where your dog can safely go off leash at times, you can reward her with permission to do just that. If your door opens onto a suburban or city street, though, you'll need a different reward. You'll also want to mix up the rewards if it's sometimes okay for your dog to go out without a leash, but sometimes not. For most dogs, praise isn't going to cut it as compensation for giving up a chance at the great outdoors. Use delicious treats, such as plain boiled chicken, or toss a ball. If you can, end the training session with an on-leash walk.

Remember, what your dog knows in one place, he may not know in another. If you move or bring your dog along to visit friends, plan to give him a quick refresher course.

TAKE THIS SKILL ON THE ROAD

Although your dog should be harnessed or crated when riding in a car, it's easy and potentially lifesaving to also teach her to stay put when you open the car door or crate door. You do exactly the same thing as you did to teach her not to bolt when you open the house door: Reach for the handle; if she so much as twitches toward the about-to-open door, take your hand away. Practice, practice, practice. If she's in a crate, she stays in the crate till you leash her and give her the okay to step out; if she's in a safety harness, she stays put while you attach her leash to her collar and unfasten the harness from the seatbelt of the car, and continues to stay put until you're standing by the car door with her leash in your hand and giving the okay. Take a few sessions to teach this and you won't have to body-block her when you're at that busy highway rest stop and want to give her a toilet break.

Teaching a Down

For most people, lure-and-reward is probably the easiest way to teach a down. With your dog sitting, put a treat in front of her nose and bring it *straight* down in front of her, between her forepaws. Many dogs will follow the treat all the way down the first time; click and deliver the treat the second her elbows hit the floor. If your dog gets "stuck" partway down, that's okay. Just do a few reps, each time luring her down a little farther. Deliver the treat low, so she doesn't have to stretch up to get it.

After a few reps, your dog will probably be dropping to the ground confidently. Now have her track your hand down, but without a treat in it. When her elbows hit the floor, click and deliver the treat with your *other* hand. Food in your hand will no longer be part of the picture.

At this point, you can start to say your cue—usually, well, "Dogalini, down," and please don't let me hear you repeat it; if you hear yourself saying it more than once per rep, go back to practicing without a cue, until you can tell when your dog is really truly about to lie down. (See Chapter 3, "Anything but 'Obedience,'" if you need a refresher on when to add a cue to a behavior you're teaching.) Begin to fade away the luring gesture. Make your hand movements smaller and smaller; stand up, if you're not standing already. Also, remember that, as with everything you teach, you'll need to practice in several different situations and places to help your dog understand that "Down" means the same thing no matter what the circumstances are.

You can also shape a down, by clicking and treating for the movements that make up the process of lying down. Start with a nose dip, then click/treat bigger nose dips, then the paws moving forward and the shoulders dropping . . . Shaping a down is much harder to describe than it is to do, so let's go to the video. On this book's Web site, www.TheDog TrainerBook.com, you'll find links to video of me teaching a dog to lie down as well as to YouTube videos of other trainers working with their own dogs.

TROUBLESHOOTING

If your dog lowers his head for the treat lure but gets up out of the sit, try working with him in a corner. Or shape instead of luring. If your dog lies down slowly and reluctantly, watch to see how he moves when he lies down at other times. If he moves slowly then, too, think about a vet check; he may be uncomfortable for some reason. Speaking of comfort, make sure you are not asking him to lie down anyplace cold or wet.

Small dogs seem to get stuck with the down more often than big dogs. Be sure not to loom over a small dog; sit on the floor, or have your dog on a large, stable, elevated surface. If you've been luring, try shaping. You can also try luring a small dog under your bent knee while you sit on the floor.

Teaching a Stay

A stay (remember, you can call it anything you want, since Dogalini doesn't speak English, French, or Urdu) isn't just good for preventing your dog from jumping up or waiting before rushing out the door; it's also handy for parking your dog and keeping him out of your hair while you check that leak under the sink or sit on the floor to wrap large birthday presents. Sadly, many people wind up backing away from their dog, palm out, chanting, "Stay, stay, stay," only to have said dog get up again. But work slowly and patiently enough, and you can dance the limbo and Hula-hoop all evening while your dog stays.

Start with your dog in the position you want her to hold, whether it's a sit or a down.* For most purposes, it doesn't matter which you choose, but bear in mind your dog's comfort. A sit may be physically harder to maintain after a few minutes, whereas a dog lying down may feel more vulnerable in some situations. Lying down with a hip over and the rear legs out to the side is generally considered a more relaxed position than the "sphinx" down, from which a dog can easily spring up. I wouldn't ask a dog to remain in place on a hot, wet, or icy surface. Also, small and short-haired dogs can feel miserable on a cold floor, while your Siberian Husky will likely revel in it.

Arbitrarily, let's work through the down-stay, but the procedure will be the same if you choose a sit. Because the whole point of a stay is that your dog stays put till you let her know she's free to move, you'll need a "release cue," a word or gesture that means the stay is done. "Free," "Banana," "On your bike!"—it doesn't matter. Many people find that "Okay" gets them into trouble because when they say it in conversation their dog thinks the stay is done. I use "Okay" and haven't had this problem, maybe because I look at the dog and speak in an artificially bright tone.

THE HOW-TO

To work on your dog's stay, pick a time when she's relaxed and well exercised. That applies especially to puppies and bouncy young dogs. (I don't have to spell out the reasoning, right?)

Ask your dog to lie down, but instead of delivering a treat as soon as she hits the floor, hold off for one second. Click and give her a treat. Or, if your dog tends to bounce up again instantly, have two treats ready. Feed the first one right away, before he has time to move; then click, and feed the second treat. You'll need to move fast enough that your dog is

---

* You can either teach a stay separately, or make staying put a built-in part of the sit or down. Many trainers reasonably point out that there's hardly ever a time when you ask your dog to sit or lie down but don't want her to stay put for a while. On the other hand, the whole point of teaching a stay is that your dog does stay put till you give the cue that means "Feel free to move around now," so if "Sit" and "Down" always mean "Sit and remain sitting" or "Lie down and remain down," you have to remember to give your release cue or your well-trained dog will never move from the spot again. I don't always want to be bothered. For example, if my Juniper has sat to greet a child, I have no problem with him getting up on his own initiative as soon as the kid has moved on to other entertainments.

Avoid This Mistake

Quick and Dirty Tip

A common newbie mistake is to deliver the treat slowly and high up. Result, your dog sees the treat coming and, since she doesn't know the stay game yet, she gets up to meet the food en route. Solve this problem by bringing the treat toward your dog quickly and low—the best place to deliver it is right between her front paws. If you're working on a sit-stay, give the treat at chest height.

---

still in the down position. Once you've delivered the treats, immediately give your release cue and encourage your dog to get up. Then do another rep. Over a dozen or so reps, begin waiting a little longer before the click plus the second treat. By this time, too, a dog who tends to bounce up will almost certainly be remaining in place long enough for you to begin delaying the first treat—just for a moment, now. Build the delay slowly.

MAKE YOUR PRACTICE MORE CHALLENGING

When your dog can stay for about five seconds—that's an arbitrary number, of course—start to add a little distance. At first you'll walk backward, because your dog is likelier to get up to follow you if you turn away. Take one single step, then return to your dog, click, and deliver a treat. Give her the okay to get up immediately, even if five seconds haven't passed.

Here's why. The stay gets harder and harder for your dog depending on how long it is, how far away you are, and what else is going on around her. Trainer shorthand is "distance, duration, distraction." For best success in teaching a stay, work on one factor at a time. Whenever you make one factor more difficult, ease up on the others at first, then build them back up. That's why, when you take that first step back from your dog, adding *distance,* you should cut the *duration* of the stay.

Or suppose you've made a lot of progress and your dog is able to lie quietly for one minute while you stand ten feet away from her. On your next rep, you plan to *distract* her with a bouncing ball. Stand five feet from your dog and bounce the ball just once or twice. A rock-solid stay is mostly a matter of working slowly and patiently to start with—the ideal is that your dog never makes a mistake and breaks her stay.

It used to be thought that mistakes were beneficial, because they gave you the opportunity to "correct" your dog—as I saw one old-school trainer do, to haul him back to his stay spot, shove him down, and then cuff him under the chin to really drive the point home. In the first place, way to suck the fun out of learning and teaching. (And possibly to make your dog fear your approach.) In the second place, practice is often most efficient when it includes the fewest mistakes. If you've ever played a musical instrument, you may have noticed how once you hit a wrong note, you tend to repeat the error. The same goes for your dog learning a new behavior.

If Dogalini does get up, take a breath and then give her a short refresher, starting at a point somewhat easier than whatever you were working on when she broke. Or consider that she may be tired—maybe she's learned as much as she can for now. In that case, ask her to do one very easy rep at a level where she's letter perfect, and then call it a day.

Building duration is, for my money, the dull part of teaching a stay. Apart from watching your dog carefully to make sure you're not pushing her past her skill level, and slipping her the occasional treat and some praise, there isn't a whole lot to do. The good news is that if you've worked on those first few minutes of the stay and made them rock solid, longer periods will go quickly.

Cooking up distractions, on the other hand, is kind of fun. Dance a jig. Ring a bell. Answer the phone. Roll a ball or squeak a toy. Brandish your dog's tug rope. Walk in a circle around your dog. (A lot of dogs have trouble holding their stay when someone's behind them, by the way. Work on that circle one short segment at a time.) Distance, too, is kind of fun. Dog trainers get a little thrill at the point in teaching a stay when we first step out of sight. Come back in view within a nanosecond that first time, please.

HOW TO USE THE STAY CUE

Usually, we add a cue for a behavior when the dog has already learned the behavior well. The reason is that we want the dog to associate the cue strongly with the polished form of the behavior, not with a rough approximation.* But a perfect stay could last anywhere from a few sec-

---

* Some trainers question whether it really weakens the cue to use it before the behavior you're teaching is well polished, as long as the dog is responding in approximately the right way. I'm not certain who's right on this point, or whether the truth may vary from dog to dog.

onds to half an hour or more, depending on the situation. So if you're careful to keep your training free of mistakes, your dog's performance of stay will be near perfect from the get-go. For that reason, you can introduce the stay cue early on—as soon as you have seen your teaching succeed. The confidence you feel because of your success will help you avoid the chant of "Stay . . . stay . . . stay" you often hear when someone is worried that their dog's about to get up.

Don't use the stay cue in situations where complying is impossible or unpleasant for your dog. For instance, avoid telling her to stay as you close the door behind you on your way to work. Nor should you cue her to hold still and then clip her nails, unless you've taught her to enjoy nail clipping. ("Enjoy" means "revel in," not "put up with patiently.") Finally, I wouldn't use stay to keep a dog in a scary or volatile situation. As for parking her while you take the roast out of the oven, absolutely yes! And let me suggest you make it worth her while by slipping her a crispy bit from the bottom of the pan.

7

Leaving Stuff Alone, Stealing It, Giving It Up Again, and a Deep, Dark Dog-Trainer Secret

Biologists generally agree that dogs evolved as scavengers near human settlements. The scavenger's rule of life is, If it smells like food and it's lying around, eat it. So our dogs snarf our fallen sandwiches at home and dive for fast-food wrappers on the street. Dogs also love to chew and they love to play games. Sometimes their spot cleaning of the kitchen floor is convenient, and heaven knows half the fun of having a dog is in their playfulness, but sometimes we need to back our Zippys and Dogalinis off from items that are valuable, dangerous, or repulsive. In this chapter you'll learn how to teach your dog to leave your stuff alone—and also what to do in those inevitable moments when evolution takes over and Zippy snags the pot roast. Or your shoe.

How to Teach Your Dog to Leave Things Alone

The cue I use when asking my dog to leave something alone is "Leave it," but as always, yours can be whatever you want—"Off" or "Back up" or "Banana peel." Your dog won't care. I know some trainers who use "Mine" because to their ear that word comes out sounding pleasanter, less boot-camp-like, than the usual "Off" or "Leave it." If you tend to fall into that old-school Command Voice, choose a mild, pleasant cue for this behavior.

To begin teaching the leave it, you'll need your clicker, a hard, fairly boring dog biscuit, and an array of fingernail-size, delectable treats: something in the meaty-fishy-cheesy-soft-and-stinky line. The dry biscuit will tempt your dog; the delicious treats will reward her for resisting the temptation. Wear closed-toe shoes—why will become obvious in a moment. Keep lessons short and fun; ten or fifteen reps is plenty for most dogs. If you feel ambitious, add more training sessions rather than longer ones.

Have the deluxe treats handy, perhaps in a waist pouch or on a nearby table. Show your dog the dry biscuit and put it on the floor. Cover the biscuit with your foot, so your dog can smell it but can't get her mouth on it. She will probably paw and push at your foot, trying to get at the treat. (This is why you're wearing closed-toe shoes.) Say nothing, because the words will mean nothing to your dog. Just quietly watch her and wait. Sooner or later, when she can't get to the temptation, she will back off.

This first backing-off behavior may be so tiny and fast you barely see it. Your dog may turn her head away from the biscuit for a moment, or take half a step backward. Try mightily to catch that instant when she's doing *anything* other than trying to get at the biscuit. Immediately click, and immediately deliver one of the superdeluxe treats.

Show your dog the biscuit again, and again cover it with your foot. Again, wait quietly till she does anything other than mug your foot. Mark that behavior with a click and deliver a treat. Many dogs start getting the picture after four or five repetitions. They'll refuse to go after the biscuit at all; some make a big production of looking away from your foot or even turning their whole body aside.

At that point, you're ready for the second step. Show your dog the biscuit, but now set it on the floor right next to your foot, where you can cover it quickly if your dog dives for it. She probably will. Cover the biscuit, wait for her to quit mugging, and then take your foot off the biscuit again. Keep trying until your dog hesitates instead of immediately going for that vulnerable uncovered biscuit. Click/treat. Do several reps. Then begin leaving the biscuit uncovered for a bit longer. See if you can work up to five or six seconds in a couple of brief lessons.

MAKE YOUR PRACTICE MORE CHALLENGING

Now your dog has begun to get the idea that ignoring a so-so treat will earn her a much, much better treat. As you continue training, make it a bit more difficult. Move the biscuit around with your foot. Drop it from a few inches up, then from table height. Toss it gently. Throw it. Set it down near your dog. Replace the biscuit with something your dog likes a bit better, then with something she likes better still. Work your way up to using a leftover chicken wing. Practice in the kitchen, in the dining room, on the sidewalk, and in your backyard next to the barbecue the same way—with a temptation and a superdeluxe reward.

You can also set up a series of temptations along your block, and then practice walking your dog past them. Because you'll have your dog on leash, you'll be able to prevent her from getting the tempting item. Then you can reward her for backing off. As you train in all of these settings and with different tempting treats, your lessons will look more and more like real life, so you and your dog will be ready for the day the pot roast falls.

When your dog responds correctly 90 percent of the time at any given level of difficulty, you can add your verbal cue to that level of difficulty. Say your cue, then present the temptation. At that point, the "leave it" *behavior* will pretty much always follow your cue, so your dog can learn to associate that cue with her behavior. Expect this learning to take a couple of dozen reps.

For maximum success, go up a level in difficulty only when your dog is responding correctly 90 percent of the time at the level you're already at. Also, make lessons harder one factor at a time. Suppose you're introducing a stronger temptation than a dry biscuit. This is not the lesson in which you also begin putting the temptation between your dog's front paws. Begin each lesson with a quick refresher of the one before—don't expect to pick up exactly where you left off. Some stages are especially challenging; for instance, holding back from a thrown temptation is difficult for many dogs. Tether or leash your dog for the first few reps, so she can't reach the temptation if she makes a break for it. And if she does make a mistake, don't get your undies in a bunch or yank her leash (it's just a failsafe, not a punishment device). Just go back a couple of steps in training and work your way up again.

Usually, I wean dogs off regular food rewards once a behavior is well learned. With a leave it, though, you're often asking your dog to give up something she wants a *lot*. For that reason, it's wise to reward lavishly whenever possible. There will be times when you don't have treats on you; those are exactly the times when past generosity pays off.

How to Get Your Dog to Stop "Stealing" Your Stuff

I'd bet a lot of money that every pet dog with the power of locomotion has gotten in trouble at home for "stealing" socks, shoes, plastic soda bottles, counter sponges, and other ordinary and not-so-ordinary household items. Dogs have their reasons for what they do, but fortunately we can direct their time and energy to activities we like better (or dislike less). There are also important things *not* to do unless you want to turn normal dog behavior into a serious problem.

WHY DOGS "STEAL" AND HOW TO FIX IT

First, the why. One thing about dogs, you never have to look for deep, dark motivations. They act like rascals because they've got unburned energy lying around. They're a little bit bored and want some action. They're a little bit lonely and want some attention. The item they nab smells like you. The item they nab smells like food. The item they nab has just the right chewy texture.

That list of whys, conveniently enough, turns right into a list of problem-solving tactics.

FIX NO. 1: EXERCISE

If you've got an active young dog, be sure to provide a solid hour of aerobic exercise every day. The meaning of "young" varies from breed to breed and individual to individual. Though large dogs tend to have shorter life spans than small dogs, they may remain puppylike for several years. Dogs with a working or hunting heritage—Border Collies and German Shorthaired Pointers, for two—were bred for sustained activity and will go stir-crazy if they spend all day lying on the couch. Let me rephrase that: They *won't* spend all day lying on the couch, and they *will* go crazy looking for something to do.

FIX NO. 2: MENTAL STIMULATION AND ATTENTION

Exercise is half the cure for boredom; mental stimulation is the other half. Many people notice that their puppy's or dog's shoe-stealing evil twin appears at more or less the same time every day. Scheduling a five- or ten-minute session of reward-based training just *before* that time often preempts the witching hour entirely. It also meets your dog's need for attention—and attention *is* a need; dogs are social animals. Nobody enjoys a bored dog's pestering, but it's reasonable for our dogs to want some of our time, focus, and affection every day.

Also great for burning off mental steam: food-dispensing toys. Why should dinner take 4.5 seconds? Pack a fifty fifty mix of canned and dry food in a hollow rubber toy such as the Kong, freeze it overnight, and welcome your dog to the Slow Food movement. Extracting his food will carry him right through that time of the evening when he would otherwise be checking out your kitchen counters and the dirty laundry. And remember the smells-like-food and chewy-texture motivators for object-nabbing? You've just taken care of those, too.

MAKE SURE YOU'RE DOING YOUR PART: PREVENTION

While you're enriching your puppy's or dog's life, don't overlook plain old management as a training tool. Shoes go in the closet. Dirty laundry goes in the laundry bag. Clean laundry gets put away. Tupperware containers bearing traces of last night's pasta salad need not remain on the dining room table while you zone out in front of the TV. Remember what I said at the beginning of this chapter: That inquisitive animal who lives with you evolved as a scavenger, and if you leave interesting stuff around, she will sooner or later scavenge it. A puppy who grows up focused on exercise, legal chewies, and training time with you may rarely or never feel the need to poke around looking for snacks and fun. But once a snatch-and-grab habit has taken root, it's as hard to shake as cigarettes. Prevent access, provide alternative outlets, and don't blame your dog for her occasional lapses.

WHAT TO DO WHEN YOUR DOG "STEALS"

What to do about those lapses? (Let's assume you haven't already worked through the next section, about teaching your dog to give things up on cue.). First, take a deep breath and keep your cool. Shouting at your dog and rushing her to grab her prize is likely to produce a game of keep-away at best. At worst, she perceives a threat and gets scared and defensive. This is especially likely if you grab her, roll her over, and pry her jaws open to take whatever it is away. From your dog's point of view, such behavior is socially peculiar, to say the least. Imagine how you'd feel if out of the blue a close friend punched you and seized your wallet. Dogs repeatedly subjected to this kind of behavior may escalate from object "stealing" to object guarding. Human approach now constitutes a threat, and the canine response to a threat is often to growl, snap, or even bite.

If the object Dogalini's gotten hold of is harmless and inexpensive, your best bet is to ignore her. No agitation, and no attention given to that attention-seeking grab-and-snatch. But if that's your favorite shoe she's got, or a potentially toxic food, go with distraction and bribery. Suddenly discover something fascinating at the other end of the room. Throw a ball. Pick up the leash and invite Dogalini for a walk. Or walk up to her quietly and trade her a bit of cheese or meat for whatever she has nabbed. Yes, the lesson for Dogalini is that stealing your socks induces you to part with your cheese or take her on a surprise inspection of the local fire hydrants. Never mind; you're in damage control mode. "My people will give treats in exchange for my prize finds" is a much better lesson than "My people get weird and scary when they want something I've got." As for you, review your canine theft-prevention exercises and remember to put away your shoes.

Teach Your Dog to Give Up Items

The starting point for teaching dogs to give up items they've already got hold of looks like the emergency bribery just described, but you'll quickly morph it. And you'll be thankful for the work you put in when Dogalini has Great-Uncle Oliver's hand-knitted pill dispenser between her slavering jaws.

STEP 1

Give your dog a toy or chew he *likes* and let him get into it. You can also have a training session when he's become absorbed in a toy or chew on his own. Either way, the toy or chew should be one your dog enjoys but isn't completely crazy over. While your dog's getting busy with his goody, arm yourself with your clicker and a few delicious treats—tiny pieces of chicken or cheese or whatever else your dog just *loves*.

Silently offer your dog one of the treats. He will probably drop the toy or chew to take the treat. At that moment, click, then give the treat as you pick up the toy/chew. When your dog has finished eating the treat, give back the toy/chew.

You'll probably find that after a few repetitions, your dog no longer wants to take the toy/chew. That's fine; you can end the training session with a bonus treat, or go on to work on another behavior you're training. At this stage of the proceedings, your dog's just learning that when he's got something good and you approach, something better may be on its way along with you.

TROUBLESHOOTING

If your dog doesn't drop the toy/chew to take the treat, then either he likes the toy/chew a lot more than you thought, or he likes the treat a lot less, or both. With respect to treats, soft, moist, smelly, and meaty usually trumps dry and odorless.

STEP 2

Once again, set your dog up with something he likes and let him get into it, or pick a time when he's already occupied with a chew. Get your treats and clicker and do one or two warm-ups in which you show your dog the treat up front, as in Step I.

It helps to keep clickers and stashes of treats here and there around the house, so you don't have to do any obvious prep that will clue your dog in to a training session about to start. The sooner the scenario starts looking to him like real life instead of a training session, the better.

Next, bring your hand forward as if to take the toy/chew, but this time your reaching hand is empty. Have a treat ready in your other hand, or conveniently nearby. Because of the earlier practice and your warm-up, your dog will probably drop the toy/chew when your hand comes forward. Immediately click and give him one of your hidden treats. Hold the toy/chew while he eats the treat; then give it back to him. Repeat a few times or until your dog will no longer retake the toy/chew; then end the training session as above.

TROUBLESHOOTING

If your dog doesn't drop the toy/chew when you present your hand, do two or three more practice sessions at the first stage of training, then try again.

STEP 3

Practice with different toys/chews, working up to ones your dog likes more and more. Practice in several different locations, including outside. Start using things your dog might actually find on her own and want to hang on to—for example, used tissues and pork-chop bones. Every time you change objects or locations, start with a practice session in which you offer the dog your "trade treat" up front. And always use high-quality treats.

When your dog is reliably, happily dropping the toy or chew (that means nine times out of ten) as soon you reach for it, you can add a word cue. Say the cue just before you bring your hand forward to take the object from your dog.

TROUBLESHOOTING

If your dog seems reluctant to give up whatever he's got, or doesn't seem to register that you're asking him to do something, hold a couple of practice sessions with an "easier" object, then try again. If you've started giving a word cue but your dog doesn't respond to it, stop using the cue and practice for at least a few days without it.

Finally, if at any stage in teaching a Give/Drop, your dog is stiffening, curling his lip, growling, or behaving in any other way that makes you uncomfortable or suggests that he is uncomfortable, get professional help. See Chapter 12, "Stuff Dogs Do That Worries People," for guidance on hiring someone competent.

Is Keep-away Really the Work of the Devil?

Trainers pretty much universally advise you not to join your dog's game of keep-away. If your dog nabs something, ignore her or trade for it—just the advice I give above. And now I'll confess: I play keep-away with my dog all the time. He will grab some item—one of my shoes, one of his toys, an empty plastic soda bottle—and zoom around the house with it, galumph galumph galumph, all bright-eyed, scattering cats as he goes. (He's not chasing them; they just prefer to watch from higher ground.) I am powerless to resist this game. So is my partner. One or both of us will make Scary Monster Face and growl "I'm gonna get you!" and run after him windmilling our arms until he collapses in a heap on his bed with the shoe or toy or bottle between his feet. Why, you ask, is this okay?

Why indeed. *It's okay because everybody's having fun.* No one physically frail lives in our house. When our old dog Izzy was still alive, she'd stand or lie to one side during keep-away; I don't remember Juni ever colliding with her. We also have a rule that chewing a shoe, rather than just carrying it around or resting his head on it, results in a forfeit. But the most important factor that makes keep-away fun is that there's no aggressive edge. If Juniper had a history of resource guarding against humans, or if being chased by Scary Monsters really frightened him, we wouldn't play this game. As it is, his body language is loose and silly and he wears a huge grin; when he earns a forfeit, he gives up the shoe quietly and politely.

Take into account the context and emotional quality of your dog's behavior, as well as your own feelings about it, before you decide that you have to fix it and put an end to this game. If your dog is "unruly" but isn't hurting anyone, frightening anyone, or causing damage, and if you both find his behavior entertaining, turn it into a game, set boundaries that will keep it fun, and go to town.

Polite Leash Walking

8

How pleasant to take a long walk with your dog beside you!

Or not. Many of the dogs and people I see going for walks seem to be connected to each other only by a taut leash. The younger the dog, the tighter the leash. Communication between the two consists of the dog pulling hard in the direction she wants to go, and the person yanking back.

You and your dog can do better. But I will admit, right off the bat, that in my opinion walking politely on leash is the most difficult of the basic pet-manners skills. And for good reason.

Housetraining isn't a stretch for most dogs—they don't, as a rule, care to soil their living space. It can be a challenge to teach a dog to come to you promptly when a squirrel is in view, but we and our dogs are social partners, and (assuming we're nice to them) it doesn't go against the grain for them to choose to be with us. Walking on leash, though, involves a whole suite of behaviors that make *absolutely no sense* from a dog's point of view: moving from point to point in a straight line; remaining parallel to your companion; moving at a consistent pace instead of trotting, running, walking, rolling; moving, for that matter, at a consistent pace that's slower than most dogs' natural speed. The human and canine agendas diverge, too. We want to get from place to place and maybe get some exercise; they want to chase squirrels and smell fire hydrants.

On top of all this, dogs have an "opposition reflex," meaning that their normal response to being pulled in a given direction is to pull in the opposite direction, so their default when the leash is tight is to pull it even tighter.

Frustration and anger often arise when we think our dogs should automatically know something, or can acquire a skill easily, or are behaving in such and such a way in order to thwart or dominate us. So, paradoxically, understanding why polite leash walking is hard for dogs to learn may make it easier to teach. It's easier to be patient when you know why a task is challenging for your student; easier to be generous when you know that what looks from a human point of view like minimal progress is really a big deal for your dog. There are practical reasons why the human in the dog-human team needs to play cruise director, but pulling on leash isn't a moral issue or a palace coup.

Ten Pointers for Leash-Walking Success

As always, "whatever your dog does is what she's learning to do"—in this context, whenever she pulls on leash, what she's learning to do is pull on leash. On the other hand, every time she takes a step with slack in the lead, she's learning to keep slack in the lead as she walks with you. Before we get to the actual how-to of walking politely on leash, take a look at the following pointers, which will help you set your dog up to succeed.

1. **Be generous.** I can't overstress the importance of this. Bear in mind everything I've said about how just plain unnatural loose-leash walking is for dogs, and reward, reward, reward, reward. When I'm first teaching a dog to walk nicely on leash I may click and treat at *every single step*. The treats may be tiny, they may be the dog's breakfast kibble, but they come fast and furious.

2. **Start with a well-exercised dog whose bowels and bladder are empty.** I live and work in New York City, so even saying this hurts my heart, because if you don't have a big yard, or in fact any yard at all, there is no such thing as practicing loose-leash walking with a tired dog. We urbanites have to head out of our houses and apartments first thing in the morning with four-month-old puppies who have one single thought in their heads and that thought is "Yippee yippee yippee gotta pee!!!!" Those of you who can take your trainee out to the backyard to eliminate and then play a fast game of fetch before you practice your leash walking: *Do it*. Use the advantages that suburban sprawl has given you. I'm not glaring at you with savage jealousy. Really, I'm not.

Aside to my fellow city dwellers: Yes, you are at a disadvantage, but it's not insurmountable. Generosity, persistence, and liberal application of the other tips here will get you the behavior you want.

3. **Reward your dog for paying attention to you—both as in the exercise below, and spontaneously on walks.** Your dog can't simultaneously check in with you and pull on the leash; besides, attention is fundamental to pretty much every other behavior we want our dogs to learn.

4. **Be generous.**

5. **Vary your pace.** As I mentioned earlier, moving at a consistent pace doesn't come naturally to dogs. Also, they get bored. Walk briskly, walk slowly, trot, run. If your dog's a natural runner, occasionally break into a fast pace as a reward for attending to you.

6. **Have a clear goal in mind.** Not your geographical destination, but a picture of the behavior you want your dog to learn—your rules for leash walking. If you know what behavior you're looking for, it becomes much easier (surprise!) to recognize it and reward it when it happens, and so to reward frequently and consistently. Also, no surprise, consistency and predictability make learning easier for your dog. Since you can't tell her what you want in words, you have to show her, as clearly as you can.

Just as an example, my leash-walking rules look something like this:

- Leash to remain slack whether I've let out all six feet of it to allow sniffing, or whether I've taken up a couple of feet and my dog and I are walking side by side

---

Want to Try an Experiment?

In the last year of my dog Izzy's life, she walked so slowly that it sometimes took us over 20 minutes to circle our block, a distance of maybe 500 yards. I loved Izzy with all my heart and I am here to tell you that keeping pace with her was agony. Not only was it boring, it was even physically uncomfortable to inhibit my natural gait for such a long stretch. Our around-the-block totters did give me time to think, and one of the things I thought about was what a fast-moving, variably gaited dog might experience when we ask her to maintain a consistent, slow pace throughout a long walk. I've got no research to back me up here, but hey, do a harmless experiment: See whether your (young, healthy) dog seems to enjoy the walk more and have an easier time focusing on you if you move at a good clip most of the time and change the pace often.

Reserve Permission to Sniff

Quick and Dirty Tip

During your initial training, it's useful to reserve "permission to go sniff" as a reward for your dog, in exchange for keeping slack in the leash. Whether you want to leave that condition in place forever is up to you. Since I live in the city, leash walks are not just toilet breaks. They're also my dog's outings: They make up most of his fun and entertainment for the day, and for dogs "fun and entertainment" means a lot of sniffing. So once any dog I live with has a good, strong loose-leash habit, I change the default: Rather than dole out sniff time as a reward, I let them sniff whenever they like, subject to my cue to get moving again (because it's too hot where we're standing, because I'm running late, because someone's dog on an extending lead is about to run up to us and that annoys me and usually my dog too). Also, if my dog pulls me toward whatever he wants to sniff, he forfeits that opportunity. He may walk toward it if it's out of leash range, but no tightening the leash.

- Dog to stop roughly at my side when I stop; whether my dog sits, stands, or lies down doesn't matter to me
- Dog walks on either my right or left side, but doesn't change sides without permission.

7. Forget about heeling. You'll notice I speak of "loose-leash walking" or "polite leash walking," not "heeling." Heeling is a formal competitive exercise, with the dog close to the handler's left leg and attentively turned toward her. It's not appropriate for an hour's afternoon stroll. To begin with, if you're the dog, never being allowed to sniff pretty much defeats the purpose. As for you, for a pleasant walk all you really need is for the leash to remain slack and for your dog to attend to you enough to turn with you and stop when you do. To me, a walk with my dog feels like holding hands.

8. Switch up the equipment. For times when you absolutely must get from Point A to Point B with your dog on leash but you have no time to train or are tired or crabby or unfocused, use different equipment if you can. For instance, if your dog wears a flat buckle collar during practice, use a front-clip harness for nontraining walks. If you're using a front-clip harness during training, switch to a conventional harness (with the clip in the middle of the dog's back) for nontraining walks.*

Hint: After "Be generous," this is the pointer my fellow urbanites should engrave most deeply on your hearts. Varying your pace (Number 5) is right up there, too.

9. Be generous.

10. Be generous.

How to Get Your Dog to Walk Politely On Leash

As I mentioned earlier, polite leash walking is, essentially, attentive leash walking: Your dog pays attention to where you are in relation to him, and he positions himself accordingly.

Have your clicker and treats ready.

STEP 1

Go to a quiet room in your house or apartment and stand with your dog on leash. Don't speak to your dog or otherwise try to attract his attention; instead, just wait. Sooner or later your dog will look at you. At that instant, click and treat. Give your dog his treat at your side, in the position he'd be in if he was walking nicely on leash.

Notice how this first step in polite leash walking resembles the exercise with which you begin teaching a dog to come when called (p. 100). Attentiveness to you lays the foundation for good manners in many contexts.

STEP 2

Since you've just done something interesting, your dog will probably keep his attention on you for a moment. Work it! As soon as you've delivered that first treat, take a step. Odds are your dog will take a step with you. Click/treat—and again, deliver the treat at your side, in the polite leash-walking position.

STEP 3

Repeat Step 2 several times. If your dog gets distracted or tightens the leash, stand quietly and wait for him to return his attention to you. When he does so, click/treat in leash-walking position.

---

* Back-clip harnesses may be workable only for smaller dogs, because they enable the dog to put his body weight and muscle power into pulling.

If your dog pulls on the leash, then turns his attention back to you (click/treat!) more than, say, twice in a row, then you've probably taught him the pattern "tighten leash, return to handler" rather than the pattern "walk next to handler." No need to fret—this is a common pitfall and easy to climb out of. Next time he tightens the leash, wait him out. When he returns to your side, *don't click*. Instead, take a quick step forward. Your dog will almost certainly fall in with you; take another step. *Now* click/treat—assuming, of course, that your dog hasn't tightened the leash again. Delaying the click/treat until your dog has taken two or three steps beside you and has kept the leash slack will break the connection between tightening the leash and getting a click/treat, and instead strengthen the connection between walking next to you and getting a click/treat.

Dogs are very quick to learn these "behavior chains." This sometimes works to our disadvantage, as it might here, but it also enables us to teach them long, complex sequences—everything from running an agility course to barking once when the doorbell rings, then dropping into a sit and waiting there while you sign for a delivery.

How far can you expect to get in your first training session? If you've started with a well-exercised, slightly hungry dog and you're working in a quiet, nondistracting environment, you may find that in just a few minutes your dog can walk next to you for half a dozen steps while getting one or two click/treats. But it's also fine if in this first session you're still clicking and treating with every step. Younger, bouncier, more distractible dogs may progress more slowly; this doesn't mean that you're doing anything wrong or that your dog is dumb or uncooperative. And if you have adopted an adolescent or older dog who has already had months or years of practice in pulling on leash, she, too, may take more time to learn new habits.

STEP 4

In your next few practice sessions, stick with the nondistracting environment. Gradually drop the frequency of your click/treat—first to an average of one click/treat per two steps, then one click/treat per three steps, and so on.

As you gradually decrease the *average* rate of clicking/treating, avoid setting up a pattern. If your dog can reliably expect a treat every fifth step but never in between, he'll stop paying attention to you between treats. If he gets a treat *on average* every fifth step but sometimes gets one every other step, sometimes every seventh step, sometimes every fifth step, he'll never know when a treat may come, so he'll keep watching you.

STEP 5

Take your practice to a slightly more distracting location—your backyard, say, or the sidewalk in front of your house. Even someplace your dog visits every day will present a step up in difficulty if he hasn't yet practiced there. You know your dog best, so you know which situations and times will be most or least distracting; make a mental hierarchy of places where it's hard for your dog to focus on you, and work your way up it. Many dogs will succeed if you restart from Step 2 in the new location, but if your dog's easily distracted, restart at Step 1.

STEP 6

As your dog's loose-leash walking becomes proficient in each location, continue practicing there but gradually thin out the number of food rewards you give.

STEP 7

Gradually practice in more and more distracting situations. Each time you bump up the level of difficulty, also bump up the rate at which you deliver rewards. When your dog has solid skills in the new, more distracting context, start thinning out the number of food rewards again.

STEP 8

Eventually, your dog's habit of walking on a loose leash will be so well entrenched that you can give food rewards quite rarely. I've found, though, that nothing makes polite leash walking fall apart faster than *ignoring* your dog.

Or, Try Polite Leash Walking Without the Leash*

If you have access to a safe fenced area (say, your backyard, for starters), you can begin teaching loose-leash walking without a leash. Bring your clicker and an ample supply of good treats. Turn your dog loose and start walking around. Your dog will very likely take off

---

* This method is an adaptation of the "Choose to Heel" technique developed by the trainer Dawn Jecs.

bounding/trotting/sniffing, especially if she's young and this happens to be the first walk of the day. We've specified that you're working in a safe place, so you need do nothing but walk—no calling your dog, no kissy noises, no following her. *Do* keep an eye on her, though, because though you seem passive you are actually Lying in Wait.

Sooner or later, your dog will break off her poking around and sniffing and look at you, or maybe even take a step toward you. That's your moment! Click, let your dog come to you for the treat, and deliver the treat at your side, where you'd like your dog to be when she's walking on leash with you. Continue walking. As you practice, your dog will begin to come to loose-leash walking position more and more often. Click and treat each time. If your dog takes several steps with you, click and treat repeatedly.

In later sessions, you can expect your dog to orient to you more quickly and stick with you longer. You can continue practicing off leash in other enclosed areas, if they're available, or introduce the leash. For some dogs, the leash changes the picture enough that they have to learn all over again to walk politely next to you; if that's your dog, try a couple of practice sessions in which she drags the leash and you don't pick it up; then graduate to holding the leash.

For many of us, the only venue where we can practice polite "leash" walking off leash is the living room, and if you've got a big dog and a small living room it's hard to accomplish much. But if you do have access to a safe off-leash area, by all means include off-leash practice in your training. It can help break you of the habit of tightening up on the leash, if you tend to do that.* Also, you can't deliver a leash correction if you're not holding a leash, so off-leash practice is especially valuable for retraining the reflexes of anyone who originally learned to train dogs using sharp jerks on the leash.

Last, off-leash practice works, so it also builds your confidence as your dog's trainer *and* as your dog's friend. Many people secretly believe that on some level manners training is grim—fallout, I expect, from the days of leash jerks, the pulley down, and the alpha roll. I don't generally get too mystical about these things, but I believe that seeing our dogs freely choose to work with us (and visibly enjoy themselves doing so), without any compulsion, chips away at that grim feeling and lightens our hearts.

---

* You can also use a leash that attaches to a waist belt. Or anchor your leash-holding hand at your navel and don't move it from that spot.

Anxious Dogs

Every so often, I have a client (or I get an e-mail from someone, or I see someone on the street) whose dog pulls frantically on leash all the time, sometimes weaving from side to side, often with ears pinned and tail tucked between her legs. Sometimes the dog's body is low, too. In a variation of this scenario, the dog has to be dragged outside for walks and moves slowly and reluctantly on the entire outbound leg of the walk, then pulls as hard as she can toward home. These dogs either ignore treats altogether, or take them but drop them, or eat them mechanically, without seeming to notice them.

They're scared. "Teaching polite leash walking" is irrelevant to them, because they are so overwhelmed by anxiety when they're outdoors that they can't learn anything (except, perhaps, that the outdoors is someplace where dogs feel scared). If I've just described your dog, never mind the polite leash walking for now; you have bigger fish to fry. Work with a qualified behavior professional to ease your dog's anxiety and build up her confidence. (See Chapter 12, "Stuff Dogs Do That Worries People," for help in finding someone.) Then you'll be able to do something about how hard she pulls on leash.

How to Use "Penalty Yards"

The world is full of a number of smelly, informative, and edible things that your dog will be tempted to pull toward. So take some time to teach her that the way to get to what she wants is to keep the leash loose en route.

Set up a goal for your dog—this could be a biscuit on the ground or a person she adores. I call this exercise "Penalty Yards," but really your job is to keep the flow of rewards fast enough that your dog succeeds in walking next to you with a loose leash as you approach the goal.

Click and treat as rapidly as you can, as long as your dog keeps the slack in the leash. The instant she draws forward and tightens the leash, say, "Oops!" and go right back to the starting point. Remember, you're not trying to deliver a "leash correction" here—the consequence of surging forward is simply that your dog winds up farther away from what she wants to reach. If your dog tends to leap forward and hit the end of the leash hard, save wear and tear on her and you by holding the leash so she only has a couple of feet to play with.

Repeat, repeat, repeat, gently delivering penalty yards whenever your dog draws the leash tight. Although this exercise requires patience (like all training!) it will go more and more quickly as you practice with different temptations and your dog gets the hang of it. The first few times you practice, while your dog is still figuring out the rules of this game, set the goal fairly close to your starting point, and pick a temptation that isn't too overwhelming (a dry biscuit, not a hamburger). This enables your dog to succeed early on without so many frustrating reps that she gives up and shuts down or gets agitated. What distance you choose as a starter depends on how energetic your dog is, how hard or easy a time she has learning self-control behaviors, and your sense of your own skills and reflexes. Also, something we often overlook in training is how encouraging it is for you, your dog's teacher, to succeed: another reason to start easy.

Some dog trainers advise coming to a dead halt whenever the leash gets tight, and just standing there till the dog returns to your side. I haven't found this effective. Even though the dog isn't moving forward anymore, her pulling has still brought her closer to whatever she was pulling toward. Many dogs stand at the end of the tight leash, huffing air and looking perfectly content. The penalty yards method works better, because it imposes a cost on pulling—the dog winds up *farther* from her goal.

To deal with tempting items that you don't want your dog to reach or get hold of, teach her the "Leave it" cue (see Chapter 7, "Leaving Stuff Alone . . .").

Teach Your Dog to Stay on One Side

When I got my first dog, Izzy, and taught her to walk politely on leash, it was no problem if she switched back and forth from my right to my left whenever she felt like it. As long as she kept that slack in the leash, our walks were comfortable. Then I got a second dog, Muggsy. Was I sorry I hadn't taught Izzy to stick to one side at a time! Not only did the leashes get tangled, but also Muggsy would try to follow Iz if she moved to the side opposite him, so I had two dogs crisscrossing in front of me. Drat. Needless to say, I changed the rules on Iz and taught Muggsy to stay on one side from the get-go.

Teaching a dog to keep to one side is simple to do. Half the battle is in teaching loose-leash walking in the first place, because you're delivering rewards at a particular spot on whichever side of you. Sooner or later, though, your dog will be attracted by something on the other side and try to crisscross. My way of dealing with this is to block the dog's movement by physically stepping in his way, and just wait. Because the attempt to cross isn't working, the dog will look up at you or take a step back or otherwise try something else, at which point you can encourage him to to move with you; click/treat as soon as he initiates that step. Notice that you prevent the dog from getting closer to what he's interested in, so his attempt to cross isn't automatically rewarded the way pulling forward on the leash is. It's still possible he'll learn a behavior chain: "I move into a crisscross, I step back, I take a step with my person." Here's how to avoid that problem: After the first two or three attempts to crisscross, start holding out for a few steps back in position, then a few more, before you click/treat.

If you observe your dog carefully, you can often learn what objects and people will tempt him to crisscross. Up the rate of reward while you're passing them so that he begins to perceive temptations as hints that it would be worth his while to pay even more attention to you.

As always, anything (anything safe!) that appeals to your dog can be deployed as a reward for behavior you like. Sometimes when I can see my dog has been tempted to crisscross but has caught himself and stayed at my side instead, I'll stop or make a U-turn and invite him to go inspect. This is the same doggy Zen you employ in teaching "Leave it"—turning away from a temptation buys the dog access to it or to something even better. If trying to crisscross doesn't work, but staying on the same side occasionally buys your dog access to the temptation, guess which behavior he will be more inclined to use?

I recommend you teach your dog not to crisscross even if you're absolutely, positively, 100 percent sure that you'll never have two dogs at the same time. Who knows, you might wind up taking care of a friend's dog while she's out of town, or someone might be taking care of your dog. Also, I was absolutely, positively, 100 percent sure I would never have two dogs at the same time, so you see what happens when you're absolutely sure of things.

Though you don't want your dog inviting herself to switch sides, it's useful to teach her to switch sides on your cue; you can keep her on the curb side whether the curb's at your left or right, for instance. You might also want to give her a little distance while passing another dog head-on, or move her away from a person who makes her uncomfortable.

If you've taught your dog to target to your hand (see Chapter 10, "Play? Training? Tricks"), this is easy as pie—just extend the hand on the side you want her to cross to and give the cue to target. Click/treat the first few times you use the targeting cue in this new context.

Teach Your Dog to Sit When You Stop

For the record, teaching your dog to sit when you stop isn't essential to a full and happy life! On the other hand, it's easy, it looks snazzy, and it's a nice courtesy if you've stopped to talk with someone who's not comfortable with dogs. Or if it's your dog who's slightly shy, having a well-rewarded task to perform can relieve her anxiety as well. Here's how to teach it.

Remember, stationary behaviors are harder for your dog to learn when he's amped and rarin' to go. So begin teaching on the homebound leg of a long walk, or at any other time when your dog has had enough exercise to be relaxed (but not so much that he's desperate to hit the hay, either). As you walk along, simply come to a stop and ask your dog to sit. Encourage him to do so at your side if he's not in position already. As soon as he sits, click/treat and begin walking. Your dog's getting two rewards here: the treat and the opportunity to move forward again.

Repeat that sequence four or five times at random intervals: Stop; cue your dog to sit; click/treat; start walking. Then stop and just wait to see what your dog does; say nothing. Give him a slow count of five to think about it. Odds are, he'll sit. Click/treat and start walking again. Repeat two or three more times, not giving a cue but waiting for your dog to figure out what to do.

TROUBLESHOOTING

If your dog doesn't get the sit-when-you-stop skill quickly, no worries! Some dogs are more cautious than others in offering behaviors. And the dog who's slow to offer a sit may be quick to learn to jump through a hoop. Do another half-dozen reps in which you give your dog a word cue, and after that try a rep in which you wait for him to figure it out again.

Second practice session: Try just two or three reps in which you give your dog the cue to sit; on the next rep, say nothing and wait him out. By this time, you can probably expect that he'll sit quickly.

Third practice session: No more word cues! Just wait for your dog to sit when you stop. Now just the fact that you've stopped has become your dog's cue to sit. Click/treat, and start walking.

Further practice sessions: You can omit the click now, but still deliver a treat every time. But pause a couple of seconds before you give the treat. (Then start walking again.) If your dog has had a lot of sit/stay practice in other contexts, you can lengthen the sit quickly in this context. If not, build up slowly. Remember to keep the duration of this sit random, so your dog never quite knows when the treat may come.

Using this behavior "for real" (as you stop and talk to someone, for instance) makes it a new and different situation. The first few times that new situation comes up, ask your dog to sit instead of waiting for him to figure it out. If he has to stay sitting for any length of time, deliver occasional treats as he does so. As for when you should give him a chance to figure it out for himself, that depends. How excited is he today? Does he love to greet people, and does that make it harder for him to stay seated beside you rather than say hi? Did he pick up the sit-when-my-person-stops lesson in a snap?

WHEN NOT TO HAVE YOUR DOG SIT

There will be situations when your dog may not want to sit and shouldn't have to: on snowy or icy or salted pavement (don't make him stand in one place on these, either); on hot pavement (ditto); in a puddle (ditto). Also, prolonged sits become uncomfortable for many dogs; if you need to park your dog for a five- or ten-minute stretch, teach him to lie down instead, or just let him stand. If your dog has hip or other joint problems, talk to your vet about what position may be most comfortable for him. Finally, if you teach your two-year-old dog to sit when you stop, she does so happily for years, and then she starts doing it slowly or reluctantly or not at all as she gets older, respect her creakiness and consult your vet.

How to Handle Dog Meetings On Leash

Dogs vary in their greeting styles, in how comfortable they are with new canine acquaintances, and in how they respond to strange dogs getting into their personal space. Being on leash can complicate these factors. A tight leash pulls a dog's body upward, so that her posture may appear challenging to other dogs. Many dogs respond tensely to a direct frontal approach by another dog—but two people walking their dogs will often pass or greet each other head-on. Finally, people don't always recognize canine signals of unease or even imminent explosion.

The stage can be set for dog-dog greetings that rapidly turn into arguments or even fights, which is no fun for anybody. And for some dogs, especially those who were a bit shy or touchy to begin with, such encounters may have long-term behavioral effects. Many clients have reported to me that their dog's reactive on-leash barking and lunging at other dogs got its start after a dog-dog greeting that went south.

You have two main lines of defense. Alas, the one I prefer really rains on people's parades: Don't have on-leash meetings with dogs, period. A high-quality manners class using reward-based methods will help you teach your dog to focus on you even when other dogs are around, and so can your own solo practice with the attention exercise earlier in this chapter.

Besides lowering the odds that your dog will learn unfortunate lessons, a no-greetings policy helps keep life simple for her. A single rule—"When I'm on leash, other dogs are irrelevant"—is easier to learn and potentially less frustrating than "Sometimes you can and sometimes you can't." Life may also be simpler for you if you don't need to make a decision about every dog you encounter on every walk you take.

Mind you, I'm not saying that dogs shouldn't meet other dogs and spend time with them. If they enjoy other dogs' company, of course they should have dog-dog time! Visit a well-run dog park or day care, or set playdates with friends, or go on country rambles with your human friends and their dogs. (See Chapter 2, "Socialization," for guidance on choosing dog parks, and whether your dog should go at all.)

Of course, my universal rule has a sub-paragraph for those of you whose response is "But what about my dog's friends?" Oh, all right. If your dog has doggy friends whom she's already met frequently on leash with a good time had by all, they can continue meeting. But please make your dog trainer happy—don't just let your dog drag you over to her buds. Play the "Penalty Yards" game described earlier, to teach her that if she wants to visit a friend, she needs to keep that leash loose all the way.

Also bear in mind that dogs' behavior may change as they mature. The dog who was your dog's best pal when they were pups may grow up to be standoffish or even testy with his peers. Or that newly standoffish dog might be your own. Don't say I didn't warn you.

GREET CANINE STRANGERS AS SAFELY AS POSSIBLE

If you speed on the freeway, I hope you're at least putting on your seat belt and turning off the cell phone while you do it. And if I haven't persuaded you to skip the on-leash dog greetings, then do the following to keep them trouble free. Learn to read dog body language (see Chapter 9, "The Parallel Universe") and know what a relaxed greeting looks like. You can certainly ask the other dog's handler whether her dog likes meeting other dogs, but it's surprising how many people are either clueless or in denial. I have a vivid memory of walking a friend's dog into the street one day to avoid an oncoming dog whose handler insisted that he was friendly. Ah, not so much—not with that high, tight posture and arcing tail, those dilated pupils, that hard stare, and the ears and corners of the lips pushed forward. That dog wasn't even subtle!

Conversely, if your dog's interested in another dog, and that dog strikes you as friendly but her handler looks anxious or tries to wave you off, steer clear. My clients report having the same conversation over and over when walking their well-trained reactive dogs.* "Please keep your distance," they beg of the stranger whose dog is dragging her rapidly closer. "Oh, he's friendly!" the stranger replies, and by now it's too late for my client to say, "But my dog isn't!" Cue explosions both canine and human. Don't be that stranger, okay? It's hard on the reactive dog and his person, and it's not much fun for your dog to be snarked at, either.

---

* "Reactive" is trainer-speak for "Barks and lunges at other dogs" (or when startled for other reasons).

9

The Parallel Universe

DOG BODY LANGUAGE AND COMMUNICATION

Dog body language is rich, complicated, subtle, and endlessly interesting; as you learn about it, another world opens up, a parallel universe of dogs' lives, taking place right next to ours and often completely outside our notice. Eyes, ears, lips, foreheads, tails, backs, and even feet—every single part of a dog's body has something to tell us. How quickly or slowly is she moving? In a straight line or in an arc? Does he stop and sniff the ground?

But maybe any encouragement to study dogs' body language should come with a warning. The better you get at reading dogs' social signals, the more you'll see how much unkindness we inflict on them without meaning to. You don't have to be much of a sensitive plant to start flinching at the anxiety written all over the hunched body and tucked tail of a dog left tied up outside a store, the lip-licking, ear-pinning attempts to appease a human who's just given an old-school "collar correction," the sidelong glances and muscle tension of a dog being walked by his oblivious handler past another dog who's snarling and lunging.

On the upside, it's marvelous to watch a socially skilled dog look away from an uneasy one and then find something else to do, as the stiffness disappears from the body of the socially inept dog. Dog play will blow you away—the quick breaks, the lightning-fast butt-high, front-end-low play bows, the you-chase-me-I-chase-you reciprocity. When you can "hear" what your own dog is telling you, you can teach her more effectively because you will know what puzzles, intrigues, or worries her. You and your family—human and canine—will even be safer, because you'll know when the person telling you his dog is friendly knows what he's talking about, and when he really, really doesn't.

Several good book and DVD atlases of dog behavior and body language are on the market now; they're hours and hundreds of pages long. This chapter will get you started, and, I hope, in spite of the sad-making downside, hooked. A list of further resources, including links to some excellent YouTube videos, appears on this book's Web site, www. The DogTrainerBook.com.

How to Read Your Dog's Body Language

The following tour of your dog's body isn't exactly a dictionary of dog body language, because very few given movements or positions have a fixed meaning. For instance, pinned-back ears mean one thing when paired with a "play face" and a wiggly butt, something else when the dog is crouched on the ground, unmoving. Plus, some things that hint at dogs' feelings aren't really "behaviors," unless you think of shedding and paw sweat as behaviors. I'll put all those body parts and physiological phenomena in context to give you a picture of what dogs usually look like in certain emotional states—relaxed and excited friendliness; anxiety and stress; "guilt"; imminent aggression. And we'll talk about dog-dog interactions and how to tell good play from an encounter that is, or is about to be, Not Good.

HOW TO READ YOUR DOG'S HEAD AND FACE

Look at your dog's head as a whole: Is he carrying it low or at normal height? Or is his neck straight up, with head held high and still? The higher and more tense his head and neck, the more alert he is. Ask yourself what he's so alert about: A squirrel? The mail carrier? Another dog?

Watch his ears: Are they forward, straight up and down, somewhat back, pinned tight against his head? In general, the more forward and

---

Train Yourself

Quick and Dirty Tip

Dog body language is quick. To train your eye, pick a body part—the ears, say—and just watch that one part for a while, on every dog you see. Next time, watch another body part. If you're really getting your behavior geek on, try watching random YouTube videos of dogs, hitting Replay over and over and focusing on a different body part every time. In no time at all you'll be headdesking just like a dog trainer, wailing at people's misinterpretations of their dogs. Good times!

tense a dog's ears, the more tense the dog. He could be all keyed up about that squirrel, or he might perceive a threat. Floppy ears are harder to read for humans (and probably for dogs, too); watch the *base* of the ear for clues about position. Cropped ears and ears that have been taped to stand up straight all the time may send wrong signals ("I am tense!") that interfere with dog-dog communication.

A dog squinting, the way you might squint when you smile, probably feels relaxed or happily excited. Dilated pupils, though, suggest anger or fear or both. (Unless, of course, they're dilated because of that squirrel mentioned above.) And watch for the whites of a dog's eyes. Sometimes they're visible just incidentally—for instance, a resting dog may be disinclined to move his head to look at whatever's caught his interest. More often, though, a dog showing the whites of his eyes is anxious and may even be about to snap. Trainers call this look "whale eye." The whole package includes tense facial muscles; the dog's mouth may be tightly closed, or you may see teeth, with a curled lip or a snarl. Commonly, whale eye marks a dog who's been backed into a corner or who's guarding a food bowl or a prize chew. Approach only if a dog bite is on your shortlist of experiences you'd like to have that day.

How does your dog respond to eye contact from you? Between dogs, direct eye contact or staring signals challenge, even threat. Most of our pets, fortunately, seem to have figured out that we crazy primates don't mean to be rude when we stare at dogs, but if your dog's body language is telling you he's tense, you may as well not pick that moment to gaze into his eyes. And here's a common shy-dog scenario: The dog approaches you to sniff. Her body weight is back over her haunches, rather than being evenly distributed or toward her front legs, and she stretches her neck in your direction. You look down, your eyes meet hers, and all of a sudden she's backing up, barking fiercely. (For more about shy dogs, see Chapter 12, "Stuff Dogs Do That Worries People.")

A wrinkly forehead hints at tension. A tightly closed mouth says tension loud and clear. If your dog naturally carries her mouth closed, but the muscles of her lips and muzzle are soft, you needn't be concerned. And not all tension is bad from the dog's point of view, of course. You may notice your smiley dog's jaws close up when she draws a bead on a squirrel, for example. In that particular heightened state, your dog probably feels pretty good. The squirrel's opinion may differ.

How you respond to the sight of your dog's mouth going from open to shut should depend on what elicited the change. If your dog is just

Teaching Eye Contact

Quick and Dirty Tip

It's a good idea to teach your dog or puppy to look into your eyes and hold your gaze. Children and adults who are anxious about dogs often freeze up and stare at them; a well-socialized dog who's learned to be comfortable with human eye contact is less likely to react untowardly.

One way to teach comfortable eye contact is to catch your dog's eye, then instantly click and treat. As your dog figures out that making eye contact earns a click/treat, she'll meet your gaze more quickly, and you can start holding out for longer intervals of gazing. If your dog is already jumpy about eye contact, though, odds are she has some other social "issues" as well; don't just jump in without professional help.

watching something with close interest, no biggie. But suppose, for example, your dog lunges at other dogs on leash. When his mouth goes from open to shut, he's near the limit of his self-control, too close to a dog he finds provocative. Next, the corners of his lips will move forward, and then watch out! Thar he blows. Increase distance from the other dog at the first sign of tension on your dog's face, and save both of you a lot of stress.

It's always worth watching the corners of dogs' lips—the commissures. These are such revealing body parts, and few people know how to read them. A tense dog whose commissures push forward is heading for the offensive. If you see commissures pushed back, think fear. Aggression isn't *necessarily* imminent, either way, but be aware of what emotional tone you're dealing with.

Finally, a tensely closed mouth may indicate physical discomfort. I knew my old, arthritic dog was having an especially good day when she didn't hold her mouth shut but instead let it open softly on our walks.

Lip licks are distinct from a dog's satisfied licking of her chops after she eats something tasty. A quick in-and-out flick of a dog's tongue over her lips is generally an appeasement signal. Watch a dog being walked on a choke collar or being trained by the old-school leash-pop method. You'll probably see the dog lick her lips every time the collar tightens abruptly or the trainer jerks on the leash. Appeasement isn't a bad thing in every context, and some dogs offer it much more readily than others. But appeasement gestures delivered over and over and over again, in any context, tell you that something in the situation is producing an unhappy dog.

Is your dog panting although the ambient temperature is comfortable for him and he hasn't been exercising vigorously? When you see fast, shallow pants, think stress.

Last but not least, watch for profuse drool not elicited by a nearby barbecue. Constant profuse drool suggests that your dog is a Mastiff or maybe that he needs to see a vet. But acute drooling that isn't typical for your dog may indicate significant fear.

And the happy dog face? Think relaxed, smiley, squinty, blinky. In sleepy contentment, your dog's facial muscles will be soft and quiet, never tense and stiff. In happy excitement, her face may be full of movement. Does somebody want to play? Have her ears mooshed? Or just say hi? Who's got a big old face right on the end of her head?

HOW TO READ YOUR DOG'S TAIL

Famous last words: "But he was wagging his tail!"

The canine tail is maybe the prime example of a body part often misread and read out of context. So, to be clear, just because your dog's tail is moving doesn't mean everything's A-OK. If he's standing stiffly, with his gaze fixed, holding his tail tight and high in a C curve and moving it slowly back and forth, he's in the classic "But he was wagging his tail!" position; a dog who's approached when sending this offensive signal is probably going to lunge, at the very least, if whatever he's "pointed at" comes closer.

But all curved tails are not alike. Some tails are set relatively high on the dog's back, or hold a C curve even when the dog's relaxed. My late dog Izzy's tail normally hung in a soft wave down to her hocks. When it went up over her back, I knew she was amped. But my Juniper's tail is set high and makes a nearly perfect C unless he's scared. When he's relaxed, the C swings and bounces with every step. When he's tense, it stiffens up and the curve of the C grows tighter. The tip of the C moves forward over his back.

A tail that's lowered but not tucked may just mean the dog is super relaxed. But a dog whose tail is clamped down, maybe even tucked between his back legs, is not having a good time. Sometimes you see a clamped tail in a fairly benign situation, for example on a dog who's trying to avoid another dog's attempts to sniff his butt or mount him. If that's your dog, bail him out. The encounter may not lead to trouble, but still, why should he have to put up with a dog who won't take no for an answer?

Dogs also lower their tails when afraid. If I've failed to smell the ozone, I can still tell a thunderstorm is on the way: The droop in Juniper's tail informs me that it's time for his antianxiety meds.

A friendly wag—unmistakably friendly—often involves your dog's whole back end. Her tail moves sweepingly back and forth. If she's really excited about the person or dog she's greeting, she may even wag in big, fast circles. Butt wiggles also come into play. The whole friendly-dog package usually includes a slightly lowered body, open mouth, squinty eyes, and ears somewhat back—body language that's about as close as you can get to a safety guarantee. (Except for the risk of being knocked down if you haven't taught her polite greetings!)

Tail amputation for cosmetic purposes is banned in several countries but still routine in the United States for many breeds. Obviously, it's harder to read a tail that isn't there; watch the position and movement of the stump.

HOW TO READ YOUR DOG'S BODY

It's surprising how much you can learn from your dog's torso and legs. Where is she putting her body weight? Body weight forward indicates likely approach; body weight back suggests she'd prefer to retreat. How high is she carrying herself? As with the head and the tail, high body posture signals arousal and tension. A tense dog isn't necessarily about to aggress, but proceed with caution until you know for sure what's up. The same goes for allover stiffness and stillness; a moment of stillness (dog people say a "freeze") often immediately precedes a snap, a bite, or a doggy scuffle. (Does your dog freeze up over her food bowl? When petted? Read Chapter 12, "Stuff Dogs Do That Worries People," right now.)

When the hair over your dog's shoulders and spine (sometimes all the way down to his tail) stands on end, he's excited or agitated. Aggression isn't necessarily imminent—some dogs' hackles go up this way when they play—but it's on the shortlist of Things That May Happen Next. Consider redirecting your dog from whatever she's involved in, just in case.

Dog Behavior May Change in Different Contexts

Dogs behave differently in different contexts—sometimes very differently. A dog who butt-wiggles when she meets you on the street may snarl and lunge when you come through her front door. And the dog who barks and snarls at passersby through the partly open window of a parked car may be thrilled to see those very same people as soon as her owner lets her out.

STRESS SIGNALS

Most people who live with dogs recognize some of the bigger clues that a dog's anxious, uncomfortable, or outright scared—cowering, whining, and a tucked tail, to name just three. It pays to learn to notice more subtle signs. They generally don't reflect full-blown panic, but they tell you that all's not quite right in Dogalini World. And it's bad policy to repeatedly march your dog into situations that are too much for her to handle. Even boneheaded, happy-go-lucky types sometimes get overwhelmed. Come to think of it, watching them closely may reveal that they're not such boneheads after all.

SIGNS YOUR DOG IS WORRIED

Of course, you don't need to intervene every time your dog experiences stress. For instance, he might startle easily at the sound of a car backfiring, then relax and go back to sniffing the hydrant a few seconds later. There's probably no big issue here. On the other hand, I'd be rich if I had a dollar for every client who told me a bite came out of the blue and then went on to describe in clear detail the half-dozen signs of distress her dog gave her. The human saw them all, but didn't understand.

A dog who's slightly worried about a person, another animal, or a situation may turn her head away. Commonly, you'll be able to see the whites of her eyes at the same time, as she looks sidelong at whatever the problem is. As I mentioned above, you should never, ever touch or even approach a dog who's gone still and shows the whites of her eyes, because five will get you ten she's on the verge of exploding with a lunge, a snap, or even a bite.

A True Dog Story: Jack

I often remember an aging dog named Jack whose humans noticed that he *always* retreated from their toddler's approach. They thought nothing of it, so Jack's repeated nonaggressive signals that he disliked kiddy-style handling didn't get through. Jack finally bit. The child had to have stitches, and Jack lost his home (and probably his life; I never heard back from his people on that score). Had Jack's guardians understood his attempts to communicate, they might have been able to manage the situation to keep everyone comfortable and safe; at the very least, they'd have had a better chance of finding him a new home, something that becomes nearly impossible once a dog has bitten a child.

A related but less potentially explosive behavior is ignoring—just what it sounds like. I used to take regular walks with a colleague, Jenny Chun-Ossowski, to help her dog, Lucy, gain some canine social skills. My boy Juni isn't socially adept by any means, but Lucy makes him look like Perez Hilton. As we walked side by side, Jenny and I could see Lucy glancing at Juni out of the corners of her eyes, over and over and over again. After a minute or two, she'd veer off and start ostentatiously sniffing . . . something. You could almost see the thought balloon: "Dog? What dog? I don't see any dog. Ni ni ni ni."

Lucy wasn't showing bad leash manners or blowing Jenny off. Her sniffing in this particular situation was what's called a "displacement behavior." Displacement behaviors are completely normal but turn up out of context or when an animal experiences conflict between two motivations. In Lucy's case, probably she was both socially interested in Juni and anxious about close contact with him. She'd keep an eye on him till she couldn't stand it anymore, and then she *just had to* sniff.

A surprising array of behaviors show up as displacements: humping, yawning, barking, and even going to sleep. Like Lucy's ostentatious sniffing, these are often subject to human interpretation as "blowing the trainer (or whomever) off." Nope. When you see a normal behavior but it seems weirdly out of context or like an inappropriate response to whatever's going on, think stress.

SIGNS OF DEFERENCE

You'll often see a dog sniffing the ground as he makes his way sloooowly back to a person who's yelling at him to *get over here right now!* Here, the sniffing is probably not a displacement behavior—combined with the slow approach, it directly signals appeasement and deference. The dog is saying, in effect, "I mean you no harm, I offer no challenge, see how I don't just rush right up to you rudely while staring in your face?" If you're recognizing yourself here, why, stop yelling, Yelling Person, and show your dog some happy-voice love.

Another common appeasement signal is a raised forepaw. You may see the body weight back, the entire front of the dog's body turned aside, one front foot hanging loose in the air. Humans tend to read this trifecta as guilt—read more about that on pages 154–55, in this chapter. Sneak preview: It almost certainly ain't.

SIGNS OF ANXIETY

A surprising number of clues to anxiety involve stuff coming off the dog's body. Drool? Check, though drool may also suggest nausea or dental problems. Paw sweat? Check. Watch the floor tile at the vet's office, for instance. Shedding? Check. To stick with the example of the vet's office, there's a reason you come home from Dogalini's annual checkup with even more hair on your clothes than usual. Dogs shed copiously when nervous.

While we're on the subject of stuff coming off the dog's body, consider urine. You've probably met puppies who dribble when they're excited or intimidated—that's not news. But if you have a reactive dog, male or female, who urine-marks, watch what happens immediately after he blows up at another dog. Often, the reactive dog heads for the nearest vertical surface and lifts leg. I don't think anyone knows exactly what this behavior means in this context. It's probably not much use as a signal to the other dog, who's gone by then. My rough guess is that it somehow closes the episode or brings the curtain down. Maybe it's a dog's way of saying "Phew! That's over with." Or maybe the stress that induced the blow-up also triggers the urge to mark.

We've all heard the old joke about why dogs lick their genitals. Who knows, the joke reason may even be for real. Dogs also lick their genitals to clean them, of course, and licking turns up as a displacement behavior in moments of anxiety or conflict as well. One common scenario: A person walking his dog stops to talk to a friend. They talk about the dog. They look at the dog fixedly for a long time. All of a sudden the dog sits back and licks his penis or her vulva. If penis, the bright red crown pokes out of the sheath. The dog's guardian says, "Sheesh, Zippy, way to pick your moment!" and everybody laughs. The Dog Trainer points out that prolonged gazing can elicit anxiety in dogs. Hence the out-of-context erection and personal-grooming moves. Just be grateful your dog doesn't head for a bikini wax when he feels a little bit on edge.

Dear Dog Trainer

Q. *Our Lab was on a chair that was covered with a blanket. Our daughter tugged the blanket from under him and, wap! he broke the skin on her finger. We have a nine-month-old puppy who arrived at eight weeks. He is a stressor for our grown dog but was not in the room when this happened. Otherwise the older dog has been good with the kids.*

A. This situation cries out for in-person help—aggressive behavior almost always does, and that goes double when a child's involved. You don't mention your daughter's age or the age of your Lab. Is she old enough to regulate her own behavior around your dogs, or is she still at an age where she needs constant supervision because she doesn't fully understand that dogs are alive and have feelings? As for the Lab, the breed commonly suffers from joint problems, and many older dogs of all breeds and mixes have arthritis; it's possible that when your daughter pulled the blanket, she inadvertently caused pain. Since you know the adolescent dog is a stressor for the older dog, a good plan to prevent further bites will include managing the younger dog's behavior—is he pestering the older dog? Does he need more exercise and playtime with dogs his own age? Finally, you mention that your older Lab has always been "good with the kids," but there is a big difference between "is crazy about kids" and "puts up with kids." An expert can teach you to decode your dogs' body language so that you can be sure when they really are at ease, and when they've just about had enough.

Do Dogs Look Guilty?

So, you come home after a long day at work to find your couch stuffing all over the floor, and ditto the kitchen garbage. "Rover!" you exclaim in dismay and anger. Sure enough, Rover slinks over to you, belly low, tail tucked, ears pinned back. Obviously, he knows he did wrong.

Or does he? Alexandra Horowitz, of the Barnard College psychology department, designed an experiment to test whether dogs act guilty because they've done something their guardian disapproves of, or whether they're responding to our voice and body language.[1]

Guardians first had to demonstrate that their dog would perform two behaviors: sit and stay for ten seconds and, when told not to eat a treat, leave the treat alone for ten seconds. Then, in the experiment, each person asked his or her dog to sit and stay, then showed the dog a treat and told the dog to leave the treat alone. The guardian then set the treat on the floor, in a spot where the dog could see it but not reach it. And then the guardian left the room for twenty seconds. The experimenter stayed.

During that time, one of two things happened. The experimenter either picked up the treat and handed it to the dog—who ate it; surprise!—or the experimenter took the treat away. Then the guardian came back in and the experimenter told him whether his dog ate the treat. If the experimenter said that the dog ate the treat, the guardian scolded the dog. If the experimenter said that the dog didn't eat the treat, the guardian just greeted the dog normally.

Here's the punch line: Sometimes the experimenter lied. She told the guardian that the dog had eaten the treat when actually the dog hadn't eaten it. Or vice versa.

The dogs offered significantly more "guilty" behaviors when they were scolded, regardless of whether they'd eaten the treat. And—drumroll— dogs who *didn't* eat the treat showed as many guilty-looking behaviors as dogs who *did* eat it. In other words, how guilty the dogs acted had no connection with their actual "guilt." In fact, the dogs who acted guiltiest of all were the "innocent" ones being scolded.

You won't be surprised by any of the actions on the list of guilty-looking behaviors. Among other things, dogs dropped to the ground and showed their bellies; they pinned their ears back and looked away from their guardians; their tails dropped low; they avoided their guardians. Dr. Horowitz, the researcher, points out in her paper that the list of "guilty" behaviors overlaps with the array of behaviors canid ethologists associate with fear and submission. Since the dogs acted "guiltier" when scolded, regardless of what they'd actually done, Dr. Horowitz suggests that they may have been offering submissive behaviors because the scolding made them expect a punishment. "What the guilty look may be," she writes, "is a look of fearful anticipation of punishment." And check this out: Three of the guardians in the study had a history of using physical reprimands—forcing the dog down to the ground, grabbing them, even hitting them. Their three dogs were among the four who offered the highest rate of "guilty" behavior.

Now, the study had only fourteen subjects in all. (This is typical of behavioral studies, by the way—few of them include large numbers of dogs.) We certainly can't draw firm conclusions from such a small sample, much less from the behavior of three dog-human pairs. And the study doesn't prove that dogs *don't* feel guilty. But it does strongly suggest that actual "guilt"—whatever "guilt" is if you have a forebrain as small as a dog's—and looking "guilty" aren't linked. Fear might have more to do with it.

How to Decode Body Language During Play

Common dog-park scenario Number 1: People watch while two dogs play. Suddenly, the dogs are snapping and snarling at each other. The dispute ends quickly and nobody gets hurt, but the humans are shaken. None of them saw that canine argument coming.

Common dog-park scenario Number 2: Two dogs bounce and wrestle. They never stop moving, flashing their teeth at each other, snarling, growling. Their people watch them anxiously, then wade in to break up the "fight."

In the first scenario, the humans missed the signs of escalating tension between their dogs. In the second scenario, they missed the dogs' mutual signals that all the roughhousing and horrible noises were play. Knowing how dogs communicate playful intentions, what play styles different dogs enjoy, and how to tell when the game may be about to go awry will save wear and tear on your psyche and probably your dog's.

You probably already know that play often starts with a "play bow"— front end low, butt wiggling in the air, goofy openmouthed smile. Behavior nerds call the play bow a metasignal, meaning it tells the recipient how to interpret what comes next. When Dogalini offers Spike a play bow, she's communicating that subsequent lunges, growls, bounces, and snaps aren't real threats. When two dogs know each other well, they may barely sketch the play bow. Alexandra Horowitz calls the result a "play slap"—exactly what it sounds like, a fast slap with the forepaws of the ground in front of the dog.[2]

Dogs may also laugh to initiate play. The behaviorist Patricia Simonet describes the laugh as a "pronounced forced, breathy exhalation"—panting, but a particular kind of panting, with a broader frequency range.[3] In Simonet's small study, puppies who heard recorded pant-laughs often picked up a toy or approached people and other dogs who were present.

Another puppy-typical play invitation is the face-paw—Puppy A swipes a forepaw at Puppy B's face. Or, as one scientific paper puts it, "This action involves extension of one of the forelimbs toward the face of the other animal."[4] That really doesn't quite convey the cute, does it? Some adult dogs paw-swipe, but my observations suggest that it doesn't always go over so well, especially when a big galoot directs his paw-swipe to a smaller dog.

Play itself can be lightning fast, one reason humans often find it difficult to interpret. Video is a *brilliant* learning tool; you'll find links to some good videos on the Web site for this book, www.TheDogTrainer Book.com. Chase, wrestling, and tug are a few common forms of play, and dogs have individual preferences and play styles. A personal favorite of mine is "face fighting," where two dogs stand or lie face-to-face with their teeth bared, scissoring their heads back and forth and snarling ferociously. Our late dogs Isabella, a herding mix, and Muggsy Malone, a Pit Bull mix, used to grab any loose skin they could get hold of and drag each other around our apartment. Play that intense can easily devolve into fighting, but Izzy and Muggsy were especially close friends, and rarely did their play go wrong.

PLAY GONE RIGHT

How can you tell when play, especially intense play, is going right? Look for constant, fluid, loose movement. As the play goes on, you may see the dogs take turns being on the bottom or being chaser and chasee. Surprisingly, though, the only observational study of play between pairs of dogs found that switching off rarely produced a 50–50 balance between the dogs. The same study, by Erika Bauer and Barbara Smuts of the University of Michigan, found that younger and smaller dogs generally did the most self-handicapping and offered the most play signals. These also seemed to be subordinate dogs. Bauer and Smuts suggest that perhaps it's important for subordinates to make it especially clear that play aggression doesn't reflect a serious challenge.[5]

Watch the dogs' faces. Look for open mouths. You may see teeth and hear snarls and growls, but again these will be in the context of fluid movement and lots of change—the dogs won't lock into any one position. Their ears and the corners of their mouths will likely be back rather than forward. The growls you hear will be lighter and less rough in tone than growls that signify real threat.

PLAY GONE WRONG

On the other hand, if you see brief freezes, or if the dogs are stiffening up, making more staccato movements, it's definitely time to interrupt. If the players are vocal types, listen for growling that grows deeper and more intense. Boxing, with the dogs standing on their hind legs face-to-face, can be benign or can mark the prelude to a fight.

Much depends on the individual dogs—some deescalate easily, whereas others get more and more amped until suddenly it's toddlers out of control on the playground and you've got a fight. Pit Bulls and various terriers often seem to have hair triggers, especially with dogs they don't know well. (But dogs are individuals; in any breed, you find mellow dogs and dogs quick to rile.) If you've got such a dog, the crowding and random mingling at dog parks probably aren't well suited for her—playdates and hikes with compatible dogs would be a better choice.

Play does sometimes turn into a squabble even between socially skilled dogs and even between good friends. So the fact that you've had to break two dogs up doesn't necessarily mean they shouldn't meet and play again. Give them a breather from direct interaction—the humans should step away to open up the space around the dogs, and maybe take a stroll together. Then see what develops. These dogs may become friendly or indifferent non-playmates, or they may just have had some differences to work out. If play goes south repeatedly, though, the simplest response is to help the two dogs to steer clear of each other. You don't get along with every person you meet, and rare is the dog who gets along with every other dog.

You don't necessarily have to intervene every time play goes wrong. Even socially skilled dogs who are good friends sometimes make mistakes—nipping a little too hard, for instance, or body-slamming with just that bit too much enthusiasm. Usually they'll de-escalate all by themselves. The dog on the receiving end of the mistake will yelp or snap, and the dog who made the mistake will move out of the other dog's space. One or both dogs will probably "shake off," as if shaking off water. Next may come a renewed invitation to play, which may or may not be accepted. Either way, the dogs have handled the situation just fine; unless this scenario takes place over and over again, there's no call for humans to step in.

THE BEST WAY TO PLAY

Dogs play best in pairs; when a third dog joins the mix, whether in chase or wrestling, two often gang up on the third. Alexandra Horowitz offers the plausible explanation that with multiple dogs it's easy for those "we're just playing" signals to get lost in the mix.[6] Often one dog winds up lying on his back with his tail tucked between his legs and his neck exposed, while the others stand over him, stiff and tense. Or the victim dog will stand at bay, also with tucked tail. The others dart in and out, nipping. Or a chase game suddenly goes from "Yippee!" to "Uh-oh, they're really after me!" Again, you'll likely see the chasee's tail tucked, and if the chasers catch up with her they may body-slam her and then stand over her if she drops to the ground.

These ganging-up scenes are a pet peeve of mine. People often seem oblivious to the victim dog's distress and will allow the bullying to continue until the victim explodes—at which point, guess which dog gets blamed? Fortunately, the more we learn about body language and behavior, the better we can respond to difficult situations.

10

Play? Training? Tricks?

So, there's training, and then there's playing with your dog and teaching her tricks. One's a grind, the other's fun. At least, that was the impression I had when I first got a dog. I have to admit that teaching a dog to wait for permission to go through an open door is less sheerly entertaining than teaching her to jump through a hoop. And whether your dog comes to you reliably when you call her has more serious implications for her safety than whether you can teach her to stick her head in a paper bag on the cue "Where's your lunch?"

But there's more to the mental gulf between training on the one hand, tricks and play on the other. Many of us have been sold a bill of goods about "obedience" reflecting our "alpha status" and the "respect" our dogs have for us. Supposedly our dogs barge through doors to assert their rank, while missing a jump through a hoop has nothing to do with who's the alpha wolf. In short, we're led to believe that one array of behaviors that we teach dogs is on some deep level about winning a contest with them, while another array of behaviors is just relationship-enhancing fun.

This makes no sense of any kind. In Chapter 3, "Anything but 'Obedience,'" I explained how the dominance and rank paradigm arose and why it's neither helpful nor scientifically supported. To my great pleasure, there's also evidence that play and affection may enhance our dogs' attentiveness to us and improve their response to our cues. Can I even say this without sucking the fun out of tricks and games? I hope so. Play, training, our relationships with our dogs, the quality of our lives together—they're inextricably linked.

Why Dog Play Is Important

Dogs and other animals play because playing is fun—this seems obvious. As an explanation of play, though, fun puts the cart before the horse. Behaviors, like body parts, evolve because they confer a reproductive advantage; that's how natural selection works. The experience of fun probably makes an animal more likely to play. But what advantages might play offer? And how can we use scientific knowledge about play to improve our relationships with our dogs?

People usually recognize play when we see it, but an explicit definition can help us bring what we're seeing into sharper focus. Here's a definition I like: Play is "an apparently purposeless activity with no immediate adaptive goal, utilizing species-typical motor programs that are exaggerated in intensity or number of repetitions, or misordered compared to mature behavior, or mixed together with behavior appropriate to different contexts."[1] Oh-kay. In other words: Play has no immediately obvious purpose; playing animals do things that are typical of their species, such as chasing and leaping, but they do those things in exaggerated and mixed-up ways, and they do them out of the usual context. Chasing, for example—outside of play, it's usually a food-getting behavior. But if playmates wind up eating each other, you know the play went seriously wrong.

So, why do this crazy, mixed-up, apparently pointless thing called play? One early hypothesis was that young animals play to burn off steam and because they're bored.[2] There might be something to this if we're talking about our pet dogs, who mostly get their food for free. Animals living on their own, though, rarely have surplus calories to waste.[3] Indeed, that's probably one reason why social carnivores, like wolves and dogs, show so many conflict-avoiding behaviors, and why most aggression, like those noisy fights that scare the heck out of the humans at the dog park, results in little or no injury. A hurt animal has a tougher time getting food and must use precious energy to heal.

These days, behavioral scientists are throwing around several hypotheses about the purposes of play. One: Play develops motor and cognitive skills. Two is closely related: Play helps young animals learn to deal with physical surprises such as losing one's balance and with unpredictable behavior by other animals. The idea is that animals develop behavioral flexibility and resilience by coping with surprises in a safe context.[4] Three: Social play helps build and maintain social bonds.

Now let me astonish you. All those hypotheses seem intuitively obvious, and none of them has been proved. Any Animal Planet fans out there have probably heard of meerkats, social carnivores related to the mongoose. A researcher who studied social play among meerkats couldn't find any connection between play and social cohesion, or between play and later success in fighting.[5] On the other hand, if you're a brown bear cub, your odds of survival seem to improve with social play.[6] So maybe play has different effects in different species. We don't know—there are so many kinds of animals in the world, and it's so hard to measure the effects of play.

According to a study by Erika Bauer and Barbara Smuts, play between pairs of unrelated adult dogs reflected existing rank relationships between those dogs.[7] (But other researchers have found dog-dog status mutable and hard to assess.) Studies of rats, squirrel monkeys, and human beings suggest that the same applies to them.[8] Relatively little of the play the dog researchers observed was what we'd call fair with respect to "who's on top."

"Uh-oh," you might be thinking, "if play reflects rank relationships, I'm in trouble! My dog always hangs on to the ball when we're done playing fetch. He even carries it home." Or "My dog wins an awful lot of our games of tug."

Here, a little detour. My dogs generally cooperate with my house rules, the most important being that goodies—such as treats, walks, and attention—become available to those who do as I ask, when I ask them to. But do they think I'm the Alpha Dog Queen of England or the village goatherd? Beats me—their behavior seems deferential, but I can't read their minds. Many dog trainers and behavior specialists state with certainty that dogs perceive humans as more or less exalted dogs. But—and here comes one of the most important statements in this book—*there is no evidence that dogs perceive people, or their relationships with us, the way they perceive their relationships with other dogs.*[9] If we want to develop insight into how our dogs perceive humans, then it's their behavior toward humans we need to study. And, ultimately, it's only their behavior that we can know.

Nicola Rooney and her colleagues in England have been studying dogs' behavior toward people in the context of play. Some findings from one of their studies: Access to play with dogs didn't spoil dogs' appetite for play with humans. This suggests that play with dogs and play with humans may have different motivations. Dogs playing with people were more likely to present a tug toy to their play partner than dogs playing with other dogs. In other words, they seemed more eager to engage a human play partner. Dogs playing with people were also more likely to give up the tug toy. They hung on to the toy longer when their play partner was another dog.[10]

Wait, there's more! In a study of how play affected the dog-human relationship, Rooney and her colleague John Bradshaw assessed confident, supposedly dominant behaviors in a group of Golden Retrievers before and after 20 rounds of tug in which the dogs mostly won or mostly lost. Then they did the experiment backward, letting the dogs win if they'd lost in the first round, and vice versa. Important note: The experimenters used Goldens because this breed has a rep for owner-directed aggression. (Yes, you read that right.) So if winning at tug causes trouble, you might expect these to be the dogs it caused trouble in.

The researchers found no significant change in confidence or "dominance" whether the dogs won or lost. The "dogs scored higher for *obedient attentiveness*" after the tug games than before. Whether they won or lost, they did become more demanding of attention as the tests went on, and the most playful dogs in the study group showed more "playful attention seeking."[11]

MORE RESEARCH NEEDS TO BE DONE

The experimenters carefully note the limits of their work. They studied a small number of Labs and Golden Retrievers. Surveys by other researchers of mixed-breeds came up with similar results, but the various full breeds differ behaviorally. So follow-up experiments should use other breeds. And do we *know* for sure that you can relax and play with your dog, no worries about who wins or loses and whether there's going to be a palace coup? We don't.

Behavioral science, unlike pop experts, rarely has definitive answers to give. Caution's in order if your dog has aggression problems, especially if she guards her food or toys. But the best evidence we have suggests that for most of us, the hypothesis that play builds social bonds is right on target. Reward yourself for taking all this science on board—go forth and have fun with your dog!

MAKE TRAINING PLAY FOR YOUR DOG

When it comes to training our dogs, "It's all tricks to them"*—or it can be, if we bring the same spirit of play and pleasure to teaching "Leave it" as we do to "Where's your lunch?" Trained behavior can become a form of play.[12] And if you like, you can teach tricks to as precise a standard as any formal or competitive behavior. Just keep your undies unbunched.

Also, I've presented the instructions for each trick as a continuous series of steps. That doesn't mean you need to teach the whole trick in just one lesson! Take as much time and as many sessions as you and your dog need.

How to Teach Your Dog Targeting

Targeting is trainer-speak for touching things. It's not a part of the traditional "obedience" curriculum, but it's one of the most useful, versatile skills you can teach your dog.

Targeting takes advantage of dogs' natural impulse to investigate novel objects, or familiar objects that have appeared in novel positions. Nose touches and front-paw touches are easiest for most dogs to learn; you may notice that your dog prefers one paw over the other or that she touches with her nose in preference to using her paw, or vice versa. It's worth teaching your dog to target to both your hand and a target stick, which can be as simple as a foot-long half-inch dowel or as fancy as a telescoping wand with a spongy bulb on one end.

NOSE TARGETING: HOW TO

Start with a slightly hungry dog and a dozen or so tiny, savory treats.

Step 1: Place your target (your hand or your target stick) directly in front of your dog's nose, say half an inch or an inch away. Most dogs will sniff the target and in doing so will touch it. Catch the moment just as nose touches target, or a nanosecond *before*; immediately click/treat.

---

* Some famous trainer said this. Or maybe more than one famous trainer has said it. I'll happily credit the source if I ever find it.

> If your dog doesn't seem to notice your hand or *Quick and Dirty Tip* the stick, or if she looks away, put your hand/stick behind your back, wait a second or two, then show her the hand/stick again. This time bring it a bit closer to her. If that still doesn't work, rub a treat against the hand/stick where you'd like your dog's nose to go. Amazingly enough, the aroma of food reliably attracts sniffing.

Step 2: Repeat the process, with your target item at different angles but always right up close to your dog's nose. Switch from right to left hand as randomly as you can, so your dog learns to target to both.

If your dog is more inclined to paw the hand or stick than to nose it, try presenting it higher up. And if your dog shies away or otherwise seems fearful of the hand or stick coming close to her face, you can shape nose targeting using a stationary object that you set on the floor.

Step 3: Over a couple of dozen reps in one or two training sessions, your dog will learn to reach forward briskly and bump your target. Increase the distance to the target, a little at a time. Go to three inches, then six inches, a foot, two feet. Remember to vary the angle and location of the target, and to practice in different places, to teach your dog that targeting works everywhere. In each new place, do a quick refresher with the target close to your dog. You'll be able to increase the distance quickly.

Tricks That Build on Targeting

JUMP THROUGH A HOOP

An old classic. Hoop, dog, dog jumps through hoop. Has that circus-trick feel without the animal cruelty of actual circuses. If you happen to have a cat handy, you can clicker train her, too, and impress the neighbors, or at least those under the age of ten, by having Dogalini and Kittychai take turns through the hoop.

Equipment: a child's hula hoop; an assistant to hold the hoop, or a brace to hold the hoop steady; clicker/treats; a dog. For a target, you can use either a stick or your hand. If your dog is large, a long target stick is preferable, because your dog will be well clear of the hoop when he touches it and you click. If he hears the click when he's still close to the hoop, he may stop with his back legs knocking into the hoop.

Caution: Dogs whose skeletons aren't fully mature shouldn't jump more than a few inches and shouldn't jump repeatedly. The age of maturity varies from breed to breed and from dog to dog, so if you have any doubts, ask your vet. If your dog has, or may have, orthopedic problems, ask your vet whether it's safe to teach him tricks that involve jumping. You can teach the first steps (where the dog is walking through the hoop) on any surface the dog can comfortably walk on, but once you introduce any jumping at all you should work only on resilient surfaces that offer traction. Carpet is okay; cement is not.

Remember, how many repetitions you do at each step, and how many steps you go through in a given training session, is up to you and your dog. Go by how fluidly, confidently, and eagerly your dog *and* you are performing. A confident dog who's had a lot of clicker-training experience may be jumping through the hoop on the first training session; a dog who's new to training or who's a bit timid may need a couple of sessions to learn to walk through the hoop.

Step 1: You'll begin by teaching your dog to walk through the hoop, so set it up or have your helper hold it so that the bottom edge is on the ground. Let your dog investigate the hoop if he wishes.

Step 2: Present the target just in front of the hoop. Click/treat your dog for touching the target. Do about half a dozen reps. You'll probably want your dog to learn to jump through the hoop from either direction, so alternate sides.

Why oh why, you wonder, am I telling you to start here instead of by presenting the target so your dog has to walk all the way through the hoop to touch it? Because if you present the target far from the hoop, your dog may walk around the hoop rather than through it. It's better to practice so that he gets it right every time.

Step 3: Present the target just barely on the far side of the hoop from where your dog is, so he has to stick his nose through the hoop to touch the target. Click/treat each touch.

Step 4: Present the target at enough of a distance on the far side of the hoop that your dog has to step halfway through the hoop to touch it. Click/treat each touch.

Step 5: Present the target so that your dog has to walk all the way through the hoop in order to touch it. Click/treat each touch.

If your dog hesitates or tries to walk around the hoop instead of walking through, lower the hoop and/or give your dog a refresher from Step 3 on.

Step 6: Raise the hoop a bit off the floor. For a tiny dog, an inch is a good start; for a larger dog, you could raise the hoop as much as three or four inches. You're looking for a height at which the dog doesn't yet have to jump but needs to lift his feet a bit higher than in a normal walk.

With the hoop raised this small amount, repeat Step 5. Click/treat!

Step 7: When your dog is walking through the slightly raised hoop with confidence, raise it a bit more; each time you raise it, practice at that level until your dog is passing through confidently and quickly from either side of the hoop.

Step 8: Time to lose the target! Present the hoop by itself, just off the ground. Your dog may hesitate; one option is to wait him out, or try a sweeping hand gesture in the direction you want him to go. As soon as his back legs clear the hoop, click/treat.

Step 9: Over a couple of dozen reps, in however many sessions you need, gradually raise the hoop till your dog is jumping through easily and confidently.

Step 10: If you used a hand gesture in Step 8, that may already have become a cue to your dog that it's time to jump through the hoop. You can also add a verbal cue if you want: Choose the word you'd like to use and say it just before your dog jumps through the hoop. Expect that it'll take your dog a couple of dozen reps to associate the word with the jump.

Once your dog's jumping through the hoop confidently on cue, you're done teaching and can stop delivering a click/treat at every successful rep. But always reward! You can use praise, laughter, scritches, and applause, and do sometimes give a treat as well.

To teach your dog to run through your legs on cue, just practice Steps 2 through 5 with yourself in place of the hoop. If your dog is small enough, or you're tall enough, you can build on this to teach him to dart through your legs repeatedly as you walk bowlegged.

CLOSE A DOOR OR A DRAWER

This skill is commonly taught to service dogs for people with limited mobility or strength, but it can come in handy for anyone. Say you've just taken a couple of pots and pans out of a low kitchen cabinet and have your hands full—well, hey! Ask your dog to close the door for you. Or she can shut the front door behind you when you've just come in with the baby or a couple of bags of groceries.

Equipment: clicker/treats; a dog who knows how to target to your hand; and a pad of sticky notes in a color that contrasts with the color of the door or drawer you want to teach your dog to close. (Remember, dogs are red-green color-blind.)

Plan in advance what you'd like your dog to close for you. For instance, if you expect to use this trick with small lightweight doors such as those on kitchen cabinets, she can comfortably do it with her nose. But if you think you might like her to close a full-size door, it's probably better to train for a paw whack/push than for a nose push. If you're teaching your dog to do paw pushes, just read "paw" in the directions where I say "nose." Oh, and if the drawer is sticky, fix it before you start.

Step 1: Present the sticky pad close to your dog in your open flat hand. Click/treat when she touches it.

Step 2: Repeat several times with the pad in different positions. You're ready for the next step when your dog is bumping the pad confidently, rather than your hand.

Step 3: Hold the pad in the air for your dog to target. This will help make it even more clear to her that she is getting the click/treat for touching the pad itself. You can also position your hand holding the pad so that the pad is right in front of the drawer or door you want your dog to close. Make sure your dog can see it easily. Once again, you're ready for the next step when your dog is bumping the pad confidently.

Step 4: Slightly open the drawer or door you'd like your dog to close. Take a note off the pad and stick it to the drawer or door where your dog can see it easily. (If you're like me and buy the cheapest sticky notes you can find, you may need to tape the note to the drawer.) At this point, since your hand is out of the picture, your dog may hesitate. Give her a few seconds—say, a slow count of five—to think. If she's really confused, you can finger-tap the note to draw her attention to it. Click/treat for even a light, tentative touch to the note. Do half a dozen to a dozen reps.

Step 5: As your dog learns that the note is her target even when it's not in your hand, her nose touches will become stronger. Some of the touches may move the drawer or door a bit. When you see that your dog is bumping the note confidently, start clicking only those bumps that move the drawer or door. She probably won't be closing it yet, but encourage vigorous pushes. Return the drawer or door to its original slightly open position between reps, so you can more easily track your dog's progress.

Step 6: When those nose bumps get reliably vigorous, start picking out the ones that actually close the drawer or door, and click and treat only for those.

Step 7: When your dog's confidently closing the drawer or door almost every time, do reps with it open a bit farther, then a bit farther again, clicking/treating for closing the drawer. If your dog pushes the drawer or door partly shut, wait a sec—then click and treat if she goes back and finishes the job.

Step 8: Take a couple of rounds of practice to get rid of your sticky-note target: Cut it in half; then cut your half in half; then let your drawer go bare.

Step 9: Teach your dog the cue you want to use, by speaking it or making the gesture just before she closes the door or drawer. I like a finger point as a cue for drawer/door closing. Once you put the behavior on cue, click/treat only when you've used the cue, so that your dog doesn't wind up closing every drawer or door you ever leave open!

SPIN

Or "Chase Your Tail." Or "Turn in a Circle." The faster the better. Work up to three or four rotations at a time. You get the picture. Why is it so cute when dogs do this? IDK.

"Nips" is "Spin" backward, of course.

Caution: Canine compulsive disorder commonly takes the form of spinning. Don't teach your dog this trick if she already has a diagnosis of CCD or even if you think she might; also stay away from it if your dog is a Bull Terrier, like Spuds MacKenzie, because this breed is prone to CCD and, specifically, to spinning as a symptom.

Equipment: a target stick or your hand; clicker/treats; a dog.

Step 1: With your dog in front of you, hold the target stick so he has to turn his head and (if he targets confidently) his shoulders a bit in order to touch it. As he turns toward it, click/treat. Note that the *move-*

ment is what you're after here, so try to click before your do,
touches the target, while he's still in motion.

Step 2: Repeat Step 1 a few times, gradually moving the targe
so that your dog has to turn farther and farther in order to reac.
With a dog who targets confidently, you can get to the midpoint of t.
turn within a half-dozen or a dozen reps.

Step 3: Just after the midpoint of the turn, your dog may take a
shortcut and circle in the opposite direction—the closer route to the
target stick. It's best not to "practice" mistakes. To avoid this one, do
several reps with your dog turning halfway around the circle, then
move the target stick just an inch or two farther along the circle. Continue to work in *small* increments, and do more reps at each increment.
It may take longer to teach the second half of the turn than it did to
teach the first half.

If your dog does take a shortcut, give him a quick refresher, starting from the very first step.

Step 4: When your dog reliably circles 360 degrees to touch the target (hand or stick), you can put the spin on cue. One way is to make
smaller and smaller gestures with your hand or target stick—continue to
click/treat for every correct response—till you wind up with a little
hand-wave as your "Spin" cue. (If you go on to teach "Nips," the reverse
process leaves you with a hand-wave in the opposite direction as your
cue.) Develop a word cue by saying "Spin" ("Nips") just before your
hand-wave, so that the word reliably predicts the gesture that your dog
already knows. Once your dog knows the word cue, you can drop the
gesture cue if you like. But there probably isn't any practical reason to
do so, the way there is with a wait or down.

RINGING A BELL

This trick is an "interact with object" trick, which calls on a dog's impulse to investigate new things. Hot tip for all such tricks: If your dog
isn't paying any attention to the item you want him to do something to,
put the item behind your back, wait a few seconds, and then bring the
item out again.

Some dogs are sensitive enough to sound that this trick will be unpleasant for them to perform. If you suspect your dog might be one of them, ring the bell yourself first and watch your dog's reaction. If he startles a bit but then recovers quickly and is curious about the source of the sound, ring the bell where he can see it a couple of times over a day or two. When he no longer startles, you're good to go. On the other hand, if your dog is significantly frightened, go for quieter tricks!

Equipment: a desktop bell or a hanging bell; clicker/treats; a dog.

Decide before you start whether you'd like your dog to use his paw or his nose to ring the bell, so you know what you're going to click/treat for when he does it. If you have a big, bouncy, enthusiastic dog like my Juni, go for the nose touch, or you'll wind up with the version of this trick that I inadvertently taught, where the dog sends the bell flying across the room with his paw whacks. Not that that isn't good for a laugh.

Step 1: Be ready with your clicker and treats before you bring out the bell. Place the bell close to your dog on the floor, or hold it in front of her.

Step 2: Click/treat *anything* your dog does that indicates attention to the bell, even if it's just a look. Most non-shy dogs will sniff it; dogs who have a lot of experience in learning to interact with novel items are likely to nose it or paw at it or both.

Step 3: Click/treat closer approaches to the bell, or more confident sniffs or paw touches—whatever your dog is doing that's headed in the direction of ringing the bell.

Step 4: As more and more of your dog's touches actually ring the bell, start holding out for that; click and treat only if the bell rings.

Step 5: When your dog is confidently ringing the bell with almost every touch, add your cue. "Service!" maybe? Or "Suppertime!"

You can use exactly the same procedure to teach your dog to press a big floor pedal/button like the kind that some lamps have. That's not the tip, though. This is the tip:
If you teach your dog the lamp trick, make sure the on/off button is out of reach between demonstrations. Some dogs, not naming names here, will quickly discover how easy it is to liven up an evening by hitting the lights at random times.

Quick and Dirty Tip

WHERE'S YOUR LUNCH?

Dogs are always hungry, right? So if your dog sees a brown paper bag such as might have his lunch in it, he'll look inside for his lunch, right? ("Juni, where's your lunch?" "I'm lookin' for it right here in this bag, aren't I?")

Equipment: a paper bag big enough for your dog's head to fit with room to spare; clicker/treats; a dog; an optional weight for the bottom of the bag to keep it in place once you set it on the floor.

Fold over the top of the bag to help it stay open.

Step 1: Have your clicker and treats ready. Show your dog the open bag and click/treat any move to nose or sniff it. Ignore any paw movement. If your dog happens to stick her nose inside the bag the first time, great! Many dogs who've had experience finding goodies in paper bags will do just that.

Why not put a treat in the bottom of the bag for your dog to find, so as to speed up the process of getting her to put her head in? Well, the clicker police will not come to your house and arrest you if you do this, but it actually may be a little easier to teach your dog to *keep* her head inside the bag for a few seconds if she's focused on what behavior got you to click and treat, instead of focused on getting and eating the treat in the bag. (The technical term for this kind of interference is "overshadowing.")

If your dog is "footy" (if she tends to whack the bag with her paw rather than nose it), present the bag at head height rather than on the ground.

Step 2: As your dog learns to confidently target the opening of the bag, look out for reps in which she's actually sticking her nose in, or sticking it farther into the bag than she did at first. Begin to click and treat only those reps.

Step 3: When your dog is confidently sticking her head all the way into the bag on every rep, start holding off on the click for a fraction of a second. Now you'll be rewarding her for leaving her head in the bag for a bit.

Step 4: Gradually withhold the click for longer periods, until your dog leaves her head in the bag long enough that someone seeing the trick might imagine she's looking for her lunch in there. In my experience, two or three seconds is long enough to get a laugh.

Step 5: Long before this point, the bag itself has become a cue for your dog to put her head inside. Now add your word cue: Say, "Where's your lunch?" just before you show her the bag. From this point on, you won't click/treat unless you've given her the cue.

If you have a tiny dog and a large bag, you can teach your dog to walk her whole body in.

TAKE A BOW* (FOR EXTRA CREDIT)

Take a Bow is not only a super cute trick but also a nifty example of the sheer coolness of clicker training. If you suspect that you're becoming a training junkie, you may want to take the long road here and first get some video of your dog play-bowing or giving his morning stretch. You don't need this to teach a bow, obviously—people have been teaching dogs to take a bow as long as people have been teaching dogs tricks, i.e., long before there were video cameras. But using the video as a guide will enhance your understanding of the clicker training process called shaping, which makes serious trainers' hearts go pitter-patter.

In shaping, you click/treat for successive approximations of the behavior you want to teach, until your learner dog is doing the whole enchilada. Many of the tricks in this section use shaping, but in teaching Take a Bow you won't use a target stick or a prop; you'll work purely with the movements your dog chooses to make. Yes, it really, really works. And yes, until you and your dog get the hang of it, it can be slow going. The payoff for learning how to shape is terrific, though; if you want proof, head for YouTube and check out KikoPup's channel, or search for "clicker training" + "shaping." But back to our main event.

In a play bow or a stretch, the dog's front end goes down and his heinie goes up and back, while his rear feet stay planted and his front legs stretch forward. To shape a bow, you start with the first movement in the sequence; then, when your dog's confidently offering that movement, you start holding out for a little bit more.

Equipment: clicker/treats; a dog.

Step 1: Wait for your dog to do something. Watch like a hawk for the tiniest dip down of the nose.

---

* YouTube video of Boxer learning to bow: http://bit.ly/l7JG1Y. Nice because you can see the trainer feeding low, and because a second behavior creeps in and muddies up the training briefly. At the end, the Boxer gets the bow anyway.

Step 2: Tiny nose dip, click/treat. When your dog is confidently offering tiny nose dips, hold out for a . . .

Step 3: . . . slightly bigger nose dip; click/treat. When your dog is confidently offering slightly bigger nose dips, hold out for a . . .

Step 4: . . . slight head dip; click/treat . . .

Step 5: . . . bigger head dip; click/treat . . .

Step 6: . . . bigger head dip yet; click/treat . . .

Step 7: . . . head dip big enough that the shoulders drop a fraction; click/treat . . .

Step 8: . . . deeper head dip and shoulder drop; click/treat . . .

Step 9: . . . and front paws begin to move forward as the heinie starts to rise; click/treat . . .

Step 10: . . . and the head dips more, the shoulders drop more, the front paws move forward, the heinie rises; click/treat . . . and it's a . . .

Step 11: . . . bow!

Now, I've called this 11 steps, but obviously a bow or stretch is one long continuous motion, so the steps are like points on a line—you can count any arbitrary number of them. The important thing is to make the increments small enough so your dog doesn't give up, and also large enough that you can distinguish between them clearly. (That way you can keep track of what you want to click/treat for at each stage of teaching.) The advantage of video is that it enables you to study the order of your particular dog's movements as he stretches/bows, which in turn tells you what you should be clicking/treating for at each step of teaching this trick.

Deliver the treats low, at least as low as the stage of the bow/stretch that your dog has reached. You might remember that when you taught your dog to walk nicely on leash, you delivered the food rewards at your side, in the position where you wanted your dog to be—here, you're applying the same idea. There's a famous trainer axiom: Click for action, feed for position.* It'll speed up your training hugely.

How long to spend on each step depends on how fast-moving and confident your dog is, on how much practice he's had offering behaviors in clicker training sessions, and on how easily this process comes to you. One rule of thumb is that when a dog is confidently offering the behavior in a given step eight out of ten times, you can start holding out for the next step.

---

* All hail Bob Bailey, the last survivor of the trio Keller Breland/Marian Breland Bailey/Bob Bailey, perhaps the greatest animal trainers ever.

Fun Fact

First, go check out the discussion of extinction bursts in the "Barking" section of Chapter 11, "Stuff Dogs Do That Annoys People." Then come back here for the fun fact:

In shaping, when you hold out for the next step in a behavior, such as a bigger head dip, you're essentially waiting for an extinction burst. Your dog is frustrated, because that tiny head dip, which was working so well to get you to give him treats, suddenly isn't working as well anymore! What gives? Hey, dude, do you see *this whacking huge head dip I'm showing you? Huh? Huh?* Click/treat.

Now whack your own head against your desk as you realize how much time you've already spent shaping your dog's behaviors unintentionally. And perhaps not exactly as you might have wished, if you'd been paying attention.

Of course we professional dog trainers never fall into this trap. Ahem.

By the way, I do use the cue Take a Bow, but you may want to choose something without the "ow" sound that "bow" shares with "down." Less confusing for your dog!

Games for Training

Chapter 5, "Total Recall," includes games you can play to enhance your dog's motivation to stick close to you off leash and to come like a rocket when you call her. Other games, including fetch, tug, and Go Wild and Freeze, can help your dog develop self-control and learn to attend to your cues even when he's excited.

FETCH

So, you throw the ball. Your dog runs after it and brings it back, then bounces and leaps and barks until you throw it again. If this describes your games of fetch, then every time you throw the ball you're rewarding that bounce/leap/bark.

If bouncing and leaping and barking are okay with you, and if your dog's lively behavior doesn't present problems in other contexts, then bouncing and leaping and barking it shall be: No need to fix what isn't broken.

But often the dog who's bouncy/leapy/barky when she wants you to throw her ball gets a bit in-your-face when she wants other things in other contexts as well: attention; dinner; a walk, perhaps? Fetch gives you a great opportunity to teach her to get what she wants by offering quiet, polite behavior instead. What she learns in fetch won't automatically translate to other situations, but it will make the lesson easier to learn.

So here's the deal. When your dog brings the ball back and starts the barkybouncyleapy thing, you just . . . stand there. Do nothing. Say nothing. Watch your dog without giving her any overt attention. And the instant she falls quiet or sits or lies down or does anything else other than bark and bounce, *throw the ball*. Congratulations, you just rewarded her—and powerfully, I might add—for a bit of polite behavior.

Keep this up consistently and over time your dog will learn to offer the new behavior faster and faster. If you like, you can ask her for other behaviors—a down, a favorite trick, a quick touch of her nose to your hand—and use the ball throw as a reward for those. You can build a powerful stay by giving her your "Stay" cue, then walking away from her a few feet and back again before you release her to chase the ball as you throw it. (This is pretty advanced stay practice, by the way.)

Here's a quick tip: If you stop rewarding the bouncy behavior and your dog reacts by growling at you or mouthing you, get in touch with a competent behavior counselor. See Chapter 12, "Stuff Dogs Do That Worries People," for how to evaluate candidates.

TUG-OF-WAR

If you're tempted to play tug with your dog but have been holding back because you've heard that tug-of-war makes dogs aggressive, good news! It ain't necessarily so. In fact, it really ain't so at all.

Played by the rules, tug will strengthen your dog's self-control and teach her to respond to you even when she's amped. The consequence for breaking a rule is that the game ends, so dogs who love tug generally learn the rules PDQ.

Two quick cautions before the fun: If your dog acts possessive over food, toys, or space, consult a behavior specialist before you play tug. In fact, these behaviors should lead you to consult a behavior specialist anyway. Also, if your dog mouths hard when excited, keep tug-of-war games brief and low-key. Interrupt play often.

TUG-OF-WAR RULE NUMBER 1
The dog releases the tug toy on cue.

Since dogs aren't born knowing what you mean by "Drop!" or "Give!" or "Dammit, Spot!" you'll need to teach the cue. Here's how to do so in the context of tug.

When you want your dog to release, stop tugging, but keep your grip on the toy. At the same time, gently take hold of your dog's collar. Now wait patiently. Your dog can't get much action going by herself, so sooner or later, she'll get bored; she'll open her mouth and release the toy. Immediately let go of her collar and encourage her to grab the toy again. With repetition, your dog will learn that releasing the toy almost always restarts the game. (Almost always, because you've got to go to work sometime.) She'll also begin to release the toy as soon as you touch her collar, because the touch becomes a cue.

You can leave it at that, or you can add a word cue if you want. Choose a release word and say it every time, just before you touch her collar. Eventually your dog will learn that the word consistently predicts the collar touch—the release cue she already knows. At that point, she'll drop the toy when she hears the word.

Since you're teaching this rule while you play, your dog's release won't be fast at first. That's okay. As you practice, she'll learn to release the toy promptly. Remember that the more excited your dog is, the harder it will be for her to even notice that you want her to do something, so adjust your strictness about this rule to allow for how much practice your dog has had and how hot the particular game is. Do 50 or more fluid repetitions over the course of a dozen or so games before you expect an instant release.

TUG-OF-WAR RULE NUMBER 2
The dog grabs her end of the toy again only on your okay.

Choose a cue to give her permission to grab the toy. Whatever word comes naturally to you is fine. Keep the game low-key at first. When your dog releases the toy, ask her to sit while you hide the toy behind your back. Bring the toy out slowly so as not to tease with fast movement. Say your permission cue and offer her the toy. You're rewarding her sit by letting her play. If she does break the sit before your cue, immediately say, "Oops" or "Too bad"—or whatever comes to your lips; just keep it consistent. Hearing the same marker whenever she makes a mistake will help her figure out what she did wrong. Drop the toy, walk away, and ignore your dog until she gives up on the game. Then you can pick up the toy and offer it to her again.

As your dog gets good at waiting for permission to grab the toy, you can up the ante. Wait a little longer before you okay her to take it, move the toy a little faster, ask for a different behavior such as a down or a brief stay. There you have it: doggy self-control, wrapped up in a bunch of fun.

TUG-OF-WAR RULE NUMBER 3

If the dog's teeth touch your clothes or skin, even by accident, the game ends.

In Chapter 9, "The Parallel Universe," I describe those dog arguments that sound as if all hell is breaking loose; the dogs' jaws fly everywhere. Usually neither party to the squabble winds up with even a scratch. And those are *angry* dogs. They are that precise with their teeth. Your dog can certainly learn to show you the same care in play. I'm not a fan of zero-tolerance policies as a rule, but I make an exception here. Sloppy tooth manners can cost a dog her life if someone decides that the careless mouthing an owner has tolerated in play is actually a bite.

Mark every tooth mistake with a calm "Oops" or "Too bad," just as you would if your dog grabbed the toy without your okay. Drop the tug toy and walk away, ignoring your dog. Leave the room if you have to. Even end the game altogether for that hour or that day.

TUG-OF-WAR RULE NUMBER 4

The human keeps custody of the tug toy and always initiates play.

This rule is important for pesty attention-seekers and for dogs who for whatever reason need more structure in their lives than most. You should also put the toy away between games if you're using tug formally as a training reward. Otherwise, this rule is optional if you've got no problems with your dog.

A few last pointers. Many dogs get growly during tug. Look at your dog's body overall: Is he wiggly? Are his eyes soft? Does he look happy and playful? Good. Also, as a rule of thumb, play growls are relatively throaty and high-pitched; growls that mean business are deep and come from the chest. Finally, play gently with a puppy or adolescent: No pulling upward; keep the toy at the level of the dog's head or lower. Skip tug altogether while your pup is teething.

GO WILD AND FREEZE

A famous game is Go Wild and Freeze, first developed by the trainer September Morn, with variations by others. Here's one version: Start by dancing around and acting excited till your dog gets going, too. After a minute or so, you abruptly stop moving. Ask your dog to sit, or down, or do another behavior she knows well. The moment she does it, start dancing around again; when your dog joins in, stop, ask for that sit or down again, and reward her by restarting the party.

Mix things up by varying what behaviors you ask for and how long you wait before restarting the game. If your dog is excitable and likely to mouth you or ricochet off you, start with a pale-vanilla version of "going wild"—your dog's introduction to this game can be Take a Single Step and Freeze. You can also retreat behind a baby gate if need be.

Go Wild and Freeze is not only fun, it helps teach your dog self-control as she learns to respond to your cues even when excited. End the game clearly, for example by saying "All done!" and sitting down with a book. If you say the same phrase every time, your dog will learn that it signifies the end of play for now. Ignore any attempts to reel you back in; otherwise, she'll learn that pestering works.

You can use Go Wild and Freeze to teach your puppy that your kids aren't mobile tug toys. *Start with the pale-vanilla version and always play the game with an adult in charge.*

Games for Shut-ins and the Elderly

Bad weather; recovery from surgery; old age—outdoor exercise and play might be limited for many reasons. Young dogs whose physical activity is restricted for some reason need something to keep them busy. Otherwise they'll make up their own projects, usually ones you're not happy with. Old dogs may not so much mind substantial downtime, but it's good caretaking to keep them mentally limber and engaged.

Scent-based games make especially good choices for old dogs whose diminished sight and hearing make it a challenge to communicate with them. But if your dog's senses are intact, it's easy to keep up her reward-based training. Not only is it a cliché to say that old dogs can't learn new tricks, it's even a cliché to point out that the cliché is nonsense. Your old dog may not learn as quickly as she did in puppyhood, but unless she's suffering from canine cognitive disorder, she can learn, and she'll have fun doing it.

Caution: The following food-based games aren't appropriate for dogs who bite, snap, growl, or even stiffen up over food. If that's your dog, go directly to Chapter 12, "Stuff Dogs Do That Worries People."

THE MUFFIN TIN GAME

Amy Samida of the Naughty Dog Café in Ann Arbor told me about the Muffin Tin Game. Amy found it online and we'd both love to hear from its inventor, so we can sing his or her praises. Take a six-muffin tin and put a treat in each cup. Place tennis balls or other "obstacles" in about half the cups. Once a dog has found the uncovered treats, he usually figures out that knocking away the tennis balls reveals more goodies. As your dog gains experience, you can start hiding treats under only some of the tennis balls and using a twelve-muffin or twenty-four-muffin tin. Some dogs, Amy tells me, find it's the most fun to smack the muffin tin and send all the balls and treats flying—which you could go with, assuming your breakables are somewhere else. Or you could take Amy's suggestion of screwing the muffin tin to a large piece of plywood. Keep your dog hard at work!

NOBLE CANINE FORAGER

The most ridiculously easy game of all to play with dogs is just to scatter dry dog food on the floor or in the backyard. That is so simple and obvious that it almost never occurs to humans to do, mainly, I suspect, because we'd be bored by it. Dogs, not so much. Most dogs will happily pick food up off the floor for what feels like hours.

It's not inconceivable, though, that your dog may need a bit of training. A dog who's not used to hunting up her food may give up if she can't find it all right away, especially if you're starting outdoors. Make it easy for her at first by tossing a few pieces of food at a time, right in front of her. As she develops skill and confidence, you can scatter the pieces more widely. I know trainers who deliver all of their dog's dry food by tossing handfuls into the backyard.

THREE-YOGURT-CUP MONTE

In the canine version of three-card monte, the player never loses.

You need three (or, hey, more!) clean, empty yogurt cups. Punch a few small holes in the base of each yogurt cup, then get comfy on the floor with the cups and a handful of small, smelly treats. Have your dog watch as you cover one of the treats with a cup, and then give him the okay to go after it. Probably he'll need about 1.5 seconds to push the cup over and get the treat.

Next step: Put three yogurt cups upside down on the floor and have your dog watch as you put a treat under just one of the cups. Move the cups around as in a game of monte, then give your dog the okay to find the treat. He may make a beeline for the correct cup, he may sniff at each in turn and then go for the correct one, or he may just knock them all over—the Visigoth approach. Whichever method he chooses, he will be happy to do it again and again and again.

SCAVENGER HUNT

Hide an array of food and treats in and under any items you have handy—yogurt cups, clean takeout containers, and empty cereal boxes work; so do pieces of paper, folded to make a little arch so they're easier for your dog to push aside. Have your dog stay while you set up the treat-finding course, or close a door between you. When the course is ready, scatter a few treats on the floor as freebies, then turn your dog loose to poke and hunt. Get as elaborate as you want—use a dozen treats or your dog's whole dinner. If your dog eats homemade or canned food, you could feed him a meal this way just before you intend to wash the floor anyhow.

BOX O' RANDOM STUFF

A favorite foraging game in my house comes from a wonderful book called *Playtime for Your Dog,* by Christina Sondermann. Take a cardboard box and fill it with crumpled newspaper, then toss in some dry food and treats. Choose a box whose size works well for your dog. A shoebox might suit an old dog of any size who can't clamber. For a large, healthy dog, a liquor-store box could be just right.

You can make this game more challenging. Take squares of newspaper or waxed paper and tightly wrap four or five pieces of dry food in each, like hard candy. Save clean plastic takeout containers and put a few pieces of food in each of those, then close the lid. Empty cracker and cereal boxes, ditto. Then everything goes in the big box, and your dog goes to town.

When he's done, the floor will be littered with shredded paper and pieces of takeout container. However, the snorting and snuffling and general joy are well worth the cleanup afterward. Same goes for the deep sleep many dogs fall into after all that hard work.

Playtime for Convalescent Dogs

Energetic dogs whose activity must be restricted while they recover from illness or surgery need something to occupy them so they don't go flat-out nuts (and take you with them). I imagine you could develop one hell of a down-stay during a couple of weeks' convalescence, but the idea of practicing a single stationary behavior has limited appeal. Try shaping low-key behaviors that involve little movement:

- cross forepaws ("Who's a lady?"—and remember, dogs don't care if you gender-bend)
- open mouth and leave it open ("Are you a slacker?")
- nod head ("Are you handsome?" or "Are you naughty?")
- rest chin on human's hand or leg (I dunno, it's just cute)
- rest biscuit on nose till human gives the cue to flip biscuit and eat it
- wear a porkpie hat and Ray-Bans ("Who's cool?")

For a dog who can walk around but shouldn't run or jump, the possibilities expand. Many of the tricks and games in this chapter are suitable, and you might also try these:

- back up when you move forward/move forward when you walk backward
- "Bang! You're dead!"
- limp ("Does your foot hurt?")
- pivot rear end with forelegs held still ("Pivot," I guess!)
- fetch the remote (or that old classic, the slippers)
- 101 Things to Do with a Box (a famous clicker-trainer game, in which you present a dog with an object such as a cardboard box and riff off whatever behaviors he offers to teach him to push it, bite it, stand in it, fold the flaps back over . . .)

Finally, you can use convalescence as an opportunity to practice "Leave it" with significant temptations, or to work on handling issues such as nail clipping and ear cleaning.

Mental exercise can't compensate entirely for lack of physical exercise, but it sure helps. Supplement by delivering meals only in food-dispensing toys such as the Kong and the Monster Mouth.

11

Stuff Dogs Do That Annoys People

First, a few words to the wise. Many of the doggy behaviors that annoy us arise out of boredom, pent-up energy, and plain old loneliness. If you proactively teach your dog good manners (that is, behavior that pleases and amuses you), give her enough attention and affection, and provide exercise appropriate to her age and physical abilities, you may not much need this chapter. Odds also are that you'll need *something* here sometime, though, because dogs are clever (so they invent things to do) and because some of the behaviors that drive us craziest (digging and poop eating, for two) come so naturally to them.

Barking

Dogs may bark to get our attention, to drive off people or other dogs, to solicit play, or because they are stressed or bored; they may bark when startled or excited; they bark to alert their social partners (that's us and other dogs, usually) that something's up. If your dog's barking defensively or aggressively, head for Chapter 12, "Stuff Dogs Do That Worries People," including the section on how to choose a behavior consultant.

BARKING FOR ATTENTION

The big huge problem with barking for attention is that *any attention at all constitutes a reward.* That includes shushing the dog, reprimanding the dog, smacking the dog, laughing at the dog, giving the dog a cue to perform some other behavior (besides, usually the dog can do whatever it is and keep right on barking), and even glancing at the dog. Tough one, right?

To deal with attention barking, take a twofold approach. First, make barking unsuccessful. Your motto is "Barking dogs do not exist." Don't acknowledge the barking at all; either ignore the dog completely or walk away. Leave the room if you have to.

Second, bear in mind that attention is a legitimate need. Dogs are social, we're social, it gets lonely when nobody's engaging with you. Offer your dog enough attention—play, petting, training, walks—to meet her genuine needs. (How much attention is enough? Depends on the dog. Some are more independent sorts; some like to be nearby but not in the middle of things; some like to spend as much time in amongst us as they can get. Some are off the scale and might benefit from learning to enjoy independent activities such as excavating food-stuffed toys.) Pick your moment: If you offer your dog attention at a time when she's hanging out quietly, she will eventually learn that hanging out quietly is a good way to get attention. From the human point of view, this is usually a great improvement over barking or stealing socks.

On the other hand, it's also not a crime for a dog to actively solicit attention. Take a look at what other attention-seeking behaviors your dog has in her repertoire, and pick one or two that don't annoy you. I'm a sucker for a dog laying his head on my thigh while I sit at the computer, for instance, and can almost always be counted on to deliver chin, ear, and butt scratches in exchange. If I had smaller dogs I might

Teach Your Dog to "Ask"

Quick and Dirty Tip

When you've decided which of your dog's attention-seeking behaviors you're willing to respond to, give your dog attention for that behavior either within a few seconds or not at all. The idea is that your dog can "ask," and get a yes or no answer; what you don't want to teach him to do is pester. If you sometimes respond right away, sometimes after five seconds, sometimes after half a minute, et cetera, you've become a slot machine, and your dog will learn to keep putting money in (asking for attention) until you pay out, even if it takes ages.

It's also useful to teach a cut-off signal, meaning that you're going back to whatever you were doing before and the interaction is over. I use "All done," showing my dog my empty hands—the same formula I use to mark the end of a training session. The end of the interaction should be final, again so you don't become a slot machine.

go for the head resting on my foot instead. Pawing, not so much, because dog nails hurt.

My clients almost all live in apartments, and when I tell them that the best response to attention barking is no response at all, their hearts are not gladdened. The gloom deepens if their dogs have gotten into the habit of barking to get them out of bed bright and early; these are people whose neighbors may already be leaving notes on the door. Their hearts then shatter into little pieces when I go on to explain about extinction bursts and spontaneous recovery.

"Extinction burst" is learning-theory-speak for "It'll get worse before it gets better." Here's the deal. Barking has been working pretty well for your attention-seeking dog. Sometimes it works right away; sometimes it takes a while. There was that one time when you held out for twenty minutes before you threw a box of tissues at her, remember? All these experiences have taught your dog that if barking doesn't work right off the bat, she should keep trying. And trying. And trying. She'll hit that twenty-minute mark and plow on past it, and then, right before she gives up, she will give barking a big SUPERDUPER COLOSSAL EFFORT AS LOUD AS SHE CAN. *That* is an extinction burst. And with a well-established behavior, there may be more than one.

The good news is that you can expect each successive burst to be weaker than the one before. The other good news is that if you can soldier on through the extinction burst(s), you will have hugely weakened the barking. The bad news is that if you break down during an extinction burst, your goose is cooked, because you will have taught your dog that *that* is the new standard for how hard and how long and how loud she has to bark to get your attention.

As for spontaneous recovery: again, learning-theory-speak, this time translating as "Once in the repertoire, always in the repertoire." In a week or a month or a year, your attention-seeking barker will try that old favorite again. It's tempting to visualize the lightbulb going on over his head: "Oh, hey! There was that thing I used to do. Huh. I haven't tried that in a while. I wonder . . ." Spontaneous recovery is the bad news. The good news is that every time an old behavior pops up, it's weaker and easier to get rid of—as long as you don't fall into the trap of rewarding it.

Phew.

Here is what I tell my stunned, weeping clients: Get yourself some really good earplugs. Buy earplugs for all the neighbors within hearing distance, too. While you're shopping, get the neighbors a little present—some nice chocolate, an inspirational boxed set of the first five seasons of *Dexter,* something of that sort. Write them an apologetic note explaining what is about to happen to their eardrums, why, and how long it will go on. (If you absolutely positively follow the no-attention program, and make it a point to give your dog attention in exchange for acceptable behavior, the problem barking will drop off steeply within a few days. For those of you with Christian backgrounds, think Purgatory, not Hell.)

I make a joke of this, but seriously, it works—not only the earplugs, which help enormously with the ignoring, but also the note to the neighbors. People go crazy when they believe you're being inconsiderate; if they know that some annoyance is temporary and that you're working to fix it, they will usually cut you the slack you need.

Another option, depending on when and in what circumstances your dog barks for attention, may be just to cave. My dog Juniper, aka Dr. Let's Try This Experiment, discovered when he was about six that if he barked suddenly I would jump and look at him. Worse yet, sometimes I laugh. And if *I* somehow manage not to reinforce the barking, someone else usually does. So I've taken the lazy way out: I give Juni what he wants. When he barks, I say, "What what what? What?" and every time I say, "What?" Juni barks, and usually within a minute or so he's had enough of this game that I can give him his "Quiet" cue and he'll settle down. (See the next section, "Barking at the Doorbell," for info on how to teach a "Quiet" cue.) I live in a row house, but the neighbor to one side is a jazz drummer, and the neighbors to the other side have three adolescent boys who play in rock bands, so nobody has a leg to stand on with respect to noise complaints.

Which leads me to another point. If your dog's behavior is harmless and doesn't really trouble anyone, consider whether you want or need to make the effort to change it. The project will be especially tough if you (not so) secretly find the behavior entertaining. Juniper is quite predatory toward cats and I have put a ton of effort into teaching him to respond to ours socially rather than as snacks. If the barking got my goat or drove my neighbors up a wall, I'd grit my teeth and deal with it, but as things stand, it isn't a priority for me. It's you who live with your dog, so work on what really matters to you.

BARKING AT THE DOORBELL (OR THE BUZZER, OR THE SOUND OF KNOCKING)

First, a word to those people whose dog doesn't bark when the doorbell rings. A high proportion of you lucky ones have a young puppy, or a dog you adopted within the past couple of weeks. Many a puppy won't offer that first tentative doorbell bark until early adolescence. And dogs in new surroundings often seem to take a while to settle in before they bring out their whole repertoire of behaviors.

The trainer's trick here is simple: Notice quiet "nonbehavior," and don't take it for granted. If the doorbell rings and your puppy or dog remains quiet, praise her and slip her a treat. Speak slowly and softly to help maintain a calm atmosphere. The idea is to counter excitement about the sudden noise and/or the imminent guest. Treats reward your dog's quiet response to the bell, of course, but they have another function, too. If the sound of the doorbell consistently predicts treats, your dog will come to like the sound. That emotional association is a building block of friendliness to guests.

If your dog already barks at the doorbell, your options depend on the behavior's intensity. Many dogs respond well to a gentle interruption—expressly *not* a shaker can, a sharp, stern voice, or an electric shock. The idea here is not to scare or hurt your dog, only to distract her from barking. Then you can reward whatever she does instead. Incidentally, you'll be teaching her a cue that means "Please hush now."

Lie in wait with a stash of small, delicious treats. You'll use these to reward your dog's quiet instantly, before she has a chance to start barking again.

TACTIC NUMBER 1

When your dog barks, get up quietly and calmly, walk over to her, say a soft "Thanks, Dogalini," quickly feed her several treats, and then deal with whoever's at the door. This barely even qualifies as training, but a surprising number of dogs will settle down almost at once. I hesitate to get into the head of anyone who can't talk to me in words, but my impression is that once some dogs know they've delivered the alert, they're done.

TACTIC NUMBER 2

If you've been struggling with canine doorbell mania for a while, you may have noticed that raising your own voice generally doesn't help. But a soft whisper may succeed where sharp reprimands fail, perhaps because a whisper stands out from the sharp, staccato, even piercing sounds of bells, buzzers, knocks, and barks. I like "Hush," because it makes a natural cue for "Be quiet now." Again, be ready with clicker and treats to reward a halt in the barking. The sequence might go like this:

1. Doorbell rings.
2. Dog barks.
3. You whisper, "Hush."
4. Dog is briefly distracted.
5. You take advantage of the distraction: Click and quickly feed several treats.

As your dog comes to associate the interruption with treats, she will orient to you more and more readily when you get up and thank her or whisper a "Hush." As far as I'm concerned, you're welcome to spend the rest of your dog's life rewarding every quiet with a bunch of treats. But if you want to get fancy, you can begin to stretch out the interval between treats. You can also hold out for longer and longer periods of quiet before delivering the first treat. Eventually you can give

---

Combine Lessons

Quick and Dirty Tip

Once you've taught a quiet cue, you can combine it with waiting for permission to go through a door (see Chapter 6, "How to Park a Dog . . . ," for how to teach this) to create a dog who barks when the bell rings, then drops into a sit while you deal with whoever's there. Your Zippy may be a friend to all the world (and I hope he is!), but if he's medium size or larger, the combination of a few barks + quiet on cue + an attentive sit near the open door turns him into a Genuine Imitation Gold-Tone Lamé Guard Dog. An out-of-control dog can scare away villains just as well, of course, but has the disadvantage of scaring away UPS and also the cute guy down the block who wants to invite you to his barbecue.

food rewards only occasionally. But always be generous with calm, warm praise.

HELP FOR BIGGER-TIME BARKERS

If your dog is a hard-to-distract barker, practice—say, a minimum of fifty times—when there's no barking for you to interrupt. Go through the motions of answering the door just as if someone were actually there. Your dog will learn that your "Thanks" or your "Hush" means it's time to look to you for tasty treats. Having learned that lesson solidly in a calm situation, he will be more likely to respond to you when excited. Practicing without actual guests is also the starting point in teaching any dog to stay while you get the door. When you do have actual guests, ask them to call or text from outside, so as to avoid unplanned doorbell frenzy.

Some dogs can't be distracted. They always resume barking after they eat the treats, or they're in such an overexcited state that they won't eat the treats at all. Often these dogs react strongly to many sounds both at home and outdoors. They may belong to an especially vocal breed—Shelties and Min Pins come to mind, but there are quite a few others.

If this sounds like your situation, try lowering your dog's overall excitability by providing plenty of exercise early in the day. Also, cut back the amount of noise your dog's exposed to. Close the front windows, perhaps; turn down the ringer on the phone. If you live in an apartment and your dog reacts to hallway sounds, run a fan or a white-noise machine by the door. One of my clients had a computerized doorbell, so I had her pick a new sound, teach her dog to associate it with treats, then change her doorbell to the new sound. I don't recommend punishment. It doesn't teach your dog what you *do* want, and it does bupkes to relieve any underlying stress.

HELP FOR EVEN BIGGER-TIME BARKERS

What if your dog is barking at guests, not for attention but in a state that might best be described as defensive and anxious? Such barking, which tends to go on for a long time and usually starts up again whenever the visitor moves around, teeters on the edge of aggression; sometimes it falls right in. If your dog never quite relaxes while someone's visiting, or if her barks are mixed with growls, or if she advances and retreats to and from the visitor, or if she ever snaps, nips, or outright bites, what follows may be a good start but you should also head for

Chapter 12, "Stuff Dogs Do That Worries People," where I explain how to find competent professional help. The same goes if people never quite seem to become familiar to her—if the same person can come over a half-dozen times but Dogalini always responds with as much agitation as if this were the first time she'd ever seen him. (See Chapter 2, "Socialization," for more on how such behavior may arise.)

If your dog is mildly uneasy with people entering the house, try meeting visitors outside and taking a short walk together—to the end of the block and back is often enough. Send your visitor into your house ahead of you, give her a couple of minutes to get settled, then bring your dog in.

Many dogs seem to feel more threatened when a visitor enters their space than they do if they enter to find the visitor already there. We tend to ascribe their response to territoriality, but I think it might also connect with anxiety about being stuck in an enclosed space while a potential threat approaches. Whatever the reason, for some percentage of dogs who are leery of visitors, the outdoor meeting plus having the visitor go inside first is enough to settle their nerves and help them relax. The same tactic works wonders for friendly but extremely excitable dogs, by the way.

Once your visitor and your dog are both inside, check out your dog's body language. Is he holding his body loose and comfortable, or is he still tense? Is he approaching your visitor with squinty eyes, a softly open mouth, and easy wags or fast butt wiggles? Or is he pacing at a distance? Has he lain down, but facing your guest head-on and vigilant? Did he start to bark when your visitor said hi?

If your dog's showing some friendly interest but isn't quite relaxed, your guest should completely ignore her. Kind humans tend to respond to anxious dogs by trying to engage them and make friends; unfortunately, anxious dogs usually respond to that form of attention by getting more anxious still. Left to herself, a slightly shy dog may eventually check out your guest with soft, friendly body language; at that point, the guest might feed her a treat or offer a little scritch under the chin. No looming over the shy dog, please, and no grabbing her or following her if she retreats.

You should also manage the situation for everyone's comfort and safety if your dog is still acting overtly tense. Consider crating him in another room.

This may feel like you're exiling him, but think about it from your dog's point of view. If he's in the living room or wherever with an unfamiliar guest, he's tense and on guard, ever ready to spring into barking action when the worrisome invader-type person makes a move. What he's *not* is relaxed and enjoying the time spent hanging with his humans.

On the other hand, you have of course taught him that his crate is a comfy refuge where delectably stuffed chew toys are commonly had. So your dog has two scenarios available: tense vigilance, or quiet time with the canine equivalent of an Xbox. If that's not quite enough to reframe the picture for you, try this: Unless you live in a mansion and your dog's crate is half a mile from the living room, he will be well aware of the visitor's presence. The difference is that instead of practicing tense, reactive behavior when you have guests, he'll be practicing the much more desirable behavior of lying down absorbed in his chew. In short, you're taking baby steps to change your dog's response to having guests. Honestly, the visit will be pleasanter for you, too, if you don't have to worry about how your dog is going to act.

Another possibility is to give your dog a job. This coping method has a few prerequisites. Your dog needs a solid reward-based grounding in at least a couple of behaviors—a sit, a down, targeting to your hand. Walking politely on leash will work, if the room you're in is big enough. Tricks are fine too. By "a solid grounding," I mean that she has to know these behaviors well enough to perform them even when she's a bit anxious and distracted. As for you, you need to be on and clearly focused, and you also need your guest's cooperation. (Got guests who are anxious about dogs? Then it's crate time. Their tense body language may worry your dog further: instant vicious circle.)

Suppose your dog will pretty much settle down as long as your guest also stays put, but will default to a barkfest as soon as he stands up. Ask your guest to give you a few seconds' notice before he stands—your window of opportunity to put your dog to work. Cue her to perform one of her well-known behaviors, and deliver a tiny, tasty food reward. Now keep it up as your guest does whatever he needs to do. If you cued a down-stay, reward it generously, over and over. Or have your dog do a series of tricks, one after another after another, giving your dog one or more food rewards each time. The important thing is that your dog know these behaviors really well, so that she is able to respond to your cue in these less than optimal circumstances. Also, use behaviors that keep her focused on you and that aren't too exciting: You're trying to guide her toward calm and away from agitation.

A related idea is to use a remote-controlled treat dispenser, the Manners Minder,[1] to teach your dog to go to a comfy bed on cue and stay there. Once your dog has thoroughly learned the system, you don't need to stick close to her while your guest moves around—instead, you deliver her rewards from a distance.

Whatever strategy you use, be careful not to overtax your dog. In general, the more visitors there are, the more of them are strangers, and the bigger and louder they are, the more worried your dog will probably be. It's better to have a string of quiet successes with just a guest or two at a time than to throw your dog into situations she can't handle with ease. Also, if your dog growls at guests, snaps at them, or has ever actually bitten someone, you'll need to take additional precautions for safety's sake, and to talk with a knowledgeable professional about a program of behavior modification. See the next chapter for a guide to evaluating candidates.

Begging at the Table

I'm a firm believer in teaching dogs to beg for table scraps. Yes, your dog probably already has a method; most dogs seem to be born knowing how to put their nose in your lap while you eat. And how to paw your knee, and how to nudge your elbow at the exact moment you lift the soup spoon. Our food appeals to dogs; they want some. The truth is, too, that plenty of us enjoy sharing—otherwise, traditional training books wouldn't be so full of exclamation-pointed injunctions *NEVER to feed your dog from the table, or else!*

Given that our dogs want our food and we may even want to give it to them, we may as well teach them to ask for it unintrusively.

First, a housekeeping point. You may have heard that you shouldn't give your dog "people food." True, your table scraps won't likely supply your dog with a complete and balanced diet. But it's okay for a healthy dog to enjoy a few bites of your chicken, your pasta, your mu shu vegetables. Scrape off rich or spicy sauces unless your dog has a cast-iron stomach. And don't share the human foods that can really harm dogs: some biggies are onions, raisins, grapes, avocados, certain citrus fruits, and chocolate.* Check with your vet if your dog has any food-related medical problems.

Also, a word of caution: If your dog gets excessively mouth-on-people or seems outright aggressive when frustrated, this exercise isn't for her. Get help from a qualified behavior professional.

POLITE BEGGING

Normally, if you're using food rewards, you're better off starting with a slightly hungry dog. But ignoring your pot roast or tempeh has got to be harder for a hungry dog than a sated one. So feed your dog before your meal. You can do this training at breakfast and dinner, since most adult dogs should get two meals a day.

Next, place your dog's wonderful, comfy bed somewhere near the table. It should be far enough away so the dog isn't underfoot when lying on it, but close enough that when you throw food at the bed you won't miss.

When you sit down to eat, set aside five or ten tiny pieces of whatever you've got that your dog likes. And then be patient and ignore her.

Ignore her if she looks at you pleadingly. Ignore her if she barks. Ignore her if she rests her big sweet head on your thigh and whimpers because she's about to drop dead, she's so famished. If you smile at your dog while she's begging, push her away, reprimand her, or give her any attention at all, you're rewarding her behavior. Completely ignoring your dog will be the toughest part of the whole process. Whatever you do, don't hold out for twenty-nine minutes and then cave on the thirtieth. You will have built a dog who has learned to pester for thirty minutes, and you will want to knock yourself upside the head. And this may seem obvious, but nobody at the table should slip your dog any food during the meal.

Sooner or later, if you resolutely ignore your dog's begging, she will give up and go away. Ideally, she'll lie down on that comfy bed. But if she chooses to lie on the floor, call that good enough. The instant she lies down, toss her a piece of the food you've set aside. Lying down quietly is now the one and only behavior that will buy her table scraps.

Odds are close to 100 percent that as soon as she's eaten the treat you tossed her, she will get up and start begging again. Keep ignoring

---

* Visit the ASPCA's Animal Poison Control site for more info: http://www.aspca.org/pet-care/poison-control/. The phone number is 888-426-4435. Put it on your speed-dial right now.

her. Eventually she'll give up and go lie down again. Then toss her a scrap and repeat, repeat, repeat. Be absolutely consistent. Within a few meals she'll give up begging faster and faster, and she'll go lie down more and more readily. That brings you to the fine-tuning stage.

As your dog gets proficient at begging by lying down quietly as soon as the meal starts, you can stretch the interval between treat tosses. With enough practice, your dog can learn to wait patiently through the whole meal for a single bite. I don't bother to push that far. Our despairing dog, settling onto the floor with a deep, deep sigh, makes us laugh, and I can't resist tossing him a treat every few minutes in exchange. (As you might have noticed, I'm a sucker for basically anything my dog thinks up that makes me laugh.) The house manners that keep you and your dog happy and comfortable are the house manners that are right for you.

Here's a refinement you might like: Move the dog bed farther and farther from the table, a foot or so at each meal, until it's in the location where you'd like your dog always to rest during meals. This will also improve your aim as you practice throwing food at her.

TROUBLESHOOTING

When I know my dog has no way to get what *he* wants, and so will eventually try the behavior *I* want, I find it easiest just to wait him out. For plenty of people, that sounds miserable instead of restful; if you're one of them, try this. Put the dog bed right next to your seat and ask your dog to lie on it. As soon as he does, give him a table scrap. You can give him the cue "Stay," if and only if he already has a lot of practice at holding a stay in the face of distractions. Give him treats frequently as long as he's lying down. If he gets up, you can cue him to lie down again. But I suggest ignoring him and letting him figure it out instead. That way he'll start lying down automatically at every meal, without waiting for a cue from you.

When your dog is good at lying quietly, you can start stretching the time between treats just as with the wait-your-dog-out method I described first.

Another point to remember: How quickly you can teach your dog any habit depends on how long he's been practicing *other* habits. Expect a puppy to take a few days to learn that successful begging entails lying down. Expect an adult dog who's been mooching successfully his whole life to take a good long time to unlearn that habit.

Dear Dog Trainer

Q. *I have a four- or five-year-old Boxer. We have had her for about a year. We leave her alone from about nine a.m. to four p.m. This past week she has been getting into the garbage, ripping up anything she can find. She ate some turkey bones. We have toys and things for her to do, but she doesn't like to play with them. When we're not home she won't eat her food. How do we keep her from eating turkey bones, and also, how do we keep her entertained while we're gone?*

A. Several things could be going on here! Boxers are energetic dogs, so if your girl isn't getting at least an hour's aerobic exercise every morning, she should be. Dogs don't usually enjoy playing with toys by themselves, except for some food-dispensing toys— that might be why your dog ignores her toys. On the other hand, the fact that she won't eat when you're gone suggests she might be anxious when left alone. (See the section on separation anxiety in Chapter 12, "Stuff Dogs Do That Worries People.") Another thing to consider is that seven hours is a long time to go without access to a toilet; even though many dogs can hold it that long, doing so isn't good for their health. And, last but not least, put the garbage where she can't get to it! Dogs are scavengers, and garbage is full of things to scavenge.

Chewing

Like all young animals, puppies explore the world and ask questions about it. Human babies use words and hands; puppies use their jaws and teeth. They will experiment on anything in reach, including your furniture, your shoes, and, of course, you. Does this taste good? Will it squeak? Chewing also helps puppies develop their jaws. And it soothes the pain of teething. As for adult dogs, they may chew inappropriately for all kinds of reasons—boredom, loneliness, canine compulsive disorder—and also for no bigger reason than that they acquired the habit in puppyhood.

Notice that word "inappropriately." Chewing is a need for many dogs, an optional enjoyment for many others, low on the fun list for others still. If your dog's chewing is confined to legal chewies, and if it doesn't occupy so many waking hours as to be compulsive, you obviously don't have a problem.

As always, it's easiest to start dogs off on the right . . . uh, tooth. Make sure your puppy or newly adopted dog has appropriate outlets for the need to chew. Dogs have individual preferences in chew toys. Many, maybe most, love the hollow rubber toys that can be stuffed with food. The brand you're likeliest to see is Kong. If your puppy's easily discouraged, start with a mixture of half canned and half dry food. (You know why you've been hanging on to all those ratty old stained towels? It was to give your puppy something to lie on with her Kong.) Success at easy chewing jobs will help her learn to stay on task. As she gets better and better at excavating, you can up the ante. For maximum chewing time, wedge biscuits into the bottom of the toy, pack it with that half canned/half dry mix, then freeze it overnight.*

Use some of your puppy's food for training and feed the rest in stuffed toys. You'll have met his daily needs for chewing and mental exercise. This is also great bad-weather busywork to keep an energetic puppy or dog from climbing the walls.

Some toys aren't made for excavation; instead, you fill them with dry food. Monster Mouth and Buster Cube are brands you're likely to find in your local pet supply. The dog shakes, pushes, or tosses the toy to get the bits of kibble out. That may satisfy a puppy who's not one of the world's champion chewers.

Stay away from cooked bones, because many of them will splinter. Pet suppliers offer sterilized shank bones and marrow bones. But hard weight-bearing bones like these can break an eager chewer's teeth. If you give your puppy a rawhide chew, supervise her closely because pieces of the rawhide may break off and choke her.†

The second step in protecting your household goods is to prevent access to them. Stash your puppy or destructively chewing dog in a safe place—a puppy playpen or her crate—when you can't supervise her. By

---

* Some other good stuffing foods: low-fat cottage cheese, mashed sweet potato, peanut butter, and your leftovers minus the sauce. For puppies and small dogs, be careful not to unbalance the diet; with medium-size and large dogs, you have a lot more leeway, health and relative cast-iron-ness of stomach permitting.

† I use a lot of raw, non-weight-bearing bones, but individual vets, canine nutrition experts, and dog guardians differ strongly on which types of bone are safe or indeed whether any are safe at all. A lot of the opinions on each side are faith based rather than evidence based—this is to judge by how heated and absolute people get on the subject—but raw bones do entail some risk.

"supervise," I mean "give her your undivided attention." As an alternative to the crate or playpen, you can tether your dog. But when she's tethered, don't leave her alone.

The crate, pen, or tethering spot should be a pleasant space. Include a chew toy, a comfortable bed, and a source of water. Remember, puppies need a lot of rest. If your little friend gets enough exercise, training, and affection, and has had a recent toilet break, he's likely to spend most of his crate or playpen time sound asleep.

Clients usually ask me about taste deterrents, such as hot sauce or Grannick's Bitter Apple. Taste deterrents make a poor first line of defense; for one thing, many puppies and dogs don't mind them a bit. Besides, the time you spend coating every tempting surface is time you could have spent playing with your puppy. Save the taste deterrents for electrical cords and other dangers that you can't keep out of the way.

Coprophagy (Stool Eating)

One of my favorite training lists had a thread a few years back about poop-flavored dog treats and the guaranteed training success they would offer. If only they existed. And if only we could bring ourselves to touch them. Unlike humans, plenty of dogs just love feces, whether from cats, horses, or geese, or, most disgustingly to many people, their own feces and human feces. Now for everything dog behavior nerds know about coprophagy.

The likelihood is that different dogs eat different kinds of feces for different reasons. First, some coprophagy is probably completely normal. As everybody knows, dogs evolved from wolves—probably, current thinking goes, from wolves that spooked less easily than average.[2] Those not-so-spooky wolves got closer than others did to human bands and, later, human settlements. Finding human garbage and human excrement, the wolves chowed down. Eventually there evolved an animal rather like the wolf, except that it was smaller, it hung around people, and it mostly scavenged instead of mostly hunted. Hey presto, the domestic dog, for whom it is normal to eat anything lying around that might have some nutritional value, including human poop.

Cat feces probably attracts dogs because cat food is higher in fat and protein than dog food, and consequently cat feces is too. As for why dogs like horse and cow manure and goose droppings, your guess is as good as mine. Dogs like plenty of things we humans don't—when was the last time you rolled in a dead squirrel, grinning your fool head off the whole time? My best guess is that dogs just plain find feces tasty. (Why? *I don't know.*)

Not all coprophagy is normal or harmless. Dogs who suffer from malabsorption syndromes, such as exocrine pancreatic insufficiency, sometimes eat stool, including their own. They may be trying to recover the nutrients they can't absorb in normal digestion.

Some horrible nutrition studies have been done on dogs; I'll skip the details. Let's just say that coprophagy might develop in a dog with a history of severe nutritional deficiency.[3] "She's eating a low-quality diet" is often thrown around as an explanation for a pet dog's coprophagy, and maybe these studies are the ultimate source of that idea. I have to admit I'm a bit obsessive about my dogs' food, but leery though I am of most commercial diets, I sincerely doubt they're anything like what the dogs in these studies got. All the same, if your dog eats her own and other dogs' poop, and you're buying the 50-pound sacks of whatever chow is cheapest at your local warehouse store, food of better quality is worth a try.

You can often get a dog hot and bothered about a particular toy by taking it out, playing with it excitedly by yourself, then putting it away again. Same goes for shoe-nabbing. Guess what Zippy learns when he streaks past with your Manolo in his mouth and you start yelping? Poop, too, may suddenly increase in interestingness to your dog when the result of his tentative sniff and lick is that you shriek, drag him away, and stash the experimental material in a bag. Hmm, he thinks, there must be something to that stuff. And the next time he spots some feces, he speeds up the snatch-and-grab.

Incidentally, dogs can train other dogs by this same method. Our Isabella ignored litter boxes until we adopted Muggsy Malone. Muggsy adored cat poop and used to head for the box at a dead run whenever he saw a cat emerge. Izzy soon noticed his passion and scored a sample for herself. Even after Muggsy had been gone for many years, his legacy remained.

There are pretty well accepted behavioral explanations for dogs' eating their own stool—not that I know of any research to back them up. Pet-store puppies seem to eat their own poop more than the average dog. The reason would be the same one that makes crate training so successful: Dogs avoid soiling their nests. Dogs forced to eliminate in their cages will often try to clean up. Let this happen a few times, and a habit is born. Finally, eating feces—whether or not it's the dog's own—may succeed in getting attention for an animal who's lonely or bored.

Disgusting as it is to us, coprophagy seems to do most healthy, vaccinated dogs no harm, apart from occasional digestive upset and sometimes a parasite or two.[4] I did round up a news story about a Pug who developed pancreatitis after way overdoing it at the all-you-can-eat dog-poop buffet.[5]

HOW TO PREVENT POOP EATING

But even if a little poop won't hurt your dog, it rings the bell on your Gross-O-Meter, so herewith some tips for prevention. Let me say right up front that if your dog has access to the kind of feces she likes, she will sometimes eat some. Homeless people defecate in public parks; if your dog is off leash, your best defense is a rock-solid recall (Chapter 5) or response to a cue meaning "Leave that alone" (see Chapter 7, "Leaving Stuff Alone . . ."). Even so, your dog is better at finding feces than you are and may well get a few bites in before you notice and intervene. If you live in the country, chances are you can't control the availability of horse and cow and goose and deer droppings.

When you can control the environment, do it. If your dog's cleaning up after herself or your other dogs, tidy the yard diligently. If she's diving for her own feces as soon as she produces it, keep her on leash till she's done her business. Then stick something tasty right under her nose and lure her away with it before she has a chance to start. (Let her eat the treat once she's clear of the poop, of course.) Or gently pull her if a lure doesn't work. Try a play invitation to distract her. If she's a junkie for fetch, toss a ball the nanosecond she begins to rise from her squat, then clean up during the chase.

If possible, keep litter boxes where the dog can't reach them. I say "if possible" because your cat's behavioral needs may conflict. Many cats resist using a covered box or one that's in a small, confined space, especially if a feline housemate likes to pounce on them when they come out. Train yourself to hear those little cat feet going scritch scritch scritch, and scoop the poop as soon as Kitty's done. Even the slickest litter snacker can't eat what isn't there. Besides, a scrupulously clean box is nicer for your cat.

Some people muzzle their dogs to prevent coprophagy, but the commonest upshot is a filthy muzzle, which—well, yuck. If the poop-snack habit isn't well established, it may die away on its own, provided your dog has no further opportunities to practice it. Many puppies also seem to abandon stool-eating as they mature. If your puppy isn't one of those, prevent, prevent, prevent, and do teach that rock-solid "Leave it."

You'll notice I'm not touting hot sauce or commercial taste deterrents. Honestly, I don't see the point. The commercial taste deterrents you feed your dog have no effect on any feces but hers. Plenty of dogs feel perfectly fine about a dash of hot sauce on poop. And no matter which kind of deterrent you use, and how much your dog hates it, sooner or later he will find an untreated stash. Result: Foraging for feces is now on what's technically called a variable reinforcement schedule, which is what trainers use when they want to create an extremely persistent, durable behavior. Just what you were looking for in stool eating.

Last word? Almost no behavior makes it clearer that dogs are different from us. Feces disgust us. Not so for dogs. Eating feces is dangerous to humans, mostly not to dogs. Prevent access as much as you can, teach your dog a strong "Leave it" cue, and bear in mind that dogs are dogs and sometimes we have to shrug and say, "Oh well."

Counter Surfing (the Behavior Formerly Known as "Stealing Food")

Almost all of us who live with dogs know the sinking feeling that comes when you've been out of the kitchen for a few minutes and suddenly realize that Dogalini is licking her chops. Also, the block of artisanal Cheddar you left on the counter is either inside her or wearing a cloak of invisibility, and since we're not at Hogwarts, we know which it is.

Let's get morality out of the way. Your counter-surfing canine may annoy the heck out of you, but she isn't being "bad." Our best evidence about dogs suggests that they evolved as scavengers of human garbage and waste. Scavengers . . . scavenge. They look for edible stuff that's lying around unattended, and when they find some, they eat it. "My people are saving that artisanal Cheddar to impress their guests, so I'll leave it alone and wait for my dinner to show up"—well, just no. Animals that pass up chances to take in calories don't leave as many descendants as their better-nourished peers. Our anger can upset our dogs, sure, and they'd prefer to avoid it. But eating whatever they found is what kept their ancestors alive. That evolutionary history doesn't vanish just because *some* dogs live in houses now and get regular meals.

So how do you keep any dog who's tall enough or agile enough from looking for food on your counter? After all, sooner or later, if he has a working nose, he's going to notice the delectable smell of your Tofurkey wafting down. And, as the Los Angeles trainer Sarah Owings writes, "no matter what you do (rat traps, spray bottles, pennies in a can, a strict cleanup policy) counter surfing is still reinforced by that peekaboo glimpse . . . at what my boyfriend likes to call 'the realm of the gods.'" However, all is not lost. Your best defense combines management and training.

MANAGEMENT

"Management" means that you do your best never to give your dog access to unattended food. Clear the table or counter, or push the food back out of reach, or close the door. If you're actively cooking, manage by crating your dog, putting her behind a baby gate, or tethering her.

Sarah's right that even looking at empty counter space is rewarding—but at least it's much less rewarding than actually finding something to eat. Every single time your dog gets lucky on your kitchen counters, he becomes likelier to try again. There was a cheesecake once! There might be another someday. If your dog's experiments in vertical grazing never work out for him, he'll try them less often.

By the way, I choose the example of cheesecake for a reason—our counters and tables make such attractive foraging sites because they offer huge potential bonanzas. When you're frustrated with your dog's counter surfing, bear in mind the California Gold Rush.

TRAINING

The old-school trainer's answer to counter surfing is the booby trap—the rat-trap or penny-can array that Sarah mentioned. A high-tech version, which is to say the same-old, same-old but wearing a new dress, is an indoor shock fence with a perimeter around the kitchen and dining area. Low tech, high tech, don't waste your time. Plenty of dogs are unimpressed by booby traps, and supposing your dog is put off by yours, are you seriously going to remember (or have the energy) to set it up every single time you leave the kitchen for the rest of your dog's life? No, and eventually every dog but the most timid is going to take a chance that the world won't end if she jumps up. Besides, when you're cooking, you yourself will need that counter space.

As for that most timid dog, the one who's scared off counters forever by the rattling cans, you run the risk that clattering metal will also become scary forever. How fun for both of you when you drop your keys or take out empty cans for recycling. Shock systems cost big bucks, and even fans of these devices admit that just setting them up and turning on the juice is inhumane. Dogs need to be taught to heed the warning tone and avoid the shock. Finally, no punishment in the world can teach your dog what you *do* want. Spend your time on that instead, then pass Go and collect $200.

Decide what you'd like your dog to do when there's food around—maybe a relaxed, out-of-the-way down. The key is to remember that counter surfing is foraging; that is, your dog wants some of whatever smells so good. Therefore you, you brainy primate, must convince your dog that she can forage successfully by lying down.

I'm going to assume that your dog lies down on cue and that you've taught her a little bit of a down-stay, so you can walk around for 30 seconds or so without her getting up again. If not, that's your first step. Then come back at cooking time and set yourself up with a stash of treats. I am possibly the world's laziest trainer, so I just use tiny bits of whatever I am cooking, provided it's safe for dogs. Yes on the artisanal Cheddar (for most dogs); no on the raisins and onions, for instance. If you have a limited supply or the current ingredients are too pricey to share, choose any safe human food that your dog loves. Shreds of leftover meat or eggs or French toast should work just fine.

Have your dog lie down a bit out of the way but close enough to make treat delivery easy—you'll either be giving the treat by hand or tossing it so it lands right by her. Since lying down and staying put is the behavior you're rewarding, you don't want your dog to have to get up. *Frequently* deliver something from your morsel array. Or have a helper do so. If your dog reliably holds a down-stay for 30 seconds, keep those treats coming rapidly at first—an average of every 15 seconds wouldn't be too often, at all. Vary the interval so your dog never quite knows when a treat is coming—think of that old song "You Keep Me Hangin' On." Over days and weeks of practice, lengthen the interval between treats. But err on the side of generosity. You're building a habit for a lifetime. The more solid your early teaching, the more reliable the end result will be.

If you use a mat or bed as your dog's hangout location, and make sure that lying on it works really well as a tactic for getting hold of your succulent food, that mat or bed will become hugely attractive to him.

He'll begin to gravitate there on his own when food appears, in hopes that some of it will make its way to him. Fulfill those hopes often enough, and you'll find that, as Sarah Owings puts it, the bed "acts like a magnet." Sarah reports that her dog Zoë heads for her bed 95 percent of the time when Sarah's working in the kitchen, because "being on her bed is a guaranteed way to get paid."

Can you be sure your dog will never ever ever counter-surf? Probably not, but if you combine training and management you can get pretty darn close. As for the rest—well, chalk it up to life with a clever animal who appreciates artisanal cheese.

Digging

One size hardly ever fits all. Your Dachshund, the neighbor's mixed-breed, and the heavy-coated hundred-pound something or other down the block may each dig for different reasons. So different responses are appropriate, too.

HEAT

Let's take that big, heavy-coated dog first. If it's 85 degrees out and your dog is lounging in the pit he has excavated under the evergreen hedge, I will bet my consultation fee that he is trying to keep cool. In general, the bigger a dog is, and the denser his coat, the more uncomfortable he's likely to be in summer heat. And all of the short-nosed dogs—Pugs and English and French Bulldogs, for instance—are structurally unable to pant effectively to cool themselves.

If heat is your dog's motive for digging, your best bet for preempting the behavior is to cool him off. Some dogs may like a wading pool. Others may do fine with access to shade and plenty of cool drinking water. Or, if your dog is happy and relaxed in his dugout under the shrubbery, you can always let him stay. Help him cool down by rubbing him with ice cubes, too. In hot, humid weather, save outdoor exercise for early morning and the evening hours. Short-nosed dogs are safest in an air-conditioned room.

DOGS BRED FOR UNDERGROUND PURSUIT

If your digger's a Dachshund or one of the terriers, remember that hunters produced these breeds to go after rats, badgers, and other tunneling prey. The word "terrier" derives from the French for "earth," and *Dachs* is German for "badger." Should moles or groundhogs, or for that matter badgers, take up residence in your yard, your Dachsie or terrier will likely go after them. Who can tear up more perennials faster?

Maddening as this may be, it's hard to blame a dog for trying to do the job her breed was developed for. If you'd rather she didn't, you'll need to evict your underground tenants yourself.

When I did a podcast episode on the subject of digging, I suggested Earthdog as an outlet for terriers, Dachshunds, and other dogs originally bred for underground pursuit. In Earthdog, dogs follow a scent and navigate a tunnel to find a caged rat. I had some qualms about what the experience might be like for the rats, but was reassured by an aficionado that the rats are "quick to learn that the dogs are not a threat" and that "in training young dogs, one of the biggest problems is that the rats go to sleep." After the episode aired, however, I heard from someone with equal expertise who strongly disagreed; in her view, the rats are simply frightened out of their wits, and their apparently calm behavior reflects learned helplessness.

I know little about rat behavior, but it's certainly true of many animals that they'll go utterly still when they're seriously afraid, and I have seen plenty of dogs described as "calm" when knowledgeable scrutiny of their body language reveals that they're under extreme stress. Maybe someday a researcher will look into the respiration rates and the levels of stress hormones in Earthdog bait rats and find that the rats really are feeling mellow. I don't have independent knowledge on this point, so I can't wholeheartedly recommend the sport. Tracking and lure coursing are possible alternatives. Also, load up on the exercise and brainwork, and consider a digging pit (see the section that follows).

ESCAPE

Some dogs tunnel under fences to escape their yards. Escape artists may be motivated by general boredom and pent-up energy, or they may have a specific goal. Even a neutered male may be attracted by a female dog in heat, for instance, so if you've got a neighbor who hasn't done right by his lady dog, have a friendly chat about spaying. While we're on the subject of reproduction: Pregnant females may dig to create a nest for their pups, and so may a bitch suffering from pseudopregnancy. Pseudopregnancy can occur in females spayed at a particular phase of the heat cycle but is usually limited to unspayed bitches. Pregnancy, of course . . . well, spay your dog.

AGGRESSION

Some dogs react to passersby, and in particular to passing dogs, by charging them; if your dog is rushing the fence to lunge and bark, he may also try to dig past the barrier. Here aggression, not digging, is the real problem. No dog should be left outdoors unsupervised, and that goes double for fence-chargers. If this is your dog, he should be indoors unless you're actively working or playing with him, and you'll probably need professional help with his behavior. See Chapter 12, "Stuff Dogs Do That Worries People," for guidance on hiring.

CACHING

Dogs may cache food or toys—bury them, then go and dig them out later. I suppose all behaviors give us a glimpse of dogs' evolutionary history, but this one has always struck me as particularly vivid. Wolves and other predators cache food to protect it from scavengers—for example, vultures—who can't dig. *Call of the Wild*, anyone?

DIGGING PITS

I'm all about working with dogs, not against them. If your dog caches food or just plain loves to dig, consider letting him. Don't hyperventilate; I'm not going to tell you to turn over your whole yard. But perhaps you can give your dog a spot of his own where digging is "legal," even encouraged. Set aside a piece of ground plenty big enough for his whole busy self, and mark it off with a low garden border fence or a line of flat stones. You might want to choose a location where you already know he likes to excavate.

Give a couple of bones, chews, or favorite toys a shallow grave, bring your dog over, and let him go to town. You can dig at the ground a bit yourself, to help him get the idea. If he starts digging in some other spot, gently interrupt him and lead him to his digging pit instead.

LONELINESS AND BOREDOM

Finally, we've got the dog who's just plain lonely, bored, and underexercised. Maybe she's spending hours a day all alone in the backyard. If this sounds like you and your dog, I hardly have to tell you what to do. She might like a digging pit well enough, but what she really needs is more of your company, more mental stimulation, and more just plain fun.

(The Behavior Formerly Known as) "Disobedience"

No matter whether you adopted your very first dog six months ago or you're a longtime trainer with dozens of competition titles to your credit, there will be times when your dog doesn't sit, or takes the agility obstacles in the wrong order, or nabs the roast before your very eyes while you sputter, "Leave it!"

Let's consider that purloined roast, for starters. For a dog, leaving a dry biscuit alone on cue is the equivalent of kindergarten; turning away from a vulnerable and fragrant hunk of meat is an advanced skill, akin to an Olympic skater's triple axel. Neither skater nor dog can succeed without long and careful practice.

There you've got the first point to consider when your dog doesn't respond to a cue quickly, or at all: Have you practiced enough times, and in enough different contexts, to be sure she really knows that cue cold? Have you practiced with gradually greater distractions? To a professional trainer, thoroughly teaching a behavior means dozens, hundreds, even thousands of reps.

And just because a dog has learned to perform some behavior on cue in our living room or training area doesn't mean he will recognize it when he hears it on the street. That's not only because the street is distracting. It's also because the street is *different*.

There's a famous anecdote about the trainer and behaviorist Dr. Ian Dunbar challenging a roomful of trainers to prove their dogs could sit on cue. Of course our dogs can sit! said all the trainers—right up until Dunbar had some poor stooge give the sit cue while lying on the floor. Needless to say, the dog did not sit. Why? The scenario was too different. The dog didn't recognize even a familiar cue.

When you evaluate the thoroughness of your training, take your individual dog into account. It's a challenge to teach Afghans and other sighthounds to come reliably when called.* Terriers, who belong to a group of breeds developed precisely as tireless hunters of vermin, will find rodents even more intensely interesting than does your average dog. Miniature Pinschers are notorious for their inclination to bark. If you're finding it a slog to teach your dog a particular behavior, consider what she was originally bred to do. When you train against the grain, expect to need extra time and practice.

---

* Which is why the "Really Reliable Recall" was developed by a sighthound fan, Leslie Nelson.

It doesn't really matter, by the way, whether you know your dog's breed or mix. A squirrel-mad dog is squirrel-mad, even if we can't nod knowingly and say, "Well, yes, of course, that's because she's of Brooklyn Squirrel Chaser lineage."

That business of different contexts is closely related to a second common reason why dogs don't "obey." Your dog may indeed know the cue for a particular behavior upside down and backward—but the cue she knows may not be the one you think you taught her. We yammering primates focus on words words words, and we tend to assume that the sounds coming out of our mouths are equally significant to our dogs.

Canids do vocalize some of their communications, but they rely much more on body language. Dogs can have a hard time picking out which of the endless sounds we make have anything to do with them. From their perspective, the signal-to-noise ratio in speech is *really* low. Imagine you're trying to understand the intentions of a person who speaks a language of which you know nothing. You watch their face and hands and posture for clues, right? Our dogs do much the same.

As a result, you may think Dogalini is responding to your verbal cue when actually she's picked up on some tiny unconscious movement that you always make at the same time. If, say, you're carrying packages and can't deliver the usual body English when you speak your cue, she will have no idea what you mean. For this reason, professional trainers carefully separate gestural cues from words. Most pet guardians are understandably less meticulous, which is fine as long as we don't blame our dogs for the confusion that can result.

Plenty of nontraining reasons can also interfere with a dog's compliance. Emotions easily get in the way; a dog who's terrified of air brakes, for instance, is unlikely to respond to his name when he hears an 18-wheeler screeching to a halt. Is your dog barking and lunging at another dog? Then you can take it as a sign that he's experiencing significant distress—distress that will get in the way of his ability to respond when you tell him to sit. Help with the underlying behavior issues here will almost certainly have to precede any training fix.

What physical conditions are you working under? Does there happen to be a puddle right where Dogalini would need to put her heinie when you ask her to sit? Or consider this: Because tiny dogs tend to conserve heat poorly, they're often reluctant to lie down on a cold floor. The same goes for dogs with thin coats. Sometimes an older dog refuses to perform a behavior he's known all his life. If your grizzled old dude won't lie down on cue anymore, maybe his arthritis is acting up. Or maybe he can't hear as well as he once did; when you call him and he doesn't come, he's not ignoring you. The cue just isn't getting through. Illness can interfere with our dogs' quickness to respond to us, as well. Remember, a vet visit is in order whenever an adult dog's behavior changes suddenly.

When dogs don't do what we ask them to, we're often invited to think of them as disobedient, defiant, dominant, or dumb. Yes, one day you'll tell your diligently trained, non-hearing-impaired dog, "Let's go," but she'll keep sniffing the fire hydrant. I can't pretend that I've never gotten annoyed when this happens to me—but then, I have never been poky, distracted, immersed in what I'm doing, and consequently slow to respond to a reasonable request. And since I'm perfect, I have every right to expect my dog to be perfect, too. Ahem.

Garbage Raiding

Fundamentally, this is exactly the same behavior as counter surfing (see earlier section), and the same points about scavenging, morality, and prevention apply. Ditto the pointlessness of punishment.

If you believe your dog feels guilty when you come home and find garbage on the floor, please read the section in Chapter 9, "The Parallel Universe," describing a study of dogs' "guilty looks." Many trainers have done a similar experiment to show our clients that their dogs are reacting to human anger, not necessarily to an inner sense that garbage on the floor is Bad and Wrong. Why would a dog think garbage on the floor is Bad and Wrong? He has to get the food out *somehow*. Sheesh.

Some garbage-specific tips:

- Use a garbage can with a lid.
- Garbage cans with foot pedals foil some dogs.
- Keep the garbage can behind a closed door (room or cabinet) or elevated where your dog can't reach it.
- Use plastic grocery bags for your garbage; they're small, so you can take out the kitchen trash whenever you leave the dog alone.*

---

* You're bringing your own cloth bags when you shop, of course, but you can supply your garbage-bag needs from the store's recycling bin. Come on, you're using them for *garbage*. How clean do they have to be?

Humping

A visit from my best friend is a rare treat, since we live on opposite coasts. My Juniper adores Patti and acts thrilled when she appears. Last time he was so thrilled that he made a complete air-humping circuit of my admittedly tiny living room. Ah, humping—common, sometimes embarrassing, often misunderstood.

Mounting or humping, of course, is what male dogs do when they mate. But as I'm sure we've all seen, dogs don't mount only when mating, and they don't only mount other dogs; they may also mount furniture, other animals, stuffed toys, and people. Once a dog whose behavior I was evaluating got on the back of the sofa behind me and began to hump my head. Female dogs mount, though less frequently than males.

Apart from actual mating, dogs still find plenty of reasons to mount. Oddly enough, people often overlook the most obvious of these: sex. Even neutered and spayed dogs display sexual behavior, often accompanied with what looks to a human eye like flirtation—bouncy, playful, physically close. You may see a female dog lift her tail away from her genitals just as she would if in heat and preparing to mate. Male dogs may ejaculate after humping, though if they're neutered, of course the fluid contains no sperm. Masturbation humping is common, if I can judge by the number of clients who've told me about their dog's special relationship with a pillow or other soft object.

But physiological arousal isn't only sexual. Juniper's response to Patti reflected happy excitement; his penis was erect, though he didn't turn it in anyone's direction, so maybe there was a sexual component too. As I mentioned in the discussion of stress in Chapter 9, humping can be a displacement behavior in an anxious dog. I'm not aware of any studies of whether the behavior lowers heart rate and blood pressure or promotes muscle relaxation, but I certainly wouldn't be surprised. I also suspect that this anxious humping is the kind many popular training books explain as a status grab or an assertion of rank. For whatever reason, people tend to see high rank as the reason for showy, flamboyant dog behaviors such as humping and fighting. In fact, these often arise out of social anxiety. Something to bear in mind the next time a dog humps your leg—not an experience to look forward to, but usually not a portent of a palace coup.

Sexual humping and anxious humping can make *people* uncomfortable. Of course, if your dog is anxious, it's a kindness to alleviate that anxiety even if you don't mind him clasping leg. Also, a dog who routinely expresses social anxiety by humping fellow canines may sooner or later meet one who responds with significant aggression.

With pretty much any behavior that you wish your dog wouldn't do, consider whether he might be bored or seeking attention. Take an honest look at how much physical exercise, mental stimulation, and social interaction your dog gets. If your bored, underexercised, lonely young dog has learned he can get your attention by humping the couch cushion every evening right after dinner, the best way to stop the humping is to give him something else to occupy his time.

All that having been said, humping isn't always abnormal. In fact, it usually isn't. If your dog, like my Juniper, sometimes humps excitedly, laugh and let it go. If your dog flirts and humps, or is humped by, some of his or her dog friends, no worries. Occasional humping as anxiety relief is normal, and so is masturbating. There's no real way to put this delicately, but the fact that laundry may be unpleasant for you doesn't automatically signify that your dog has a behavior problem. If your dog humps you or other people occasionally, your best bet is to just get up and walk away.

So when should you worry? First, if your dog humps to the exclusion of other activities or constantly licks at or rubs her genitals, you might be looking at canine compulsive disorder or a medical problem. Allergies, for example, can make dogs itch like mad. Schedule a vet check ASAP.

Second, if your dog humps every visitor to your house or every dog and dogette he meets at the park, you have all the evidence you need that that social situation is too much for him. Visit the dog park only when the place is less crowded, go elsewhere altogether, or limit play-time to familiar friends. Let your dog rest in his crate with a chew toy when people visit.

You may hear the advice to use a "Leave it" cue for a humping dog; my only objection is that though it may solve your immediate manners problem, it doesn't address the cause. If you believe your dog's hump-ing arises out of anxiety about people or other dogs, consult a behavior specialist for advice. The same goes if he responds aggressively when you interrupt the behavior.

As I mentioned earlier, you'll often hear that humping is a domi-nance move. Perhaps it sometimes is, but beware of default "explana-tions" arrived at without much thought.[6] Take that dog who tried to hump my head. He repeatedly pushed into my space. He wasn't friendly. And he had a history of guarding his resting spots and his toys. So maybe when he climbed up on the sofa back behind me, he was pulling rank. On the other hand, he was a young, intact male who had never had training of any kind—in other words, a hormone-packed adolescent who'd grown up in a household with no rules. Maybe he was trying to dominate me, or maybe he was just one of them boys who don't know how to act. Either way, he needed a good reward-based dog trainer to show him some moves.

Nipping and Mouthing

Puppies nip. A lot. Usually during play. The good news is, young puppies have weak jaws and hardly ever draw blood. The bad news is, baby-dog teeth are needle sharp, so baby-dog nips hurt fiercely anyway. And puppies grow into dogs, with bigger bodies and strong jaws. So, best to prevent a nipping habit from settling in. Fortunately, it's easy to teach puppies to treat human skin with care. If you have an adolescent dog who nips and mouths in play, see "Out-of-Control Behavior" in this chapter; if the nipping and mouthing feel aggressive or at all scary, or if you have children or frail elderly persons at home, it's best to get in-person help.

Teaching puppies not to nip is a two-stage process. Step 1: Spend a couple of days on tooth pressure. Let your puppy put her teeth on you, but set limits on how hard she can press. Every time you play with her, allow a little less pressure than you did the time before.

Naturally, your puppy will break the tooth-pressure limit every so often. You'll need to convey to her what she did wrong. She also needs to know what the consequence is for this mistake. To give your puppy this information, mark the instant she makes a mistake, and immediately deliver a short time-out. It works like this.

You and your puppy are playing; she gives a hard nip. The second you feel those teeth, say, "Oops!" or "Too bad!"—that becomes your marker for mistakes. *Immediately* stop playing, fold your arms, and look away. For five or ten seconds, ignore your pup. Once she's settled down, you become friendly and fun again.

This method works well because the puppy learns that a hard nip predicts an "Oops!" and an "Oops!" predicts a quick social freeze-out.

Hard nipping kills play and makes you be no fun at all. Most puppies want to keep that human engagement going. So they quickly learn to be careful with their teeth.

A nice feature of the time-out method is that it's not harsh. There's no need to scold your puppy, pinch her, or shove your fingers down her throat. All you have to do is take away the fun and company for a few seconds. Just remember, you'll need to do this *every single time* you feel a nip. Otherwise you teach the lesson that sometimes, unpredictably, nipping is okay.

Once your puppy's learned to be careful, he's ready to learn not to use his teeth on skin or clothing at all. Now you give your puppy an "Oops" and a time-out the second his teeth touch you—even if it was an accident. That's Step 2.

You might wonder why we don't cut to the no-teeth rule in the first place. The reason is that accidents happen: People close their dogs' tails in car doors. They trip over old, arthritic dogs. They rub their dog's ears just when a painful infection has taken hold. The nicest dog in the world can wind up delivering a bite. We teach the no-teeth rule in two steps because we hope our puppies learn that (a) they shouldn't use their teeth on people, but also that (b) human skin is super delicate. So, Zippy, if you're going to bite, it won't take much force to make your point. Trainers don't know for sure that this lesson will stick in an emergency. But the two-step method is about as close as people can get to the way puppies learn similar lessons from other dogs.

Time-outs are all very well, but the first order of business is always,

---

If you've given the folded-arm social freeze-out a couple of days of consistent practice, but your puppy isn't letting up at all, maybe doesn't even quit chewing you during the freeze-out, try the tether or playpen method.

Quick and Dirty Tip

With your puppy tethered or in a playpen, engage him in play. When teeth touch skin, instantly walk away. Ignore your puppy for five or ten seconds, or until he settles down a bit, then come back and re-engage with him. Losing physical access to you protects you, prevents him from further practicing the Humans Are Chew Toys behavior, and makes the lesson clearer by ending his fun (which the folded-arm maneuver apparently didn't do).

always, always to show your puppy or dog what it *is* okay to do. Dogs often use their teeth in play with each other—that's normal and fine. For safety's sake, they shouldn't use their teeth on us or our clothes, but they can learn to bite objects instead. So, when you're hanging out with your puppy, keep a toy or a chewy edible to hand. Look for signs that your puppy's teeth are about to engage, and get that chewy in her face as fast as you can.

Out-of-Control Behavior

"Out of control" is a catch-all category for a pattern I see in many adolescent dogs, especially shelter dogs, and especially powerful, energetic dogs such as Pit Bulls, Labrador Retrievers, and their mixes. The typical picture looks something like this: The dog jumps up into people's faces and knocks their glasses off. If they push her away, she body-slams them and grabs their arms. Yelling doesn't faze her one tiny bit. In fact, *nothing* seems to faze her; people try kneeing, spray guns, alpha rolls, and everything they do seems to amp the dog up more. I'm pretty sure the reason I see this behavior so often in shelter dogs is that it's what landed the dog in the shelter in the first place. Nope, nothing to back that up with but intuition.

I hesitated over whether to put this section in the "annoying" chapter or the "worrisome" chapter. It belongs in "annoying" if, and only if, your dog is friendly (greets you, visitors, and strangers on the street with butt wiggles, squinty eyes, and a soft expression on her face), if she doesn't aggress in other contexts (for example, stiffening or growling over food or toys), and if no one in your household is afraid of her (gut feelings qualify as information here). Many dogs crank up easily and don't know how to settle down, but if you have any doubt at all about which side of the too-excited/shading-into-aggressive line your dog is on, get in-person help.

Aerobic exercise is Prescription Number 1 for out-of-control dogs. A leash walk burns about as much energy as window-shopping at the mall—not enough to take the edge off any healthy medium-size or large adolescent dog. Adequate exercise is fundamental to teaching patience, good manners, and self-control. Try for at least a solid hour of aerobic exercise every day in a safe off-leash area. Rambunctious adolescents need to run, trot, and maybe play fetch. Morning exercise is best, so that the dog starts the day pleasantly tired and relaxed.

Nevertheless, she'll be awake some of the time, looking for something to do. That's what it means to be a young animal, whether you've got four legs or two. The out-of-control behaviors a dog defaults to are clues to what activities she likes; usually, they make up some combination of mouthing, jumping, and trying to engage with people. It's fine that dogs like to use their mouths; it's fine that dogs like to move their bodies vigorously; it's fine that dogs want attention from their humans. The trick is to find outlets for these desires that everybody can enjoy.

With exercise, you've met your dog's need to move; Prescription Number 2 is to teach her to deploy her sharky mouth on something other than humans. Lose your dog's bowl. Any food she doesn't earn in training should come in food-dispensing toys such as the Kong and the Molecuball. (Make the stuffed Kong a challenge; see "Chewing," page 195, for tips.) Once the 30 seconds your dog used to spend eating breakfast and dinner stretch to 40 minutes, you have some hope that she will fall asleep afterward.

Mouthing and jumping are effective attention-getters, even if that attention comes in the form of reprimands. Anything beats feeling bored and left out, and riled-up people can be kind of exciting. Prescription Number 3 is to teach yourself to notice quiet, polite behavior, and choose those times to show your dog affection, toss her occasional treats, and invite her to go for a walk or play a game. Over time, she'll learn to seek attention by lying down quietly near someone, for example, or resting her chin on his leg.

Many attention-seeking behaviors can be reduced or eliminated if we strictly ignore them. But jumping and mouthing are unpleasant, painful, and sometimes dangerous. So ignoring them won't do the trick all by itself. Prescription Number 4 is to give a 30-second time-out whenever your dog jumps on people or mouths them. At home, have her wear a short leash, maybe two feet long. Mark any mistake with an "Oops!" and lead her to her time-out area. This can be her crate, another room, or a prepared spot where she can be tethered. Alternatively, you can walk into another room yourself, and close the door behind you. During the time-out, ignore her completely. Instead of gaining social interaction, obnoxious attention-seeking gets her briefly tossed from the party. The short leash makes it possible to lead her to her time-out spot without grabbing her and will help thwart any attempts at keep-away.

For the time-out to be effective, it must be delivered every single time the problem behavior happens. A behavior that still works occasionally will be very hard to get rid of. Time-outs should be delivered in a mild, calm, pleasant way. The lost opportunity to socialize is plenty of punishment for a sociable dog. In addition, time-outs are unfair if you don't teach your dog what behavior you *do* want in place of the behavior you're trying to get rid of. This is accomplished by giving attention and other rewards for quiet, polite behavior.

Another thing many out-of-control wild-and-crazy dogs have in common is that they're smart and bored, so it's important to tire their big brains. Prescription Number 5 is fun, reward-based training—at least two sessions a day, each about five minutes long. Manners—polite greetings, waiting for permission to go through doors, lying quietly on a comfortable bed while dinner is prepared—are a good starting point, but tricks are great for keeping the mood light.

For help with the Sneaky Thievin' Thiefy Dog, otherwise known as the Perfectly Normal Dog, see Chapter 7, "Leaving Stuff Alone . . ." and for help with your dog's persistent licking of you, the floor, the dog's own self . . . see the next chapter.

12

Stuff Dogs Do That Worries People
WHERE TO TURN FOR ADDITIONAL HELP

This chapter gets a great big right-up-front disclaimer: All I can provide here is a brief overview of some of the issues for which people most commonly consult behavior professionals: specialized dog trainers like me, veterinary behaviorists, or Certified Applied Animal Behaviorists. To give you an idea how much more there is to problem behavior than this little book can include, one standard text, Steven Lindsay's *Handbook of Applied Dog Behavior and Training,* runs to three volumes and well over a thousand pages. (And the print is oh so small.) The form I use just to take a client history is twenty pages long, and when the problem is complex and serious I collaborate with a board-certified veterinary behaviorist, because what we call "behavior" problems often have biological components as well: pain; disease; a subtle alteration in the normal balance of neurotransmitters in the brain.

I'm not saying that every problem you have with your dog calls for the Full Specialist Frontal Assault. You may be able to repair a small problem yourself, *with the help of the additional resources I suggest.* But even so, you need more than a few paragraphs in a basic book about dog training and care. Think of this chapter as a springboard for your further research, okay?

How to Find a Behavior Specialist

Get your White Pages and a scarf. Blindfold yourself. Open the White Pages and put your finger down at random. Congratulations—you've just found a legally qualified dog behaviorist. No U.S. jurisdiction sets any educational or licensing requirements for people who hire themselves out as experts on aggression, separation anxiety, and other behavior problems. Anyone can call himself a behaviorist or behavior consultant, never mind whether he so much as took Psych 101.

That is bad news. An ignorant and inept approach to your dog's problems will waste your time and money. What's worse, it may further damage your dog. Commonly, for example, hack behavior specialists tell clients that their dog's growling or biting reflects a dominance challenge, and they advise a punitive, confrontational approach. In fact, aggression can arise for many reasons. Genuine dominance aggression is believed to be rare; a much more common culprit is stress. Additionally, it's important to rule out illness and pain whenever behavior deteriorates suddenly, especially in an older dog. And behavior experts agree that alpha rolls, scruff shakes, collar jerks, and other forms of force present a high risk of backfiring. Translation: If you scare the dog enough, he may fight back.

It's imperative to find someone really competent to work with. One starting point for your search is the Certification Council for Professional Dog Trainers (http://www.ccpdt.org). You may remember this independent national body from my discussion of how to find a good trainer (p. 82).

In 2011, the CCPDT launched a certification program specifically for consultants working with behavior problems. The requirements are fairly rigorous. Even to qualify for testing, candidates must document 500 hours of work with behavior problems over the past five years or, alternatively, must hold a master's or doctoral degree in a relevant field, such as psychology or the life sciences. Candidates also have to submit five references—one each from a vet, a colleague in the field, and a client, plus two more from people in any of those three categories. The test itself covers principles of animal learning and applied behavior analysis; the evolution, biology, development, and social behavior of dogs; and professional ethics. Having sat for it, I can testify that it's not a walkover. (Yes, I passed).

But because the behavior-consultant exam is brand-new, there probably isn't a certificant near you. And, anyway, paper qualifications don't prove in-person skills. So whether or not your prospective hire is CCPDT certified, you'll need to evaluate her for yourself to make sure you're getting the right combination of experience, book learning, and insight and creativity.

Let's get experience out of the way first. Obviously, the more the better, but all experience isn't equal. Dog people specialize; you can spend a lifetime perfecting your skills at training dogs in the sport of agility, for instance. I, on the other hand, am obsessed with behavior modification; no one should ever hire me to teach their dog to run an obstacle course with speed and grace.

Beware of the "expert" who learned everything he knows twenty years ago and has been doing the same things over and over ever since. Science rarely deals in absolutes or final statements; it's a constant process of poking around and asking questions and revising what we *think* we know. The past couple of decades have seen a lot of research into how dogs' minds and bodies work and how best to apply that knowledge. Beware, too, of anyone who touts a special method all his own; cognitive scientists and behavior professionals spend years trying to understand what's up with dogs (and other animals), and I promise you that guy with the ad on the Google search page hasn't gotten ahead of them while they weren't looking.

Speaking of knowledge: A good behavior consultant will be familiar with what's called "learning theory." Learning theory is a well-established explanation, derived from observation and laboratory experiment, of important aspects of how animals learn and how best to teach them. Anyone who teaches anything to any person or animal is applying learning theory, just as when you play catch you're applying the laws of physics. But you'd probably like the designer of the airplane you're in to have explicit technical knowledge. The same should go for the person who's messing with your dog.

Your behavior consultant should be up to speed on studies of dogs' cognitive abilities—how they perceive the world and solve problems in it. A close knowledge of dogs' body language and social behavior is essential. Any spiel about wolf packs, for instance, is usually a red flag. Free-living dogs may band together temporarily to, say, run down an animal. But they don't generally live in structured, long-lasting groups, and the "wild pack" certainly isn't a good template for their life with us. Donna Hill, a training consultant with Vancouver Island Assistance Dogs whose academic background is in zoology, once pointed out to me that "interspecies group living" is a "different dynamic altogether."

Medical conditions and medications can affect behavior. Take a sweet-tempered dog who suddenly snaps when her ears are rubbed. I wouldn't even think about doing behavior work until we knew for sure that dog's ears were free of infection. A nonveterinarian can't make diagnoses or prescribe medications—that would be both stupid and unethical—but she should recognize when medical rule-outs are in order, and she should be generally familiar with common behavioral medications. Or at least know where to look them up!

Some crucial qualities are hard to judge. Call them creativity and sympathy. There is a reasonably well-established (and constantly developing) scientific basis for working with dogs, but there are millions of dogs. It's true that similar problems often call for similar approaches. For instance, when I meet a mouthy but friendly adolescent Pit Bull, odds are good I'll be advising plenty of exercise, plenty of chew toys, and attention contingent on polite behavior. But I will always want to consider that dog in the context of her home, her history of reward and punishment, and her behavior in other situations. Also, people have limited time and energy. What interventions will be easiest and most effective? Expect a good behavior consultant to ask a lot of questions, think hard, and offer advice tailored to your situation.

One last point: The world is full of people happy to blame you for your dog's problems. In fact, some dogs are born vulnerable, others astonishingly resilient. *Perhaps* you contributed to your dog's problems, but I'll bet you were doing the best you knew how at the time. Punishment is a dangerous behavioral tool, to be used sparingly and in emergencies whether on dogs or on people. Hire a consultant who's gentle with both you and your dog.

Sources for Referrals

Certification Council for Professional Dog Trainers, http://www.ccpdt .org. This group prepares and administers the *only* independent national certification program for dog trainers and behavior consultants.

International Association of Animal Behavior Consultants, http://www .iaabc.org. An umbrella group for pretty much everybody whose work involves animal behavior (dogs, cats, birds, horses, service animals . . .), the IAABC has its own certification process. As a new group, it's had some organizational and other difficulties, but the membership is in general scientifically serious, and members are ethically required to adhere to LIMA principles—to use the "least intrusive, minimally aversive" (aversive = unpleasant) technique that will get the job done. The guy with the behavior secrets all his own is not to be found here.

American Veterinary Society of Animal Behavior, http://www.avsabonline .org. Members are veterinarians with a special interest in behavior, as well as academic behaviorists with doctoral degrees; some are also board-certified veterinary behaviorists (see next listing). If you need veterinary input and don't have a vet behaviorist handy, AVSAB is your best bet for finding a behaviorally sophisticated vet. Their Web site offers valuable behavior info and position statements on punishment, "dominance theory," and puppy socialization.

American College of Veterinary Behaviorists, http://dacvb.org/. The big guns if you, your trainer, or your vet suspects a medical issue is affecting your dog's behavior, or if medication may be in order. Veterinary behavior is a specialty, like neurology or orthopedics, and boarded vets have to do a residency and then pass a scorcher of an exam. In my opinion, if your dog has a serious behavior problem, it's often best to work with a team comprising a vet behaviorist and a trainer specializing in behavior modification. Two catches: (1) This gets expensive. (2) Last time I checked, in early 2011, there were 54 board-certified vet behaviorists in the entire United States. The good news is that most of them will consult by phone with your primary-care vet at no charge.

Certified Applied Animal Behaviorists, http://www.certifiedanimalbehaviorist.com, are (mostly nonveterinarian) behavior specialists with advanced degrees. Like the vet behaviorists, they're few and far between. They're highly knowledgeable, but if I had medical concerns I'd want a vet on the case.

Excellent materials are available that can help make you an informed participant in your dog's care. I've included specific recommendations in each section of this chapter. Books, pamphlets, and most DVDs are available through Dogwise, http://www.dogwise.com; DVDs are available through Tawzer Dog Videos, http://www.tawzerdogvideos.com.

A Few Words About a Few Common Problems

AGGRESSION: GROWLING, SNAPPING, BITING

A dog's growl, snap, or bite may leave you feeling frightened, even betrayed, and not knowing what to do. As usual, the ether is full of unexamined ideas that get dogs and their people in trouble, and that make trouble worse when it does arise. Among the most pernicious unexamined ideas about aggression is the notion that there are good dogs, and then there are aggressive dogs. As a corollary, every dog is one or the other, and the two categories never overlap.

In fact, normal dogs have a huge vocabulary of aggressive behaviors, and humans often miss subtle clues to canine tension. A brief overall body stillness is one; pushing the corners of the lips forward is another. (See Chapter 9, "The Parallel Universe," for more information about body language and signaling.) The vocabulary of aggression ranges from the quickest hard glance up to all-out attack.

My dog Izzy once delivered a beautiful lesson in how to escalate. We were at the dog park, and a bouncy boy dog just wouldn't stop humping her. I was so flabbergasted by his obliviousness to her signals that I didn't intervene. The first time he got on Izzy's back, she walked out from under him—the equivalent of "Nah, I'm not into that." He came back for seconds. She whipped her head around at him—a low-key warning. Third time: She whipped her head around and curled her lip. Fourth time: Izzy whipped her head around and snapped. The fifth time Mr. Humpy got on her back, Izzy threw herself into the air with a roar and drove him off, snapping and snarling. Nobody got hurt. "Wow," said Mr. Humpy's guardian. "Your dog sure is aggressive."

Roughly speaking, the more behaviorally healthy a dog is, the more relaxed that dog is in different kinds of circumstances, and the less likely to aggress. Also, a behaviorally healthy dog delivers warnings stepwise, starting with the gentlest and proceeding—if mild warnings go unheeded—to something more Technicolor and surround sound. Usually, matters stop short of bloodshed. That's what happened with Izzy and Mr. Humpy.

So behaviorally healthy dogs take most of life in stride, and they deliver warnings when they're pushed. Those two facts together help explain why it's best to respond without confrontation to a dog's growl or snap. First, underlying almost all aggression is stress—whether that's a huge stressor in the moment or an accumulation of small stressors over an hour or a day. Bear in mind that this is stress from the dog's point of view, and that many dogs *aren't* in perfect behavioral health. No matter how much you enjoy the toddler next door, if your dog growls at her you can take it as a given that he finds something about her presence distressful.

Second, if you punish your dog for growling or snapping, you've essentially punished him for warning you that he's close to the limit of what he can stand. If your punishment is perfectly calibrated, he may never growl or snap again. Now that cute toddler can pet your dog on the head and he'll hold still. But he's not feeling okay about it. What happens when the little kid, who doesn't know any better, pulls the dog's tail or sticks a finger in his ear or runs up to him when he's eating dinner? You, the child, and your dog may well get lucky and go the dog's whole life without finding out. But I'd rather not leave everybody's safety to luck.

An outright dog attack is an emergency, of course. You must do whatever it takes to protect yourself or others. But if your dog growls or

---

Dear Dog Trainer

Q. *Our family has a male Cockapoo, Bill. In the last few months, he's been growling at us—usually at my mother and me, but we're the ones who spend the most time with him. Usually when it happens to my mom it is at night, when she enters my room or my siblings'. My mother doesn't even touch him or go near him, but he growls fiercely. Thankfully, he's never bitten anyone, but we are worried this is going to happen soon.*

I can't find any pattern in when and where he growls at me. Either he doesn't warn me, or I can't read the signs. We've had Bill for quite a few years now and my mom is thinking about giving him away because of the fear of him one day biting someone.

A. An e-mail will never, ever, ever include all the information in the behavior history form I ask all clients to complete. But three things leap out at me here: (1) You've had Bill for "quite a few years"; (2) the growling just started in the last few months; (3) Bill growls when your mother enters a room at night. How old is Bill? And how are his eyesight and hearing? Whenever we see a distinct behavior change in an adult or older dog, the first thing we think is that some age-related change or an illness may be causing the problem. A dog whose hearing and sight have deteriorated, for example, may growl or snap when people approach because he's startled and maybe a bit disoriented. The same goes for canine cognitive disorder, a doggy analogue of Alzheimer's disease.

So your first step is to get Bill a thorough veterinary checkup, including tests of his vision and hearing. If sensory deterioration is the problem here, you may be able to set up a kind of early warning system for Bill when you approach. For instance, you could stamp on the floor at a distance so he knows you're coming.

snaps, or if you've caught one of those more subtle warning signs I mentioned earlier, your best bet is to back off. Exit the situation. Take a deep breath or fifty, enough for you and your dog both to settle down. And then think. What, exactly, were the circumstances around the behavior? And can you identify any new or old stressors in your dog's life? You and your dog need professional help, and the best thing you can do right now is to gather information.

Many dogs guard their food bowls, resting places, or favorite toys. Many are on edge around big, assertive men or erratically moving children. Did your dog get beaten up at the dog park that morning, then have to go to the vet, and did you just step on his foot while he was asleep? Did some ignorant trainer tell you to jerk on your dog's leash when he lunged at another dog on the street? Is your dog old and arthritic? Is that chronic ear infection flaring up? Does the aggressive behavior reflect a sudden change, or have you sorta kinda seen a problem coming but wanted to believe everything was fine? I strongly suggest making written notes. A detailed account of the aggressive episode is golden, whether your dog needs behavior modification or medical treatment or both. Meanwhile, prevent further rehearsals of the aggression—avoid the problem situation as much as you possibly can.

ADDITIONAL INFORMATION

See "Resource Guarding," below, for materials specific to that problem. For good general information about aggression, see the DVD *Dog Aggression: Biting,* by Ian Dunbar (James & Kenneth Publishers, 1998), and Pamela Dennison's *How to Right a Dog Gone Wrong* (Alpine, 2005).

For aggression between dogs, see the short book *Fight!,* by Jean Donaldson (Dogwise, 2004), and the DVD *Dog Aggression: Fighting* (James & Kenneth Publishers, 2006), by Ian Dunbar. Also see "Reactivity," below, for resources specific to that problem.

Children are bitten more often than any other people. See, for example, Carrie M. Shuler et al., "Canine and Human Factors Related to Dog Bite Injuries," *Journal of the American Veterinary Medical Association* 232, no. 4 (Feb. 15, 2008): 542–46.

Finally, Janis Bradley's *Dogs Bite: But Balloons and House Slippers Are More Dangerous* is indispensable for putting the whole problem of dog bites into perspective.

PERSISTENT LICKING (AND OTHER PERSISTENT BEHAVIORS)

Dogs lick the floor clean when we drop the yogurt; they lick their chops after they've eaten something tasty; they lick our faces, or try to, when we come home. Once, Izzy turned her head on a crowded sidewalk and licked the knee of a woman headed in the opposite direction. I've no idea what prompted her. She'd never done that before, and she never did it again.

It's not unheard of for a dog to like the taste or smell of lotion and seek to lick it off the skin of the person using it. And dogs crave attention; if they don't get enough while hanging around in a quiet, unobtrusive way, they often learn to get it by barking, stealing shoes, or engaging in other obnoxious behaviors, such as persistent licking.

But licking can be a sign of trouble, too. An example is Molly, a Golden Retriever one of my podcast listeners wrote to me about. Molly could be kept busy with a toy or chewy in her mouth. But otherwise she licked; if she wasn't licking people, she licked and groomed her paws. When one behavior takes up that much space in a dog's life, we can be sure that something's wrong.

MEDICAL CAUSES OF EXCESSIVE LICKING

Some of the possibilities are medical, so if your dog repetitively licks a particular body part or parts, get a vet check pronto. The dog version of hay fever—inhalant allergies to pollen, dust, grasses, even human dander—can make the skin miserably itchy. Other possible itch culprits include fungal and bacterial infections of the skin.[1] Persistent licking has also been associated with cancers, bone fractures, and pain caused by thorns or other objects stuck in the flesh.[2] Some veterinarians think there may be a link with chronic gastrointestinal distress. Worse yet, the licking can cause new medical problems. Dogs who lick one spot on their bodies over and over again often develop acral lick granuloma, a weeping sore that can reach all the way down to the bone.

STEREOTYPIES AND COMPULSIVE DISORDER

Not only did I never meet Molly, but also I'm not a veterinarian, so there's no way for me to know whether her licking started with or without a medical cause. But her history did suggest another possibility. Molly had spent much of her first two years chained to a concrete slab with a doghouse. The people whose legal property she was had gotten tired of her. It's no stretch to imagine that Molly was desperately lonely and bored. Under these conditions, she may have developed what's called a stereotypy—a single, nonfunctional behavior repeated over and over again.[3] Animals kept in sterile environments, where they can't meet their basic behavioral needs, commonly develop stereotypies. For example, you may have seen a lion or tiger endlessly pacing its barred concrete cage in an old-fashioned zoo. Stereotypies can take many forms, including feather plucking, ear pulling,[4] and overgrooming.

Stereotypies can change the animal's brain chemistry, and they don't necessarily evaporate when the animal enters a richer, more appropriate environment. At that point, the stereotypy qualifies as a compulsive disorder. A dog whose licking developed as a stereotypy might well keep licking even once she was in a good home with an enriched environment; the difference would be that she had more surfaces available to lick.

Of course, most dogs with compulsive disorders haven't spent years on a chain. Anxiety can play a part: thunderphobic dogs sometimes lick themselves compulsively and may develop lick granulomas as a result.[5] Many breeds have a genetic predisposition to specific forms of compulsive disorder: Mini Schnauzers repeatedly "check" their hindquarters, whereas Doberman Pinschers may suck their flanks. Some dogs snap at the air as if trying to catch invisible flies. Trainer lore has it that nobody should ever invite their Border Collie to chase a laser pointer unless they want him compulsively chasing any moving light. Stressful life changes, like those that come with a new baby, can set off problems even in apparently stable, happy dogs.[6]

If your dog licks or performs any other behavior more often than seems normal, get help right away—that gives you and your dog the best chance of success. Treatment for compulsive disorder generally combines medication, stress reduction, and a full, interesting life with plenty of mental and physical exercise. You can also learn to spot your dog's triggers so as to derail compulsive incidents before they start.

ADDITIONAL INFORMATION
Sharon L. Crowell-Davis, "Stereotypic Behavior and Compulsive Disorder," Oct. 2007. Available at http://bit.ly/lopAv8.

"Stereotypical Behavior: A LAREF [Laboratory Animal Refinement and Enrichment Forum] Discussion," edited and expanded by Viktor Reinhardt, moderator of LAREF. In *Laboratory Primate Newsletter* 43, no. 4 (Oct. 2004): 3–4. Available at http://www.brown.edu/Research/Primate/lpn43-4.pdf.

REACTIVITY (BARKING AND LUNGING) ON LEASH

Sometimes I think I'll scream if I see one more person yank the leash and snap, "No!" or hiss loudly when their dog barks and lunges at something or other on the street. In this section, I'll discuss barking and lunging at other dogs, but what I have to say applies to any situation in which your dog blows up.

At first blush, punishment seems to make sense. Your dog is acting like a jerk, maybe scaring people as well as other dogs; you can't let him get away with that kind of behavior.

Well, yes and no. *Of course* nobody wants their dog barking and lunging. It *is* sometimes scary. If your dog is strong and fast and catches you off guard, you can wind up with a sprained shoulder or face-planted on the sidewalk. I am not going to tell you that that is an acceptable way to live. I *am* going to tell you that punishment is not your best route to change.

Think about dog body language to see why. What does your dog look like when she's having a good time? Her face muscles are soft and her mouth is probably slightly open. Her ears might be up or back. Her eyes may be squinty. Her tail is sweeping softly back and forth or, if she's excited, she may be doing a full butt wiggle along with circle wags.

Now picture your dog blowing up at the spaniel mix across the street. Her lips curl in a snarl. She barks deep and loud. She flings herself forward, muscles tight, and her tail may be tensed over her back or tucked between her legs. Yup, sure looks like a good time! Don't you want some of what she's having?

As her body language makes clear, the dog barking and lunging on the end of her leash is freaking out. To suggest a human parallel: In New York City, we have these giant cockroaches we call water bugs, and if you brought one of them up close to me while I was on a leash I would be shrieking and foaming at the mouth until that thing was gone. Yes, you could punish me hard enough to make me stop—*but you couldn't punish me into feeling good about nearby water bugs*. And although you can punish your dog hard enough to shut down her explosion, you can't punish her hard enough to make her feel the world is peachy keen in proximity to other dogs. In fact, you're likelier to accomplish the opposite: "When dogs appear, my person yanks my neck."

So bark-and-lunge explosions are stressful for your dog as well as for you. In addition, from your dog's point of view the aggressive display seems to work pretty well—after all, the other dog always goes away. That means every time your dog blows up, he becomes a little likelier to try the same tactic next time. Until you can get good professional help, keep your dog out of trouble as much as you can.

Make it your business to notice the distance at which your dog starts to tense up. Several factors can affect it—the other dog's size, appearance, and behavior, for three. A big dog with a naturally high tail and an intense stare might as well have a target painted on him—and in fact, that intense stare suggests he's a little reactive himself. How many close encounters your dog has already had that day will affect his stress level and thus his propensity to blow. On the other hand, if he's relaxed after a long game of fetch, he may ignore a dog he'd otherwise find seriously provoking.

As you get to know your dog's patterns, it becomes easier to keep him far enough away that he can keep his cool. If you need to make a sudden U-turn, hide behind a parked car, or distract him with food tossed on the ground, then do it! Your job as your dog's guardian is to look out for his welfare, and that means helping him out of tough spots. If you're blindsided—say, a dog comes around the corner—and he does explode, then just hold that leash till you can get out of Dodge. I know it's embarrassing. I know some people will be happy to give you the evil eye and tell you you should scold or hurt your dog. Remember, this is damage control till you get help.

There are a couple of scientifically sound and humane approaches to behavior modification for reactive dogs. Desensitization and counter-conditioning is the first. In this process, you start with the mildest version of the problem stimulus that your dog will notice. As soon as your dog notices it, you deliver something your dog loves—usually this will be a superdeluxe treat—roast chicken, let's say. When desensitization and counterconditioning is done right, your dog learns that the sight of other dogs reliably predicts that roast chicken appears in his face. Over time he comes to tolerate or even look forward to the proximity of other dogs, because they are such excellent predictors of succulent dead bird.

The second approach is called the Constructional Aggression Treatment, or CAT. Elements of it have been around forever, but the behaviorists Jesús Rosales-Ruiz and Kellie Snider are responsible for formulating it in a systematic way. CAT's premises are two. One is that though aggressive displays may start in a moment of panic, dogs learn over time that aggression works. As I pointed out above, the other dog pretty much always goes away. The second premise is that most dogs are friendly in some contexts—so the trick is to teach your dog to import those friendly behaviors into the problem situation. In a CAT session, the learner dog is presented with a mild version of the problem stimulus—for the purposes of this book, another dog. As soon as the learner dog offers any nonaggressive behavior, the other dog moves farther away. In effect, the learner dog learns to drive dogs away by being nice to them. Paradoxically, at some point in the procedure, the learner dog may apparently get to like the other dog for real.

The third approach, developed by Grisha Stewart of Ahimsa Dog Training, is called Behavior Adjustment Training. It combines elements of CAT and desensitization/counterconditioning along with specific trained behaviors.

All these approaches are simple in principle, subtle in practice. How much a dog improves depends on many factors, including the trainer's sensitivity and skill, the reactive dog's resiliency and quickness to learn, and the guardian's willingness and ability to work hard. Also, many dogs benefit from appropriate behavioral medication—ideally, prescribed by a vet board-certified in this specialty.

ADDITIONAL INFORMATION
"Feisty Fido," by Patricia McConnell and Karen London, discusses on-leash aggression toward other dogs. Be sure to get the new (second) edition.

Constructional Aggression Treatment: Shaping Your Way Out of Aggression, by Jesús Rosales-Ruiz and Kellie Snider (DVD).

Organic Socialization: BAT for Aggression and Fear in Dogs, by Grisha Stewart (DVD).

Pos-4-ReactiveDogs (http://pets.groups.yahoo.com/group/Pos-4-ReactiveDogs) is a Yahoo! group devoted to, you guessed it, reactive dogs.

RESOURCE GUARDING

It's "resource guarding" when a dog stares briefly at another dog who approaches while she's on her favorite bed chewing her favorite chew. It's also "resource guarding" when a dog freezes, snarls, and launches himself at your torso if you approach while he's eating. And it's "resource guarding" when Dogalini gives Zippy a dirty look if Zippy approaches while you're petting Dogalini, or if when you pet Zippy, Dogalini trots up and pushes him away.

As you can see from those examples, resource guarding covers not only a variety of behaviors but also a wide spectrum of seriousness. It is normal dog social behavior to warn another dog off your goodies with a look or a lip curl; the socially appropriate response from the other dog is to abandon the attempt to get hold of those goodies. If the two dogs generally get along well and such encounters never, or only very rarely, escalate even as far as a quick scuffle, there's no call for humans to intervene.

On the other hand, most behavior specialists would prefer to prevent or undo even the mildest resource guarding against people. I'll discuss the guarding of food, but the points I'll make apply to anything a dog might guard.

Sometimes people tell me Bowser gets a little stiff if you come within six feet of his dinner, so they just leave Bowser alone when he's eating. And there is an argument to be made that such mild guarding is normal behavior—after all, an animal won't last long in the wild if anybody can just march right up and take his food away.

The trouble with applying that argument to dogs who live in human homes is, what if the three-year-old grandkid comes to visit and gets all in Bowser's face during kibble time? From Bowser's point of view, his polite warnings that this is *his* bowl, thank you very much, were ignored, so what could he do but escalate? From the toddler's point of view, all those stitches really, really hurt. And Bowser, of course, winds up dead.

Well-accepted, scientifically sound behavior modification can help the resource-guarding dog. Some trainers have used a version of the Constructional Aggression Treatment with success (see the previous section, "Reactivity," for more about CAT), but generally you should expect a variation on the theme of counterconditioning and desensitization. It works like this: Starting with the mildest possible version of the problem situation, you teach the dog that the problem isn't actually a problem at all, but rather a predictor of yummy treats. Over time, you build up the dog's comfort level till she can handle situations that reflect normal life. A dog who growls over her food bowl when people are six feet away can learn to greet human approach with happy, relaxed wags instead.

The catch is that, as always, it takes far longer to repair problem behavior than it does to install desirable behavior in the first place. (See Chapter 2, "Socialization," for info on how to prevent resource guarding.) And it's a truism that behaviors can't be guaranteed to leave the repertoire. Mainly we hope to see them move to a waaaay back burner.

With the help of the resources listed below, you may be able to repair a *mild* problem on your own. For serious resource guarding, especially if you have children, please get professional help. Meanwhile keep everyone safe—feed your dog in a quiet area of the house and leave him alone to eat. If he guards edible chews, either stop giving them or give them only under carefully controlled circumstances.

ADDITIONAL INFORMATION

Jean Donaldson, "Assessment and Treatment of Resource Guarding." *APDT Newsletter* [now *The APDT Chronicle of the Dog*], November/December 2002. Available at http://4pawsu.com/Donaldson.pdf.

Jean Donaldson, *Mine! A Guide to Resource Guarding in Dogs* (Kinship Communications/San Francisco SPCA, 2002). This is a standard guide to counterconditioning and desensitization procedures for resource-guarding dogs.

Pat Miller, *Positive Perspectives: Love Your Dog, Train Your Dog* (Dogwise, 2004) includes an excellent short discussion of resource guarding and a protocol for modifying the behavior.

Joan Orr and Teresa Lewin, "Resource Guarding." Especially helpful on the subject of children and resource guarding. Available at http://bit .ly/j1FMdh.

SEPARATION ANXIETY

So, your dog barks nonstop after you leave for work, or not quite nonstop: He pauses long enough to tear up the house and to pee and poop in the middle of the living room floor. "Uh-oh," you think, once you're finished tearing out your hair, "Zippy has separation anxiety."

Maybe, maybe not. The disorder we call separation anxiety ranges in flavor from mild to a super-triple-extreme form that some of my colleagues prefer to call separation panic. The common element is that the dog's behavior looks, as far as we non-telepathic types can see, like an expression of distress at being left alone. And that's the key—not frustration or boredom, but distress.

Here's a typical scenario. As you get ready for work, Zippy acts more and more restless. He follows you around the house, whining occasionally. Maybe he drools. On a smooth floor, you notice his paws leave sweaty prints. When you pick up your jacket and keys, Zippy slinks off to his bed and lies down, ignoring the smoked beef tendon you left for him there.

And when you get home—whether it's an hour or five hours later—Zippy goes wild with joy, as if you'd just appeared in a helicopter to lift him off the deck of the *Titanic*. He grabs the smoked tendon and prances around with it before settling in to chew. Suddenly it's a prize, though he didn't touch it all day. Then you notice the smell. Zippy never eliminates inside when you're home, but while you were gone he left loose stool all over the kitchen floor. Oh, and hire a handyman before the landlord notices the scratch and bite marks around your front windows. Zippy's gums and paw pads are raw.

Zippy's behaviors more than meet the criteria for separation anxiety, though not every dog with separation anxiety will act the way Zippy does. Here are some common signs:

- **Your dog shows anxiety and stress around your departure**. Zippy is restless and whiny; he follows you around, his paws sweat, and he drools. These are clear, specific signs of growing stress. Another dog might demonstrate anxiety by just lying down passively, as if giving up.
- **Your dog ignores food in your absence**. Zippy doesn't touch his chew while he's alone, though once you're home he makes it clear that yes, smoked beef tendon is important in Zippy World.
- **Your dog has accidents *when left alone***. Barring illness, Zippy doesn't eliminate indoors—except when he's alone, even for just an hour. (Note: Housetraining issues can coexist with separation anxiety. If your dog eliminates indoors while you're home as well as while you're out, the inappropriate elimination could result from separation distress in combination with housetraining problems, or from housetraining problems alone . . . or, of course, from some other problem that we're not considering here.)
- **Your dog tries to escape when left alone**. Zippy focused his energy on an exit route. And he took his project seriously: He tried so hard he hurt himself.
- **Your dog vocalizes when left alone**. I've made Zippy a silent sufferer, but if he made noise it would probably involve howling or panicked-sounding barks.

Zippy's case is somewhere in the middle of the separation anxiety bell curve. When I adopted her, my Isabella was close to the mild end. Unless her bowels were absolutely empty before we left, we'd find a little pile in the living room when we got home. And we always got the Hello of Crazed Joy. But Iz didn't have diarrhea and she never chewed or pawed the windows or doors.

At the other extreme are dogs who leave oceans of drool in their crates, break teeth and nails against the metal as they struggle to get out, then cut themselves to ribbons shattering a plate glass window to escape.

By contrast, a destructive, loud dog who's bored and full of beans will snarf that beef tendon right up and then look for a garbage bin to overturn. Chewing is likely to be directed toward pleasingly fragrant items such as TV remotes and leather shoes—though these sometimes draw the attention of anxious dogs as well. As for a bored and lonely dog, I'd expect a repetitive, monotone bark bark bark. It makes you sad while it drives you crazy. If your dog is getting amped about sounds in the hallway or sights on the street, expect flurries of explosive barking, with intervals of silence between.

A dog's history is revealing, too. When I meet a young, active dog who's taken up creative redecorating, I always ask about exercise and opportunities to chew. That young, energetic dog had better be getting a solid hour of aerobic exercise first thing in the morning, plus meals given as training rewards and in food-dispensing chewable toys. Otherwise, kiss your sofa and shoes goodbye.

I made my examples pretty unmistakable—unlike real life. Most of the behaviors associated with separation anxiety can also arise for other reasons, including medical reasons. A dog may bite at doors and windows as part of a frustrated territorial display toward dogs or people passing by. Or she may defecate in your absence because some sound she hears every day at 10:15 scares the living daylights out of her. Or she may suffer not only from separation anxiety but also from allergies that make her bite at her itchy paws. And anxious dogs are still individuals—two dogs with separation anxiety may show their distress in very different ways. So talk to your vet and a skilled behavior consultant. (If you work with a board-certified veterinary behaviorist, these may be the same person.)

Treatment for separation anxiety usually combines meds with behavior modification. What to prescribe is up to your vet.[7] Many clients are uncomfortable with psychoactive medication, but bear in mind that if your dog has separation anxiety, he or she is *suffering*. And the longer any behavior problem continues, the more entrenched it becomes. Anxiety-related disorders, in particular, just trash a dog's quality of life. I strongly believe we should throw everything we've got at them.

The gold standard in behavior modification involves changing a dog's associations with your departure activities and gradually accustoming her to longer and longer absences. We usually advise clients to keep greetings and departures low-key—when your dog acts woebegone or excited, it's best to keep your demeanor matter-of-fact. Dogs read our emotions closely, so it helps to send the message that comings and goings are no big deal.

Separation anxiety is associated with "Velcro dogs," the ones who follow you from room to room and always want to be resting at your feet or pressing their heads against your leg. So some behavior specialists also suggest independence training in various forms—for instance, practicing stays at a distance.

When you and your consultant discuss the plan for your dog, try to be realistic about how much time and effort you can put in. Behavior modification for separation anxiety is effective but can be laborious, and one study found that guardians did best with the simplest, least time-intensive plans.[8]

We don't quite know what causes separation anxiety. Often, it crops up after a move or a drastic change in schedule. For this reason, dog trainers and behavior specialists often advise clients to include time alone in their puppy or dog's normal routine. Separation anxiety is commoner among dogs adopted from shelters—but are they anxious because they did time in a shelter, or did their former owners give them up because they had separation anxiety? It's commoner among dogs owned by single people, but maybe dogs in large households spend less time alone, so their problems are masked. Are male or female dogs more prone to separation anxiety? Depends on which study you read.[9]

My own guess is that separation anxiety has deep evolutionary roots. Wolves, of course, live in stable, family-based groups. Feral dogs generally don't, but the species didn't part ways all that long ago. Dogs are obviously sociable and strongly bonded to their human companions. They also depend completely on us, but have no say in our comings and goings. What a surprise it would be if they didn't get worked up about the situation from time to time!

ADDITIONAL INFORMATION

Patricia McConnell's "I'll Be Home Soon!" (Dogwise, 2000), and Chapter 23, "Don't Leave Me!," in Pat Miller's *Positive Perspectives: Love Your Dog, Train Your Dog* (Dogwise, 2004).

SHYNESS

Is it nature or nurture? In general, it's both; behavior of all kinds can be genetically inflected and then shaped by experience—for instance, Border Collies are predisposed to a sequence of behaviors that makes it relatively easy to teach them to herd sheep. Nervous dogs and shy dogs can be deliberately bred. A famous experiment at the University of Arkansas produced two genetic strains of pointers. One strain is friendly and sociable; the other strain is fearful. The fearful dogs don't explore or even move around much and they freeze up when people come near. You won't be surprised to learn that they're also hard to train.[10]

The nervous pointers are an extreme case, because their condition has been purposely accentuated. They remind us, though, that dogs—like us—have a genetic predisposition somewhere in the range between super-shy and super-outgoing. We should also remember that "has a genetic basis" is generally not code for "can't be changed."

Nurture, the other piece of the puzzle, includes your dog's life experience and also her mother's. Do a Web search on "maternal stress" plus "effects on offspring" and you'll uncover dozens of studies on rats, mice, rhesus monkeys, and humans. The human studies are retrospective, of course, meaning that women are asked about what their lives were like when they were pregnant. But many stressors have been inflicted on pregnant nonhuman animals, from unpredictable noise to random temperature changes.[11] To oversimplify the findings of a huge body of research that I have no hope of mastering, if your mother experienced significant stress during pregnancy then you are likely to grow up more anxious and reactive than the average bear. Or rat or human or dog.

It's also been found that rats whose mothers spend a lot of time licking and grooming them are less fearful and release lower levels of stress hormones in novel situations than rats whose mothers aren't so big on the licking and grooming.[12] And rat pups who are handled grow up to behave less fearfully, even if their pregnant mother was stressed.[13]

In short, your dog has better odds of growing up confident and sociable if he had an affectionate mother who didn't suffer too much stress during pregnancy, and if neither parent's genetics predisposed them to be shy or anxious.

Abuse or other trauma, such as pain from being hit by a car, can surely affect a dog's behavior as well. I've had clients tell me they suspect their shy dog was abused by, say, a man with a beard, because she hides behind the client's leg whenever bearded men appear. But trainers and behavior specialists generally believe that undersocialization is the likelier villain. In Amish, Hasidic, and hipster communities, you see a lot of beards; elsewhere, not so much. It's not that a puppy has to be exposed to men with beards, or else she grows up scared of them. Rather, a fearful response to sights and sounds that are relatively uncommon suggests a puppyhood with limited experience of the wide range of perfectly fine things in the world.

Shyness and fear are hard to shake under the best of circumstances, whereas fearful responses are easily learned. And the more time your dog spends feeling anxious or fearful, the deeper that anxious groove gets worn. So, as much as you can, protect your shy dog from things that scare her. Trainers and behaviorists use the concept of "threshold," meaning the point at which an animal just barely becomes alert to something that worries or upsets her. She might watch whatever it is, or breathe faster, or hold her breath, or give some other sign that she's less than 100 percent relaxed and happy. That's your cue to create more distance between your dog and the object of her alertness. If you live in an urban environment or if your dog is afraid of many things, you may not be able to avoid them all. Do the best you can.

After that, it probably goes without saying that you shouldn't push your dog to engage. Nor should you use food to lure her to approach something that scares her. If your offer of a treat frequently predicts situations in which she's pressured to approach scary things, you can even wind up with a dog who's afraid of treats.

You *can* feed superdeluxe treats at a distance where she's just become aware of the scary thing. This process is called counterconditioning: basically, creating a better emotional association for your dog. You turn the scary thing into a solid predictor that deluxe treats are coming, and by doing that you turn it into a not-scary thing. In behavior modification, counterconditioning is usually paired with desensitization, the process of diminishing the intensity of the dog's emotional response. Counterconditioning and desensitization are pretty simple in principle but subtle in practice; for best success, they depend on carefully controlled exposures to the scary thing, and on equally careful attention to the dog's responses, so that she is never pushed past what she can comfortably handle. If your dog has significant fears, work with a pro.

Although you shouldn't push your dog, you can encourage her. Say she's eyeballing a garbage can that's suspect because it's not in its usual place. You know her signals well and you can see that she's just teetering on the verge of worry. Try softly playful, silly talk—"Oh, my goodness, will you get a load of that garbage can? How dare it move like that?"—and then take her away from it. Dogs are exquisitely sensitive to human emotion, so in marginal situations we can often help them by taking a happy, playful tone. Keep the excitement level down, though, because excitement and fear are two sides of the same physiological coin.

Suppose one day your fearful dog chooses to investigate that nomadic garbage can. Calmly praise and encourage this exploration, while never pushing it. Once your dog's done, she's done; take her away. When an experience like this is going well, even professionals are often tempted to try "just one more time," and that's invariably when a truck backfires at the moment the brave dog sniffs the garbage can. Avoid the exploding-garbage-can effect. Always quit while your dog's ahead.

Use caution if your dog is sniffing and checking out a person who worries her. People who like dogs have a terrible time with the idea that a dog might be afraid of them; they say, "Dogs love me!" and "I've got a way with dogs," and then they bend over the dog and try to moosh her ears. If your shy dog has stepped outside her comfort zone, then human behavior like this will, at best, scare her. At worst, it can elicit a bite.

Shy and fearful dogs are often a bit inflexible or brittle; they do okay with predictable, familiar patterns, but fall to pieces when objects appear out of place or humans make sudden movements or there's a change in your household. So help your anxious dog by establishing clear routines and by directing her behavior through reward-based training. You can let a sociable, relaxed dog meet visitors without any choreography (though you may want to teach him to keep all four feet on the ground when saying hi). On the other hand, an anxious dog might feel more at ease if you carefully teach her that the doorbell is a cue to lie on her bed and stay there instead of trying to make doggy small talk.

I hesitate over human analogies, but I think it's fair to say that predictability eases your dog's worries in the same way that being dressed right and knowing what fork to use for the salad makes us less anxious about formal dinners.

If your shy or anxious dog has some confident, relaxed dog friends, try walking them together. There's evidence that an anxious animal's fears can be eased by the presence of nonfearful companions.[14] So if your dog's pals look up when they hear a truck backfire, but then immediately return to their close study of the nearest hydrant, your dog may be able to relax too, at least to some extent. These effects may not hold up when your dog's relaxed friends aren't there, and it's not likely that they'll spontaneously spread to other contexts. Still, every good experience will improve your dog's quality of life. And even a tiny confidence-building effect at least points in the right direction.

Finally, try "dog-appeasing pheromone." This manufactured version of a pheromone secreted by nursing mother dogs is supposed to ease anxiety. It's sold under the brand name Comfort Zone, and you can get it as a plug-in diffuser and also as a spray that you can put on a collar or bandanna. It's no miracle cure, but it's not expensive and there is fairly good experimental evidence that it helps some dogs.[15] By the way, I can just barely smell *something* if I plaster my nose to the diffuser, so don't worry that it'll stink up your house.

Recommendations are often made for the product called Anxiety Wrap and for flower remedies, aromatherapy, the massage-like Tellington TTouch, and on and on. Many of my colleagues swear by these, but as far as I've been able to learn there's no objective evidence to support the efficacy of any of them, except perhaps the scent of lavender.[16]

You should work with a professional if your dog has intense fears or is afraid of many things. The trainer may also wish to refer you to a board-certified veterinary behaviorist, because the right medication can relieve your dog's anxiety and maximize his progress.

ADDITIONAL INFORMATION

See "Reactivity," p. 226, for more information about the Constructional Aggression Treatment and Behavior Adjustment Training, two scientifically grounded training techniques that can be adapted for work with fearful dogs. For the "Look at That" game, useful for many anxious dogs, see Leslie McDevitt, *Control Unleashed: Creating a Focused and Confident Dog* (Clean Run Productions, 2007). Leslie McDevitt's Web site is http://controlunleashed.net.

The ASPCA's excellent "Virtual Pet Behaviorist" site, http://www.aspcabehavior.org, includes a good article about counterconditioning and desensitization. While I disagree that it is always necessary to consult a Certified Applied Animal Behaviorist or a board-certified veterinary behaviorist, it's true that dog trainers are insufficiently professionalized; evaluate prospective hires carefully, as explained at the beginning of this chapter.

The Fearful Dogs website, http://fearfuldogs.com, offers many helpful resources.

Nicole Wilde's book *Help for Your Fearful Dog: A Step-by-Step Guide to Helping Your Dog Conquer His Fears* (Phantom Publishing, 2006) has much to offer, but unfortunately includes chapters on homeopathy, flower remedies, and other modalities that have either been thoroughly debunked or for which the evidence is feeble at best. Go with the solid behavior tips and skip the woo.

There's a Yahoo! group, Shy-K9s, devoted to shy dogs, with good discussions of how to manage them and modify their behavior. Plus, you can't beat the emotional support factor—life with a shy dog can be difficult.

THUNDERSTORM PHOBIA

Why thunderstorm phobia? The best answer may be "Why not?" All animals learn certain fears more readily than others—many people are afraid of snakes, not many of postcards. Probably, evolutionary history primes organisms to learn to fear things that can harm them. Storms are dangerous: Getting wet can lead to hypothermia; heavy rains can cause flash floods; and there's always the chance of being struck by lightning. A quick escape to shelter ups the odds of surviving to reproduce. And the startle response to sudden, loud bangs is probably inborn.[17] Outright phobia of thunderstorms is the extreme case of a behavior that makes evolutionary sense. Unfortunately, such phobias are not only easy to develop, they're hard to shake.[18]

The standard therapy for fears is counterconditioning and desensitization. You start desensitization by exposing your learner to the frightening stimulus in its mildest possible form. A human who's terrified of flying might look at a picture of a plane. For dogs, we usually countercondition by pairing the scary thing with a superspecial treat. When the dog learns that a mild form of the scary thing reliably predicts the deluxe treat, she starts acting pleased by the scary thing. The trainer increases the scary thing's intensity bit by bit, always waiting for the dog to look relaxed and happy before the next step.

With thunderstorms, two factors may undermine success. First, counterconditioning and desensitization largely depend on avoiding random exposures to the scary thing. If you can control thunderstorms, a lot of dog behavior folks would love to hear from you. Second, a thunderstorm isn't just one thing. It includes a darkening sky; humid air; the smell of ozone; changes in barometric pressure; wind and rain; lightning; and thunder, including thunder so distant humans can't hear it. We can sort of replicate some of these, but not all—and what we can't replicate, we can't work with systematically.

There aren't any published studies of behavior modification alone, though, so my statements are based on my impressions and those of other behavior consultants. Few interventions for thunder phobia have been studied scientifically, few or no studies have been repeated, and what studies there are include only small numbers of dogs. Still, they offer the best information we have.

Say your dog is only mildly anxious, maybe a little restless, before and during storms. He responds to your cues, he'll eat, and he doesn't shake, salivate, or try to hide. If he also has a game that he just loves, try a fix of play. The minute you're aware that a storm is coming, bring out the ball or the tug toy. If you throw a play party whenever there's a storm, your dog may learn that storms predict good times.[19]

But you won't always be home when a storm comes, and every episode of anxiety makes it likelier the anxiety will worsen. So if you don't see clear improvement after a couple of storms, or if your dog is highly anxious, get a competent specialist to help you, and go to the intervention I recommend for almost all thunderphobic dogs: the gradual exposure and treats of counterconditioning and desensitization *plus* antianxiety medications prescribed by your vet. When this one-two punch was studied, 30 of 32 dogs improved at least somewhat.[20] Two people in the study reported that their dog's storm phobia was gone. At a four-month follow-up, the improvements had held. You'll notice these results aren't spectacular—though most dogs improved, almost none seem to have been "cured."

You may see melatonin recommended for thunder phobia. Many people, including me, have the impression that it helps their dogs, but whoops, no scientific studies exist. Melatonin may be worth trying; talk to your vet first, of course.

In a preliminary study of "dog-appeasing pheromone" (brand name Comfort Zone), nine out of twelve dogs treated with pheromone plus behavior modification showed some improvement, as reported by the owners.[21] These numbers are tiny; on the other hand, Comfort Zone is pretty cheap. I would try it.

A newish product is the Storm Defender cape, lined with metallic lamé. This is less crazy than it sounds. A veterinary behaviorist at Tufts hypothesized some years ago that pain from static electricity may contribute to thunder phobia;[22] the point of the lamé is to prevent static buildup. A 2009 study found that about two-thirds of dogs wearing Storm Defenders showed some improvement, according to their owners.[23] But—and how baffling is this?—so did about two-thirds of dogs wearing fake Storm Defenders, which looked like the real ones but minus the lamé. That might be the placebo effect at work or the owners' perceptions. Or maybe the owners' body language changed and in turn changed the dogs' behavior. Or maybe it just helps dogs to wear a cape during storms. Who doesn't feel stronger and more dashing in a cape?

While you're dressing your dog up and giving him antianxiety meds, cut out as many features of the storm as you can. Draw curtains, close windows, turn on the AC, or play soft music. If your dog wants to hide in the bathroom or sit next to you, let her. Debate rages over the effect of comforting your dog by petting and talking to her. The attitude that you and your dog have to be tough guys is laughable or sad A calm, encouraging friend can help us through an anxious hour.

ADDITIONAL INFORMATION

You may find value in the DVD *Dog Behavior, Medicine, and Training: Storm and Other Phobias,* by Nicholas Dodman (Tawzer, 2009). Some people have found the Thundershirt wrap (http://www.thundershirt .com/) and the CD *Through a Dog's Ear* (http://www.throughadogsear .com/) helpful for their dogs. To countercondition the sounds of a storm, there's the *Sounds Good Audio CD—Thunderstorms* (Legacy Canine Behavior and Training, 2004).

Conclusion

13

WHAT HAPPENED TO JUNIPER, AND HOW

When we left Juniper, he had just pinned his first puppy playmate. After that, things went from bad to worse. He got thrown out of puppy class for staring and picking fights. If I gave him unrestrained access to puppies, he usually bowled them down and then stood over them, growling, until they had lain still for a while, and then he would stiffly step away. I got some bad advice. Keep taking him to the dog park; he'll learn. Punish his behavior toward puppies; he'll learn. What do you mean there's a problem here? He acts like a perfectly normal pup.

I sympathize with my clients' denial, because every time Juniper had a positive interaction with a puppy I breathed a sigh of relief and told myself everything would be okay. Besides, Juni was a peach in so many ways. He was friendly and affectionate toward every person he met. Children, the bane of many dogs, were targets for wiggly wags. Street noises didn't bother him. I had started clicker training him the night we brought him home and I remember my pride when an older woman who'd trained dogs only in old-school ways expressed amazement at his attentiveness to me as I walked him on leash: "*How* old did you say he was?" Three months.

Juni's behavior with older dogs could only be called wormlike; he wiggled up to them almost on his belly and licked their faces till they got fed up and snapped him away. I didn't yet understand the significance of this. He kept going after puppies. The older he got, the higher the upper age limit on his victims; Juni was getting big and refining his performance.

An edge crept into his behavior toward Izzy. He wouldn't leave her alone. Izzy adored puppies, and her patience with him was inexhaustible. When we visited friends and their dog, Mercy, walked past while he was eating, Juni lunged and snapped at her. Mild resource guarding between dogs is normal, but it was worrisome for a puppy less than six months old to guard food so intensely against an adult dog. He started guarding food against Izzy, too. One day when I handed her a treat, he attacked her; in the ensuing fight, she put a few holes in his face. I tossed him in his crate and wept. He was six months old; I was pretty sure he wasn't going to make it to a year. One of his siblings had already been euthanized, for aggression toward people. Though aggression toward people and aggression toward dogs aren't linked, it wasn't a good omen.

I felt I had only a few hopeful signs. As explosive as Juni was, his aggression was mostly a sound-and-light show. He still loved all people. He was able to socialize peacefully with other dogs, even puppies, if he was introduced to them in a careful, controlled way, one small step at a time. Sarah and I agreed that if he ever injured Izzy seriously we would euthanize him, but meanwhile we'd keep trying.

I had a phone consultation with a trainer who couldn't have been nastier to me but who gave me a workable plan for defusing Juniper's aggression toward Izzy around food. Transitions and exciting moments were "hot"—for instance, Juni might attack Izzy when Sarah came home from work. (Nowadays I would say that a dog like him has trouble regulating arousal.) As his resource guarding improved, I was able to use food to reward him for going to particular spots and staying there during volatile times. We found that a Comfort Zone pheromone diffuser seemed to help him stay calm as well; sometimes Juni even went and sniffed it, which we called "saying hi to Mom." Finally, finally, I bought a clue and stopped bringing him to the dog park. Not only was it unfair to the dogs he jumped and frightened, but also I came to understand the emotional underpinnings of his behavior and to see that he was overwhelmed. His bullying of dogs his age and younger was the flip side of his obsequiousness toward adults. Both behaviors reflected his extreme social anxiety. This also explained why slow, careful introductions went so well: They gave Juni time to get past his initial feeling of threat.

My experiences with Muggsy and Izzy had already sparked my interest in training and in behavioral work. As I developed more skill in managing Juniper, I found I wanted to go further. I apprenticed with a local trainer, Barbara Giella, attending client interviews and preparing plans for less challenging cases. I read behavior texts and participated in e-mail discussions of aggression and general training. My mentor began giving me clients to work with on my own, with her as backup expert. I started learning to see where problem behaviors could be nudged in a better direction, or how a dog's fears might be eased. A client who was moving asked how she could make the process of packing less stressful for her very skittish dog. Was I thrilled when she told me how much it had helped to scatter cardboard boxes around her apartment and encourage her dog to investigate and play with them.

By the time he was a year old, Juni's attacks on Izzy had pretty much ceased, though I still gave him a time-out whenever I thought he was playing too roughly with her. To attend off-leash hours in the park was out of the question, but he desperately needed aerobic exercise, so I occasionally brought him to an isolated area, keeping a 50-foot line attached to his collar so that I could restrain him if need be. If I threw a ball for him he chased it down and then pranced around with it in his mouth instead of bringing it back for another throw. We practiced over and over having him give me the ball and then get it back again as a reward, gradually working up to short throws and then longer ones until the game we were playing was fetch instead of keep-away. Later I learned that this method of teaching, which starts with the last step in a linked series of behaviors and then works backward through the preceding steps, is called backchaining. Sophisticated trainers use it all the time; unsophisticated trainers, like me, have to reinvent the wheel.

I couldn't get enough of learning about dogs. I found seminars and workshops to go to; I mustered all my courage to attend the introductory trainer academy taught by one of my heroes, Pat Miller. Pat is a former president of the Association of Pet Dog Trainers, the author of many training and behavior books, and a powerful advocate of nonviolent dog training. A year after we adopted Izzy, when I'd read everything the public library had to offer and taught my new dog some tricks, I had thought of myself as pretty expert. My ego had gotten even bigger after Muggsy's rehabilitation went so well. Five and a half years later, though, when Juniper was four years old, I knew for sure I was an utter ignoramus about dogs, and my only excuse for taking people's money was that I was maybe, just maybe, a little less of an ignoramus than I used to be.

Fast-forward. Another sibling of Juni's was euthanized. This was the brother who most resembled him, and who had been raised by an honest-to-God dog expert. His aggression toward people kept escalating in spite of his guardian's wise and careful work with him. From this and from what I learned of Juni's other littermates, it certainly seemed his behavior had a genetic component, or at least a biological one. My boy still needed great care around dogs other than Izzy and a select few others, but his lively friendliness toward people never changed; somehow he'd dodged that bullet.

I kept working on his dog-dog social skills, but life in Brooklyn made it two steps forward, one and a half steps back. In behavior modification, we work hard to protect the dog from more intense exposure than he's ready to handle to whatever the problem is; in the city, where there's no such thing as a rousing game of fetch in your fenced backyard, controlled exposure to dogs was a lost cause. We'd meet a dog coming around a blind corner, or off leash where off-leash dogs weren't supposed to be; Juni would bark and snarl and lunge, and some portion of our hard work would be undone. Yet, all in all, he was fairly easy to live with now. He was even able to attend a clicker workshop at Pat Miller's with me, and when I took Pat's weeklong behavior modification seminar, he was my practice dog.

Fast-forward again. It was late 2007 or early 2008, and Professor Jesús Rosales-Ruiz, of the University of North Texas, his graduate student Kellie Snider, and the "Constructional Aggression Treatment" were all the buzz. CAT joined well-established behavior modification techniques with the insight that if a dog knows how to offer friendly social signals in one context, she can learn to use those same friendly signals in another—even in a context where she has previously learned to aggress. Rosalez-Ruiz and Snider had worked out a procedure for teaching dogs how to make scary things go away by acting friendly instead of by stiffening, snarling, lunging, and barking.[1] It seemed as if for at least some dogs they worked with, "acting friendly" had even turned into "feeling friendly, for reals." Could it be?

Pat, who was by now my friend and colleague as well as my teacher, wanted to try CAT but didn't care to experiment on a paying client. I leaped to volunteer Juniper. We blocked out a weekend. I can't remember how I felt at the time; probably hopeful, but trying not to be.

CAT didn't go so well at first. On the video of our initial session, Juni looks like a dog losing his mind. It needs to be said that we weren't doing the procedure right; we were constrained by space, by the need and desire to record this experiment, and also by Juniper himself: When Kellie Snider watched the video, she told Pat that Juniper was among the most difficult dogs she'd ever seen. I'm not quite sure how to feel about that! Anyway, we persevered. And . . . Juni got it. He started offering sociable signals to first one dog, and then another, and then another. On the third day of our long weekend, Juni was offering appropriate, sociable signals to five different dogs, which was about twice as many as ever before. (He was *tolerant* of many dogs, but there's a sea of difference between tolerance and friendliness.)

Back home, I enlisted my saintly dog walker, Meg, who with her other clients' permission provided dog after dog after dog for me to practice with. (It's important to note that, because of the progress Juni had already made, these dogs were never subjected to aggressive displays.) I kept logs of Juniper's behavior and although we had our bark-lunge moments, over time not only did he not regress, he continued to improve. More and more often I saw him look at other dogs with curiosity and interest instead of with the hard stare and stiff body language that are the first stages of an aggressive response.

I don't think Juni will ever be able to mingle at random with unknown dogs. But today, more than three years after we first did CAT, he can almost always pass dogs on the street with either indifference or friendly interest or at most a long look. When we meet a new dog, he greets them appropriately, although usually with some tension; more and more often, he initiates play with them. Mind you, his play style is clumsy and dorky and in general the opposite of slick, but *play!*

Juni also continues to love children, Hasidic rabbis in big fur hats, skinny white ladies in oversize sunglasses, homeless people pushing shopping carts, the truck drivers who coo over him when we stay in motels, the schizophrenic woman in our neighborhood who pets him and calls him Moose and uses him as a bridge to talk with me . . . and, well, everybody, including people I'm not so wild about myself.

If it seems as though the improvements in Juni's behavior took a long time and aren't finished—well, that's so. Not only did he come right out of the wrapper with problems, but also I made mistakes with him that I would not make again. Hindsight is 20/20. I should have kept him out of the dog park, where he was emotionally overwhelmed and where he consequently practiced aggressing over and over and over again. (I bear a heavy weight of responsibility for the dogs he frightened.) I should never have punished him; what good can that have done a puppy who was, when it came right down to it, freaking out? I should have recognized his cringing, wormy behavior toward adult dogs as the sign of social anxiety that it was. I should have concentrated on careful, controlled, one-on-one introductions to friendly dogs, to help him build up his canine social skills and confidence. All these shoulds. Many of my clients suffer from similar guilt and shame.

A difficult dog can distort your life; I used to walk in the park every morning with a group of friends and their dogs. Juni made that impossible, and I won't be able to do it again until he is dead and I have another dog, one less troubled than he. Some of my clients tell me they haven't had anyone over to their apartment in years. An acquaintance with a remarkably "interesting" dog asked me just the other day about boot camp insta-cures. Unfortunately, real-life behavior change is a matter of patience and slogging and documenting your progress to remind yourself how far you've come. And sometimes persevering isn't the right choice.

I persevered with Juni because as troubled as his behavior was, the trouble was limited in scope and I felt, very unscientifically indeed, that he was sticking with me too. There was never a more affectionate dog, or one who looked sillier having the zoomies. He sometimes follows our cats around, trying to sniff their bums. He will learn any trick as fast as I can teach it to him. Faster.

At a certain point—maybe he was four years old, maybe five or six—I realized that things had already been as bad as they were ever going to get. From here on in, barring some weird neurological disorder or a brain tumor kicking in, we were coasting. Then CAT came along, and it turned out "coasting" wasn't nearly optimistic enough.

Izzy died, old, frail, tottery, and sweet, in May 2010, at home, eating a big bowl of ice cream and falling asleep as the sedative took effect. We crated Juni during the euthanasia so he wouldn't try to eat the ice cream. Afterward he came downstairs, sniffed Izzy's body, asked for and got some ice cream, said hi to our vet, and then got on the sofa with the vet tech and climbed into his lap.

Juni has long since stopped giving me cause for tears, but there's never a day when he doesn't make me laugh.

Notes and Sources

1. So Many Dogs, So Little Time: How to Choose the Right Dog

1. The complete list of AKC-recognized breeds is at http://akc.org/breeds/complete_ breed_list.cfm; the page provides links to the official breed standard and to further information. Read with caution.

2. See I. R. Reisner, K. A. Houpt, and F. S. Shofer, "National Survey of Owner-Directed Aggression in English Springer Spaniels," *Journal of the American Veterinary Medical Association* 227, no. 10 (2005): 1594–1603. The abstract is at http://ncbi.nlm.nih.gov/ pubmed/16313036. Survey-based research is always problematic, but the abstract includes some information that will help you up your odds of finding an ESS minus the unfortunate genetic baggage.

3. Dachshund Club of America FAQ, s.v. "Do they have any funny habits?," accessed June 10, 2010, http://dachshund-dca.org/faq.html#habits. The DCA also knows why dogs do this, although scientists don't.

4. Historically, the idea of breed purity has been linked with the idea of racial purity, so I find the term "purebred" distasteful. See Mark Derr, "The Ugliness of Beauty," in *Dog's Best Friend: Annals of the Dog-Human Relationship* (Henry Holt, 1997), especially 215ff.

5. A list of breed-specific health concerns appears at http://www.akcchf.org/canine-health/breed-specific-concerns. Also see the Web site of the Canine Genetic Diseases Network, http://caninegeneticdiseases.net; Dr. Jeffrey Bragg, "Purebred Dog Breeds into the Twenty-first Century: Achieving Genetic Health for Our Dogs," http://sirius dog.com/genetic-health-dogs-bragg.htm; the Web site of the UK Royal Society for the Prevention of Cruelty to Animals, http://rspca.org.uk, with a link to the RSPCA report on the health of pedigreed dogs; Michael D. Lemonick, "A Terrible Beauty," *Time*, Dec. 12, 1994; Jean Dodds, DVM, "Guide to Hereditary and Congenital Diseases in Dogs," http://siriusdog.com/hereditary-congenital-diseases-dog.htm.

6. RSPCA report, 21. (As far as I have been able to learn, no similar research has been done in the United States.)

7. This is the problem faced by cheetahs, for example. There's a good discussion at http:// evolution.berkeley.edu/evolibrary/news/070701_cheetah.

8. For the Dalmatians and outcrossing, see Mary Straus, "Guaranteed Stone-Free Dalmatians? Yes!," *The Whole Dog Journal*, June 2010, 4. Straus detailed the UK and U.S. breed clubs' opposition in a follow-up, "Update on 'Low Uric Acid' Dalmatians," *The Whole Dog Journal*, January 2011, 4.

9. "Researchers Seek Cause of Intervertebral Disk Disease in Dachshunds," *Purina Pro Club Dachshund Update* 1, no. 1 (July 2007). Available at http://bit.ly/lAxaHo.

10. According to the Orthopedic Foundation for Animals, 72 percent of 485 Bulldogs evaluated between January 1974 and December 2010 had hip dysplasia (http://www.offa .org/stats_hip.html). Among Boston Terriers, English Bulldogs, and French Bulldogs, the rate of births by cesarean section was over 80 percent; see Katy M. Evans and Vicki J. Adams, "Proportion of Litters of Purebred Dogs Born by Caesarean Section," *Journal of Small Animal Practice* 51, no. 2 (Feb. 2010): 113–18. For digestive problems, see, for example, Valérie Freiche, DVM, and Cyrill Poncet, DVM, "Upper Airway and Gastrointestinal Syndrome in Brachycephalic Dogs," *Veterinary Focus* 17, no. 2 (2007): 4–10.

  See also Nicola Rooney and David Sargan, "Pedigree Dog Breeding in the UK: A Major Welfare Concern?," independent scientific report commissioned by the Royal Society for the Prevention of Cruelty to Animals in 2008. Both the full text and the executive summary are available at http://rspca.org.uk/allaboutanimals/pets/dogs/health/ pedigreedogs.

11. Ibid.

12. See notes 11, 12, and 13 to Chapter 12, "Stuff Dogs Do That Worries People," for some of the background on maternal stress.

13. See, for instance, Kimberly J. Sandino, "Behavioral Genetics and Child Temperament," *Journal of Developmental and Behavioral Pediatrics* 26, no. 3 (June 2005): 214–23, for a review of studies of humans.

14. There are no reliable national statistics, only guesstimates. A study by the National Council on Pet Population Study and Policy (http://petpopulation.org/statsurvey .html) covers the years 1994–1997 and, as the NCPPSP points out, has significant limitations. (That's not to say anyone else could have done any better; there are huge difficulties in collecting such data—see http://americanhumane.org/animals/stop-animal-abuse/ fact-sheets/animal-shelter-euthanasia.html.) As a sample, in 2007 New York City's municipal shelter system euthanized 15,768 cats and dogs (http://nycacc.org/images/ 2007Charts.jpg); this represents a *decline* of 55 percent over eight years.

  The NCPPSP has prepared a brief paper highlighting reasons that animals are relinquished (http://petpopulation.org/exploring.pdf). Whether people's stated reasons can be taken at face value is an open question: When people give up animals because they're moving (the Number 1 reason for dogs, Number 3 for cats), is the bond already weakened by some other household problem, so that the move provides a pretext? And what constraints inflect the decision? I would never voluntarily move to a place where I couldn't take my animals, but what would I do if I also had kids and the alternative was homelessness?

15. For example, this Canine Behavior Evaluation—http://sheltermedicine.vet.cornell.edu/ behavior/documents/CanineBehaviorEvaluationForm.pdf—based on a procedure developed by Sue Sternberg, and the SAFER "canine aggression assessment tool" (http:// emilyweiss.com/safer.html).

16. E'Lise Christensen et al., "Aggressive Behavior in Adopted Dogs That Passed a Temperament Test," *Applied Animal Behaviour Science* 106 (2007): 85–95.

17. Kelley S. Bollen and Joseph Horowitz, "Behavioral Evaluation and Demographic Information in the Assessment of Aggressiveness in Shelter Dogs," *Applied Animal Behaviour Science* 112 (2008): 120–35.

18. Bollen and Horowitz, "Aggressiveness in Shelter Dogs." See also Barbara Robertson, "Dog Is in the Details," *The Bark,* spring 2004, http://thebark.com/content/dog-details.

2. Socialization: The One Thing to Do If You Do Nothing Else at All

1. A sampling of articles: R. S. Clarke, "Individual Differences in Dogs: Preliminary Report on the Effects of Early Experience," *Canadian Journal of Psychology* 5, no. 4 (1951): 150–56; William R. Thompson and Woodburn Heron, "The Effects of Early Restriction on Activity in Dogs," *Journal of Comparative and Physiological Psychiatry* 47, no. 1 (1954): 77–82; Ronald Melzack, "The Genesis of Emotional Behavior: An Experimental Study of the Dog," *Journal of Comparative and Physiological Psychiatry* 47, no. 2 (1954): 166–68; Ronald Melzack and William R. Thompson, "Effects of Early Experience on Social Behavior," *Canadian Journal of Psychology* 10, no. 2 (1956): 82–90. Most or all are available in full text on the Internet; the easiest way to find them is to head for Google Scholar and search on the titles.

    The seminal work on puppy development and behavior is John Paul Scott and John L. Fuller, *Dog Behavior: The Genetic Basis* (originally published as *Genetics and the Social Behavior of the Dog*) (University of Chicago Press, 1965), which reports a long-term study that included various degrees of isolation and social interaction, and which also describes the work of other researchers. The discussion on pages 175–82 is especially relevant.

2. For the record, this doesn't make the dog (or the person!) racist. See Raina Kelley's superb discussion of this issue: "Your Dog Isn't Racist," *Newsweek,* July 2, 2010, http://www.newsweek.com/2010/07/02/your-dog-isn-t-racist.html.

3. M. R. Shyan, K. A. Fortune, and C. King, "Bark Parks: A Study on Interdog Aggression in a Limited-Control Environment," *Journal of Applied Animal Welfare Science* 6, no. 1 (2003): 25–32. Discussed in Karen Perusek, "A Review of Shyan . . . ," *The APDT Chronicle of the Dog,* Nov.–Dec. 2010, 14–15.

3. Anything but "Obedience": The Whys and Hows of Building a *Cooperative* Dog

1. The classic article on learned helplessness is Steven F. Maier and Martin E. Seligman, "Learned Helplessness: Theory and Evidence," *Journal of Experimental Psychology: General* 105, no. 1 (1976): 3–46. The Wikipedia article on learned helplessness is at http://en.wikipedia.org/wiki/Learned_helplessness.

2. L. David Mech, "Leadership in Wolf, *Canis lupus,* Packs," *Canadian Field-Naturalist* 114, no. 2 (2000): 259–63, http://www.npwrc.usgs.gov/resource/mammals/leader/index.htm.

3. For example, see this series of photos: http://youtube.com/watch?v=nw3q3FIv4SU.

4. Douglas Smith, quoted in Claudia Dreifus, "A Conversation with Douglas Smith: Following the Wolves, Number by Number," *The New York Times,* July 22, 2003.

5. Roberto Bonanni, Simona Cafazzo, Paola Valsecchi, and Eugenia Natoli, "Effect of Affiliative and Agonistic Relationships on Leadership Behaviour in Free-Ranging Dogs," *Animal Behaviour* 79 (2009): 981–91. Other essential reading: James Serpell, ed., *The Domestic Dog: Its Evolution, Behaviour, and Interactions with People* (Cambridge University Press, 1995); P. Jensen, ed., *The Behavioural Biology of Dogs* (CABI, 2007); Raymond Coppinger and Lorna Coppinger, *Dogs: A Startling New Understanding of Canine Origin, Behavior, and Evolution* (Scribner, 2001); and Ádám Miklósi, *Dog Behaviour, Evolution, and Cognition* (Oxford University Press, 2007).

6. A fascinating paper on this subject is John W. S. Bradshaw, Emily J. Blackwell, and Rachel A. Casey, "Dominance in Domestic Dogs—Useful Construct or Bad Habit?" *Journal of Veterinary Behavior* 4 (2009): 135–44.

7. In the wolf-wolf "non-alpha-roll" photos, the submitting wolf does leave the carcass she or he is feeding on. Observations of wolf behavior find a complicated and variable relationship between food guarding and rank. See, for instance, L. David Mech, "Alpha

Status, Dominance, and Division of Labor in Wolf Packs" (2000), http://www.mnfor sustain.org./wolf_mech_dominance_alpha_status.htm; Mech, "Leadership in Wolf, *Canis lupus,* Packs." Ádám Miklósi (op. cit.) notes that among wolves "lower-ranking animals may carry a small piece of food in front of the dominants 'provocatively' with raised tail and head" (p. 86).

8. Second ed. (Dogwise, 2002), 22. My colleague Marci Haw found this reference when I was tearing my hair out. Thank you, Marci!

5. Total Recall: Getting Your Dog to Come When Called

1. The behaviorist Patricia McConnell did her doctoral thesis on the voice pitch trainers use with animals. Apparently, no matter where you are in the world, high-pitched, rapid vocalization encourages swift movement, and slow, deep vocalization encourages slow movement. Dr. McConnell discusses her research in *The Other End of the Leash* (Ballantine, 2002).

2. Nancy Abplanalp CPDT-KA
Thinking Dogs
planalp@omsoft.com
http:/thinkingdogs.net

9. The Parallel Universe: Dog Body Language and Communication

1. Alexandra Horowitz, "Disambiguating the 'Guilty Look': Salient Prompts to a Familiar Dog Behaviour," *Behavioural Processes* 81 (2009): 447–52.

2. Alexandra Horowitz, *Inside of a Dog: What Dogs See, Smell, and Know* (Scribner, 2009), 201.

3. Susan Milius, "Don't Look Now, But Is That Dog Laughing?," *Science News,* July 28, 2001.

4. Marc Bekoff, "Social Play and Play-Soliciting by Infant Canids," *American Zoologist* 14, no. 1 (1974): 323–40.

5. Erika B. Bauer and Barbara B. Smuts, "Cooperation and Competition During Dyadic Play in Domestic Dogs, *Canis familiaris,*" *Animal Behaviour* 73, no. 3 (2007): 495, 497. Bauer and Smuts are assuming, of course, that what they call "subordinate" status accurately reflects the social structure of the dogs. This is a vexed question.

6. Horowitz, *Inside of a Dog,* 200n.

10. Play? Training? Tricks?

1. James L. Gould and Carol Grant Gould, *The Animal Mind* (Scientific American Library, 1999), 164.

2. Alex Hawes, "Jungle Gyms: The Evolution of Animal Play," *Smithsonian Zoogoer* 25, no. 1 (1996).

3. For a close discussion of the energetic costs of obtaining food, see David W. Macdonald, Scott Creel, and Michael G. L. Mills, "Canid Society," in *The Biology and Conservation of Wild Canids,* ed. David W. Macdonald and Claudio Sillero-Zubiri (Oxford University Press, 2004), 85–106.

4. Marek Špinka, Ruth C. Newberry, and Marc Bekoff, "Mammalian Play: Training for the Unexpected," *The Quarterly Review of Biology* 76, no. 2 (2001): 141–67.

5. The studies are cited in Camille Ward, Erika B. Bauer, and Barbara B. Smuts, "Partner Preferences and Asymmetries in Social Play Among Domestic Dog, *Canis lupus familiaris,* Littermates," *Animal Behaviour* 76 (2008): 1187–99.

6. Robert Fagen and Johanna Fagen, "Juvenile Survival and Benefits of Play Behaviour in Brown Bears, *Ursus arctos*," *Evolutionary Ecology Research* 6 (2004): 89–102.

7. Erika B. Bauer and Barbara B. Smuts, "Cooperation and Competition During Dyadic Play in Domestic Dogs, *Canis familiaris*," *Animal Behaviour* 73, no. 3 (2007): 489–99.

8. See citations in Nicola J. Rooney and John W. S. Bradshaw, "An Experimental Study of the Effects of Play Upon the Dog-Human Relationship," *Applied Animal Behaviour Science* 75 (2002): 161–76.

9. See the crisply worded discussion in Nicola J. Rooney, John W. S. Bradshaw, and Ian H. Robinson, "A Comparison of Dog-Dog and Dog-Human Play Behaviour," *Applied Animal Behaviour Science* 66, no. 3 (2000): 236.

10. Rooney, Bradshaw, and Robinson, "Dog-Dog and Dog-Human Play."

11. Rooney and Bradshaw, "Experimental Study of the Effects of Play."

12. In *Carrots and Sticks: Principles of Animal Training* (Cambridge University Press, 2007), Paul McGreevy and Robert Boakes discuss the pleasure animals may find in learning and how training can become a form of play—*if* it's not too heavy on the aversives (science-speak for "unpleasantness") (p. 89).

11. Stuff Dogs Do That Annoys People

1. See http://landofpuregold.com/store/p=mannersminder.htm for more information about this useful device.

2. See, for example, Raymond Coppinger and Lorna Coppinger, *Dogs: A Startling New Understanding of Canine Origin, Behavior, and Evolution* (Scribner, 2001). But Alexandra Horowitz, in her terrific book *Inside of a Dog* (Scribner, 2009), suggests that dogs didn't evolve from present-day wolves, but rather that dogs and present-day wolves had a common ancestor. Who's right? Who knows? Maybe both. There's a reason some researchers speak of "Canis soupus." See, e.g., Nina Fascione et al., "Canis soupus: Eastern Wolf Genetics and Its Implications for Wolf Recovery in the Northeast United States," *Endangered Species Update* (July 1, 2001).

3. Just for starters: D. H. Read and D. D. Harrington, "Experimentally Induced Thiamine Deficiency in Beagle Dogs: Clinical Observations," *American Journal of Veterinary Research* 42, no. 6 (1981): 984–91; Harold R. Street, George R. Cowgill, and H. M. Zimmerman, "Further Observations of Riboflavin Deficiency in the Dog," *Journal of Nutrition* 22 (1941): 7–24. Don't read them.

4. Donal McKeown, Andrew Luescher, and Mary Machum, "Coprophagia: Food for Thought," *Canadian Veterinary Journal* 29 (1988): 849–50. Can you believe somebody thought that was a clever title?

Erik Hofmeister, Melinda Cumming, and Cheryl Dhein, "Owner Documentation of Coprophagia in the Canine," undated preliminary study; available through the Wayback Machine (http://webarchive.org); shortened link http://bit.ly/ki5V8f. Unfortunately, the final study has not been published. Also see Joanne A.M. van der Borg and Lisette Graat, "Pilot Study to Identify Risk Factors for Coprophagic Behavior in Dogs," in *Proceedings of the Vlaamse Diergeneeskundige Werkgroep Ethologie International Congress on Companion Animal Behaviour and Welfare* (2006). A follow-up study is in the works (Joanne van der Borg, personal communication with author, Feb. 10, 2010).

5. Diane McCartney, "Dung Almost Deadly for Dog," *The Wichita Eagle*, Sept. 20, 2008. Pugs have a reputation as gourmands. This one weighed eight pounds and ate stool from a Labrador Retriever and a Basset Hound. I bet a comparable quantity of bacon would have made her sick, too.

6. See John W. S. Bradshaw, Emily J. Blackwell, and Rachel A. Casey, "Dominance in Domestic Dogs—Useful Construct or Bad Habit?" *Journal of Veterinary Behavior* 4 (2009): 135–44. Bradshaw and his colleagues argue provocatively that there's little empirical evidence for the existence of dominance hierarchies in domestic dogs and that behaviors commonly cited as dominance related can more parsimoniously be accounted for by associative learning. In other words, "dogs do what works." An article describing this paper appears at http://sciencedaily.com/releases/2009/05/0905211122711.htm.

12. Stuff Dogs Do That Worries People: Where to Turn for Additional Help

1. Andrew Luescher, "Compulsive Behaviour," in *BSAVA Manual of Canine and Feline Behavioural Medicine*, ed. Debra F. Horwitz, Daniel Mills, and Sarah Heath (British Small Animal Veterinary Association, 2002), 229–36.

2. G. Landsberg, W. Hunthausen, and L. Ackerman, "Stereotypic and Compulsive Disorders," in *Handbook of Behavior Problems of the Dog and Cat*, 2nd ed. (Saunders, 2003), 195–225.

3. "Excessive crate confinement or neglect has been implicated in the development of grooming and licking excesses." Steven R. Lindsay, *Handbook of Applied Dog Behavior and Training*, vol. 2, *Etiology and Assessment of Behavior Problems* (Blackwell, 2001), 144, citing S. Hetts et al., "Influence of Housing Conditions on Beagle Behavior," *Applied Animal Behaviour Science* 34 (1991): 137–55.

4. "Stereotypical Behavior: A LAREF [Laboratory Animal Refinement and Enrichment Forum] Discussion," edited and expanded by Viktor Reinhardt, in *Laboratory Primate Newsletter* 43, no. 4 (Oct. 2004), 3–4, http://www.brown.edu/Research/Primate/lpn43-4.pdf.

5. Suzanne Hetts, *Pet Behavior Protocols* (American Animal Hospital Association Press, 1999), 156.

6. Landsberg, Hunthausen, and Ackerman, "Stereotypic and Compulsive Disorders," 211 ("Case 1").

7. Probably the most commonly prescribed medication for separation anxiety is Reconcile (or the generic fluoxetine). But of course medication has to be tailored to the individual animal.

    See Barbara Sherman Simpson et al., "Effects of Reconcile (Fluoxetine) Chewable Tablets Plus Behavior Management for Canine Separation Anxiety," *Veterinary Therapeutics* 8, no. 1 (spring 2007): 18–30. This was a placebo-controlled, double-blind study with 35 participating veterinary clinics and 242 dogs, a high number for a behavioral study. All that is terrific. However, it was funded by Lilly, the manufacturer of Reconcile. Please note, I am not saying the study is a bad one. It's hard to get government funding to study medication for animals, and I would rather have a well-done manufacturer-funded study than none at all!

8. Yukari Takeuchi, Katherine A. Houpt, and Janet M. Scarlett, "Evaluation of Treatments for Separation Anxiety in Dogs," *Journal of the American Veterinary Medical Association* 217, no. 3 (Aug. 1, 2000): 342–45.

9. For the preceding discussion, I've drawn mostly on the following sources: G. Landsberg, W. Hunthausen, and L. Ackerman, *Handbook of Behavior Problems of the Dog and Cat*, 2nd ed. (Saunders, 2003), 258–67; John W. S. Bradshaw et al., "Aetiology of Separation-Related Behaviour in Domestic Dogs," *The Veterinary Record* 151, no. 2 (2002): 43–46; Gerrard Flannigan and Nicholas H. Dodman, "Risk Factors and Behav-

iors Associated with Separation Anxiety in Dogs," *Journal of the American Veterinary Medical Association* 219, no. 4 (2001): 460–66; Debra F. Horwitz, "Separation-Related Problems in Dogs," in *BSAVA Manual of Canine and Feline Behavioural Medicine,* ed. Debra F. Horwitz, Daniel Mills, and Sarah Heath (British Small Animal Veterinary Association, 2002): 154–63. There are many other scholarly publications and journal articles on the subject.

10. K.A. Houpt, "Review Article: Genetics of Canine Behavior," *Acta Veterinaria Brno* 76 (2007): 431–44. The "nervous pointers" are described on page 433; there's an extensive literature about these dogs.

11. T. Tazumi et al., "Effects of Prenatal Maternal Stress by Repeated Cold Environment on Behavioral and Emotional Development in the Rat Offspring," *Behavioral Brain Research* 162, no. 1 (2005): 153–60; A. S. Clarke and M. L. Schneider, "Prenatal Stress Has Long-Term Effects on Behavioral Responses to Stress in Juvenile Rhesus Monkeys," *Developmental Psychobiology* 26, no. 5 (1993): 293–304; Monique Vallée et al., "Prenatal Stress Induces High Anxiety and Postnatal Handling Induces Low Anxiety in Adult Offspring: Correlation with Stress-Induced Corticosterone Secretion," *Journal of Neuroscience* 17, no. 7 (1997): 2626–36.

12. A. Shekhar et al., "Summary of a National Institute of Mental Health Workshop: Developing Animal Models of Anxiety Disorders," *Psychopharmacology* 157 (Oct. 2001): 327–39. Since researchers seem to be perfectly happy using rats as a model for humans, there doesn't seem to be any reason not to use them as a model for dogs. Anyway, the research on maternal stress and maternal behavior points in the same direction whatever species happens to be subjected to experiment.

13. Vallée et al., "Prenatal Stress Induces High Anxiety."

14. See Steven R. Lindsay, *Handbook of Applied Dog Behavior and Training,* vol. 3, *Procedures and Protocols* (Blackwell, 2005), "Social Facilitation and Modeling."

15. To find abstracts, do a Google Scholar search for "dog-appeasing pheromone." There have been studies of shelter dogs, dogs going to the vet, dogs going on car trips, dogs afraid of fireworks, newly adopted puppies … In general, effects on anxiety-related behaviors seem to be small but statistically significant. I don't think any studies have found an effect on aggression or house soiling.

16. For lavender, one recent study is M. Komiya et al., "Evaluation of the Effect of Topical Application of Lavender Oil on Autonomic Nerve Activity in Dogs," *American Journal of Veterinary Research* 70, no. 6 (2009): 764–69. The authors found a lowered heart rate among five dogs treated with lavender, but besides being small, the study was sponsored by an aromatherapy organization. Another study is Deborah L. Wells, "Aromatherapy for Travel-Induced Excitement in Dogs," *Journal of the American Veterinary Medical Association* 229, no. 6 (2006): 964–67 (32 dogs; those exposed to lavender scent were quieter and rested more during car trips).

17. Steven R. Lindsay, *Handbook of Applied Dog Behavior and Training,* vol. 3, *Procedures and Protocols* (Blackwell, 2005), 158.

18. See Joseph Ledoux, *The Emotional Brain: The Mysterious Underpinnings of Emotional Life* (Simon & Schuster, 1996), 235–38, for a discussion of "preparedness theory."

19. Lindsay, *Handbook,* vol. 3, 159. See also Pat Miller, *Play with Your Dog* (Dogwise, 2008), 64–65.

20. Sharon L. Crowell-Davis, L. M. Seibert, et al., "Use of Clomipramine, Alprazolam, and Behavior Modification for Treatment of Storm Phobia in Dogs," *Journal of the American Veterinary Association* 222, no. 6 (March 15, 2003): 744–48.

21. Sharon L. Crowell-Davis and Mami Irimajiri, "Evaluation of the Efficacy of a Synthetic Pheromone Analogue in the Treatment of Storm Phobia in Dogs: A Pilot Study," proceedings of the North American Veterinary Conference, January 18, 2008.

22. Nicholas Dodman, *Dogs Behaving Badly: An A-to-Z Guide to Understanding and Curing Behavioral Problems in Dogs* (Bantam, 1999), 67–68.

23. Nicole Cottam and Nicholas H. Dodman, "Comparison of the Effectiveness of a Purported Anti-static Cape (the Storm Defender) vs. a Placebo Cape in the Treatment of Canine Thunderstorm Phobia as Assessed by Owners' Reports," *Applied Animal Behaviour Science* 119, no. 1 (2009): 78–84.

Conclusion: What Happened to Juniper, and How

1. Some people argue that Rosales-Ruiz and Snider are claiming credit for techniques that others previously used; as far as I can tell, though, they were the first to carefully study and systematize the procedure now called CAT.

Acknowledgments

Somewhere or other, in the past couple of years, I read some complainy person's complaint about the vast length of acknowledgments sections in many books. Ha! I could write a list of acknowledgments as long as this entire book, and I'd still be leaving people out. If I've forgotten you, please forgive me. I'm very nervous about this whole thing. It's my first time.

I owe a special debt to Polly Hanson, who first put a clicker and Jean Donaldson's *The Culture Clash* into my hand. The late Barbara Giella took me on as her apprentice and showered me with encouragement.

For a decade now, I've been learning from the great trainer Pat Miller, first on her e-mail list and then at her trainer seminars and workshops. I'm proud to be Pat's student, colleague, and friend. Thank you for your encouragement and input all these years, and for your kind and helpful reading of this book.

Thanks to all the Brooklyn Millerites, especially the brainy and creative Viviane Arzoumanian, who had plenty to say about Chapter 1, and to the wonderful people who share dilemmas, advice, and encouragement on the Peaceable Paws interns e-mail list. You're the best colleagues ever.

I'm grateful to my clients and their dogs, from whom I've learned so much about devotion and hard work. Meg Blitz, Juniper's dog walker, gave with extraordinary generosity of her time and effort in scheduling and participating in the CAT sessions that have made so great a difference in his life.

Kenn Russell sealed his doom by mentioning my name when Quick and Dirty Tips was looking for a dog trainer. Richard Rhorer took me on and coached me through my first stumbling scripts. Emily Rothschild's electronic red pencil was always on the mark, and no other editor will ever be as easy to amuse. Thanks to Amelie Littell and Geraldine

Van Dusen at St. Martin's Griffin, and to Anaheed Alani, who should get a special prize for making sense of my chaotic endnotes. Nancy Inglis gave me my first freelance proofreading gig ever; since no good deed goes unpunished, she also got the job of proofreading this book. Thanks, Nancy!

E'Lise Christensen, DVM, DACVB, is the best veterinary teammate a trainer could hope for and a dear friend too. Our discussions of training and behavior modification and our work together inform every chapter.

Jessica Elliott, who is much smarter than anyone has a right to be, read the manuscript closely, catching any number of mistakes and making me rethink many points. Chapter 1, in particular, was greatly improved thanks to her input. Chagrin sometimes warred with appreciation, I admit, but appreciation wins by a mile, Jess. Thank you for putting in so much time and thought.

Sarah Egan noodged me into getting a dog, which changed everything about my life except her own central place in it. Believe it or not, words fail me.

Sarah and I have had three wonderful dogs so far: Isabella, Muggsy Malone, and Juniper. Izzy was a street stray. Muggsy was left tied up on our block. Juniper's mother was taken, already pregnant, off the streets of the Bronx. What is it they say? One person's trash . . .

Index

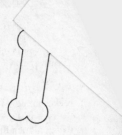

About the Author

JOLANTA BENAL had never had a dog until she was persuaded to adopt a stray in 1998. Now Jolanta is a Certified Professional Dog Trainer–Knowledge Assessed, and the host of *The Dog Trainer's Quick and Dirty Tips for Teaching and Caring for Your Pet,* which iTunes named one of the best new podcasts of 2009. She is also a professional member of the Association of Pet Dog Trainers and was a founding member of the International Association of Animal Behavior Consultants, serving as the first associate editor of its journal, *Animal Behavior Consulting: Theory and Practice.* In 2011, she became one of the first 29 trainers credentialed as a Certified Behavior Counselor Canine–Knowledge Assessed. She supports the movement to professionalize dog training and behavior consulting and put them on a sound scientific basis; she has studied with the eminent trainer Pat Miller, has taken academic courses in canine cognition and learning, and regularly attends seminars on behavior and training. Jolanta sees private clients in Brooklyn and Manhattan. For more dog training and behavior information, see her Web site at http://dogtrainer.quickanddirtytips.com and the Web site for this book, www.TheDogTrainerBook.com.